TESTING TIMES

Success, Failure and Fiasco in Education Policy in Wales Since Devolution

Welsh Academic Press – Education Series

Series Editor
Professor D. Reynolds, Southampton Education School, University of Southampton

Mission
Education and educational systems are now a matter of political, public and professional debate as never before historically. This debate concerns the ways in which schools can be improved, the nature of the schools that societies will need in the future and the deficiencies of educational systems at present.

This series aims to make available to both the professional and general reader, books that explore policy, practice, debate and controversy in education from an international perspective, and from renowned international authorities who can review fields based upon substantial knowledge and experience.

These fields will include:

Educational policy;
Educational change and transformation;
Educational practice;
Educational governance and politics;
Special educational needs.

Additionally, whilst the series will be international in nature, a particular focus will also be given to Wales and the issues related to the Welsh educational system, including Welsh medium education, the future of Higher and Further education in Wales and the more general issues in Wales about how whole national systems can be 'turned around'. This will be compared and contrasted with similar systems and educational innovations globally.

Books will be research monographs, text book reviews of particular fields/areas of education and specialist reviews in particular fields/areas.

Submissions
For further information about the series and for details on how to submit a publishing proposal, please visit our website: www.welsh-academic-press.wales

TESTING TIMES

Success, Failure and Fiasco in Education Policy in Wales Since Devolution

Philip Dixon

Welsh Academic Press

Published in Wales by Welsh Academic Press, an imprint of

Ashley Drake Publishing Ltd
PO Box 733
Cardiff
CF14 7ZY

www.welsh-academic-press.wales

First Edition – 2016

ISBN
978-1-86057-1244

British Library Cataloguing-in-Publication Data.
A CIP catalogue for this book is available from the British Library.

Typeset by Replika Press Pvt Ltd, India
Printed by Akcent Media, Czech Republic

Contents

For my nephews, Michael, Dominic, Gabriel, Reuben, Sebastian and Benedict, who have lived through these events.

Acknowledgements

One incurs great debts in writing a book and many people to thank. I can only single out a few but I hope that the many others who have taught me so much about Welsh education over the last ten years or so will realise that my thanks are given to them too.

Professor David Egan taught me when I was 12 years old. He has continued to do so in my maturity. Another professor, David Reynolds, has given me support and friendship for which I am truly grateful. His insight has changed so many of mine over the last few years. Gareth Evans of the *Western Mail* has a wisdom way beyond his years. His dedication to getting to the truth about matters has been exemplary. Anna Brychan has provided me with tremendous encouragement, and has gently but perceptively challenged many of my ideas. The writing and publishing of a book can be a gruelling task. I would like to thank Ashley Drake for being so patient and helpful in the production of a book which has had more than its fair share of challenges.

Above all I am grateful to David James, who has lived with this project for over a year without one word of complaint. His love has been invaluable.

It goes without saying that the views in this book are my own, and most definitely the mistakes.

This publication is based solely on my personal views and opinions and does not in any way reflect the views or policies of the Association of Teachers and Lecturers (ATL), which had no involvement in its publication.

List of Acronyms

ACCAC	Awdurdod Cwricwlwm ac Asesu Cymru (Qualifications, Curriculum and Assessment Authority for Wales)
ACER	Australian Council for Educational Research
ALN	Additional Learning Needs
AM	Assembly Member
ASCL	Association of School and College Leaders
ATL	Association of Teachers and Lecturers
CBI	Confederation of British Industry
CCW	Curriculum Council for Wales
CDAP	Child Development Assessment Profile
CPD	Continuing Professional Development
CWB	Central Welsh Board
CYPEC	Children, Young People and Education Committee
DCELLS	Department for Children, Education, Lifelong Learning and Skills
DfES	Department for Education and Skills
ELWa	Education and Learning Wales
EWC	Education Workforce Council
EYDAF	Early Years Development and Assessment Framework
EYFS	Early Years Foundation Stage
GTCW	General Teaching Council for Wales
GCSE	General Certificate of Secondary Education
HEFCW	Higher Education Funding Council for Wales
IEA	International Association for the Evaluation of Educational Achievement
INSET	In-Service Education for Teachers
IWA	Institute of Welsh Affairs
JCQ	Joint Council for Qualifications
LEA	Local Education Authority
LNF	Literacy and Numeracy Framework
NAHT	National Association of Head Teachers
NASUWT	National Association of Schoolmasters Union of Women Teachers
NEET	Not in Education, Employment or Training
NFER	National Foundation for Educational Research
NSP	National Support Programme

NUT	National Union of Teachers
OECD	Organisation for Economic Cooperation and Development
PFI	Private Finance Initiative
PIRLS	Progress in International Reading Literacy Study
PISA	Programme for International Student Assessment
PLCs	Professional Learning Communities
QAA	Quality Assurance Agency
SATs	Standard Attainment Tests
SEF	School Effectiveness Framework
SEN	Special Educational Needs
SHELL	Skills, Higher Education and Lifelong Learning
SSU	School Standards Unit
SQA	Scottish Qualifications Authority
TIMSS	Trends in International Mathematics and Science Study
UCAC	Undeb Cenedlaethol Athrawon Cymru
WAO	Wales Audit Office
WISERD	Wales Institute of Social and Economic Research, Data and Methods
WJEC	Welsh Joint Education Committee
WLGA	Welsh Local Government Association

Introduction

Devolution was meant to make a difference. By bringing decision making to Wales it was claimed that problems and challenges would be more closely analysed, addressed and solved. Decision taking would be brought closer to the people, who would thus have a greater say over the way in which they were governed. By forging Welsh answers to Welsh problems, things would get better.

Devolution has certainly made a difference in terms of education. In Wales there are no Academies or Free Schools, ostensibly no League Tables and no SATs. We have a curriculum and qualifications regime that looks increasingly different to that pertaining over the border in England. Devolution has made a difference, but has it made things better? With headlines that scream about our children's underperformance in GCSE exams, and our seemingly perpetual wooden spoon among the home nations in international tests, it would be a bold person who would answer that with an unequivocal 'Yes'.

At the outset I had better nail my own colours to the mast. I was an enthusiastic supporter of devolution in the late 1990s. In fact, although I didn't have the vote in the ill-fated referendum of 1979, I would have voted Yes then if I could have done. It always seemed to me that Wales deserved and needed much greater say over its own affairs, and that we were talented enough as a nation to deliver brighter and better solutions than those that were foisted on us from Whitehall.

My experience over the last ten years has been a big challenge to that position. I wish we could point to a tranche of evidence to show that Welsh children are now better off, better educated and better qualified than they would have been if we had stuck with the monolithic status quo. I wish we could, but we can't. Instead, we have evidence both internal and external that shows that the education system in Wales has not improved as well or as quickly as in other parts of the UK. Key questions this book tries to answer are why that is the case, what has gone wrong, and what we need to do to put it right.

There is an awful lot to put right. This book takes a candid view of the Welsh education system. I hope it is fair, pointing out successes as well as highlighting failures. But it does do the latter, and some of that will make for very uncomfortable reading. Those who do not like what they read might be tempted to reach for the rather facile argument that I am 'talking Wales down'. In education, as in every other area, there is a pernicious sort of patriotism which really is the last refuge of the scoundrel.

Those who are expecting, or fearing, what they might consider a standard trades union approach will also be disappointed or encouraged in equal measure. For the past ten years it has been a privilege to be the Director of the Association of Teachers and Lecturers in Wales. This has brought me into contact with thousands of teachers, heads and support staff. I have been impressed by their dedication, hard work and resilience. But I have also been saddened by the lack of support they often encounter and the lack of consistent narrative from central government, which has fundamentally undermined much of what they are trying to do. What follows are my own personal reflections on the situation here in Wales. They are not the official position of ATL. Much of what I have to say will be welcome to ATL's members, some may not. On a minor note I also hope that this book will challenge an outlook detectable in various places, including government, that trades unions are only concerned about protecting their members. If it does nothing else it hopefully serves to show that those engaged in unions can think and have something to say. It's not simply a question of huddling round a brazier whilst on strike.

In writing any book one has to decide what to leave out as much as what one needs to put in. There are big questions in what follows surrounding the nature of the legislature and the nature of the executive in the devolution model. Or to put it less theoretically: do the problems lie with devolution itself or with the party in charge? If Wales had been much less of a one party state, would our education system be better – or even worse? Or would it not have made much difference?

On occasions it has been suggested that the paucity of the initial devolution settlement, outlined in Chapter 2, meant that the National Assembly for Wales and the Welsh Government were hamstrung. Certainly any intelligent sixth form student of politics could have predicted from the start that the original corporate model of 'administrative devolution' would quickly run into the problems it did. The referendum in 2011 and subsequent Government of Wales Act put the whole settlement on a much more rational and workable footing. The Scottish experience, too, suggests that it is not devolution as such that is the problem. So perhaps it is the policies that have been pursued that need greater scrutiny, and that is what this book attempts to provide.

It has become something of a truism in certain circles that the problems that Welsh education faces are essentially to do with poor delivery mechanisms. If only we could get those right then our problems would start to clear. This book suggests that this analysis is not entirely correct. Sometimes we have simply pursued the wrong policies, as well as delivered them very badly.

Not that there has been policy stability. Far from it. With what has been effectively a one-party state, one might have expected continuity, if little else. But as this book shows, on certain key issues, such as accountability for instance, we have lurched uneasily from one extreme to another. The fact that Labour have held the ministerial portfolio from the inception of devolution until 2016 has not meant that ministers have wanted to pursue the policy of their predecessors. There has arguably been more policy stability in England, where governments of different colours have held office, than in Wales, at least in areas like accountability.

Comparisons with England are inevitable. Not only do we share a very long border with them but we also share a great deal of common educational heritage. Neither system is now where it was in 1999. The English have tried some bold, possibly even reckless, experiments with their education system. There are critiques aplenty of those, but this book is not one of them. Another facile argument trotted out is that 'at least Wales hasn't done so and so'. This book is an attempt to analyse what has been *done* in Wales, not what has not been replicated from across the border.

In terms of many of the contested issues in England, Wales can be portrayed as providing an unfortunate counter-example to those who want to argue against the policies of the current regime there. Take for instance the whole question of teacher assessment versus external testing. For a decade or more Wales had no external testing of children before they sat their GCSE exams. The experience of teacher assessment in Wales superficially gives the lie to those who claim that it can be as accurate as any external test. But the key word there is 'superficially'. Because the abolition of the SATs regime was bungled in Wales, it does not then follow that they could not be successfully abolished in England. This is just one area where I hope that by shedding light on what actually happened, policy makers elsewhere won't throw the baby out with the bath water by assuming that such courses of action don't work.

This book focusses on policy rather than personalities, though I have done some thumbnail sketches of the key players in Chapter 1. That is also when I try to situate Welsh education in the broader historical context. Chapter 2 looks at the 'Grand Narratives' that are supposed to animate the Welsh education system and attempts to analyse them on their own merits. Chapter 3 outlines what, in a nod to Dylan Thomas, I have called 'A Child's Journey in Wales'. This chapter focuses on the stages of compulsory education and the philosophies that are supposed to underpin them. Curriculum and Assessment are examined in Chapter 4. At the time of writing we are just embarking upon an ambitious programme of curriculum reform in the wake of the Donaldson Review of 2014, but this builds on previous failures and successes. Chapter 5 examines the vexed question of qualifications, in particular the path that has seen the development of the Welsh Baccalaureate, but it also tells the tale of the two GCSE English fiascos. Chapter 6 tries to bring together some of the major statistical data on which one can judge the Welsh education system to date. The final chapter gives some pointers to what must now be done.

Wales has suffered from a dearth of critical comment on its education policies. Most English writers, if they mention the country at all, do so in passing, using Wales as a counter-example to what they want to urge. We need more home-based analysis to get debate going in a more productive way. Thankfully, in the last year or so, things have begun to change. Leighton Andrews' book, *Ministering to Education: A Reformer Reports*, which appeared in autumn 2014, was ground-breaking in many ways[1]. It revealed some of the inner workings of government but also Andrews' own conception of his time in office. It is also the only book written by a former cabinet member to date – a reflection on the dearth of talent that has plagued devolution since its outset. A fascinating read, Andrews' book is inevitably partisan, though one doesn't have to do much decoding to see his contempt for the legacy he inherited. A more balanced book appeared in early 2015, written by the *Western Mail*'s young but veteran education correspondent, Gareth Evans. *A Class Apart: Learning the Lessons of Education in Post-Devolution Wales* told it all as it was, wart upon wart.[2] Evans set the ball rolling in terms of the critical assessment of the past seventeen years. My own book aims to build on these firm foundations and will hopefully also provoke the sort of critical debate that Wales so desperately needs.

In writing it I have changed my mind about several issues and on occasions had to accept that what I wanted to believe was simply not the case. Unfortunately these reflections have tended to push me in the direction of feeling less sanguine about future prospects for change. In the conclusion I outline what seems to me to be some of the absolute essential questions we must answer if we are not to languish in division three internationally, with a system which is noticeably worse than those of our neighbours on these islands.

Since 2012 there has been relentless scrutiny of most of the components of our education system in Wales. Teachers, and to some extent students, have felt scrutinised as never before. More rigid performance management and less toleration of failure have led to a number of teachers and heads being encouraged to quit the profession. Schools have fallen under the spotlight, first of Banding and now of Categorisation, and are ranked against each other in terms of outcomes. Local authorities have been probed and inspected by Estyn with a rigour hitherto unseen. But one numerically small but strategically important section of the jigsaw remains much as it did. The Department of Education has changed its name a few times and shuffled a few chairs, but little has been done to change the culture, and crucially the delivery, of national educational policy.[3] If you want to find the weakest link in Welsh education today, then look no further. If performance management measures the effectiveness of teachers, and Categorisation the effectiveness of their schools, then PISA is the measurement of the system as a whole. This year's PISA outcomes need to be seen in this light. Above all, they are a judgment on Ministers and on their Departments in providing the overarching narrative, support and direction for the entire system. The results so far are far from encouraging.

This book shines a light into the corridors of power and finds them seriously wanting. I have grown to know many of the officials quite well over the years. One or two have become good friends. By and large they are hardworking and committed to education. This book does not set out to blame individuals, apart from on the occasions when they have been extraordinarily reckless, but it does set out to expose system failure. Andrews, as you will be able to read later, famously described the Education Department as dysfunctional. It still is.

To shine this light I have concentrated on analysing high-level policies, strategies and initiatives. The chapters deal with the foundation blocks for any education system: narrative, curriculum and assessment, qualifications, and accountability. It has been a rewarding but frustrating process to go back over the debates, hopes and failures of the last seventeen years. But it has not just been a process of hindsight. In what follows I hope I show that some of the debacles and fiascos could have been avoided if more honest debate and discussion had been encouraged.

That seems to me the weakest point of the system. There are obviously enemies of devolution and there are inevitably partisan politics in play, but those of us who try to position ourselves as critical friends of the Welsh Government are growing increasingly weary of having our motivations questioned, our integrity impugned, and our advice derided. There is a lack of confidence and maturity which makes it difficult for the Department to do what a good civil service needs to do: give impartial advice to the Minister. All too often they have rubber-stamped ideas which obviously were ill thought through. Chris Llewelyn of the Welsh Local Government Association hit the nail on the head when he described Cathays Park, where the Welsh Government is based, as a 'court'. My fear is that it resembles a Bourbon court, where nothing is learned and nothing forgotten. All too often the Education Department has seemed to exemplify one of Robert Conquest's three laws of politics: 'the simplest way to explain the behaviour of any bureaucratic organisation is to assume that it is controlled by a cabal of its enemies'.

This 'court' has been more or less open, depending on its Minister and its Director General. Ironically, when it was most threatened by Andrews, who was not averse to seeking advice elsewhere and not slow in making his disagreement known, it was probably at its most open. It had to be, as it had to find friends and knew its operations were under scrutiny as never before. Under Andrews' successor, Huw Lewis, the drawbridge was pulled up once more. Nothing illustrated the change of regime more than the following anecdote. I met a senior official outside the main entrance to Cathays Park, not long after Lewis was appointed. This was someone who, when I saw him a few weeks before, looked drawn and haggard. He now looked as if he had been on a Caribbean holiday for a month. He gleefully told me the real reason for the transformation: 'We're back in charge now'. A shiver went down my spine.

I was tempted at one stage to write a simple history of the period since 1999, but that came to seem like an indulgence. Part of this book, especially the earlier sections of chapters, is inevitably retrospective. I have sought to make balanced and objective judgments about the recent past. It is abundantly clear, I think, that I do not share the view that the Davidson era was some sort of golden age. Far from it. I think that many, but not all, of our current problems have arisen from the seeds sown in the opening years of devolution. Within the chapters we then make progress to the debates and issue of the present. I also lay down what I think are some of the critical markers for assessing these new departures. The concluding chapter is very much my understanding of what must be done.

I suspect this book will get a mixed reception within the Welsh Government itself. Some will feel very annoyed at the narrative it presents. There will be others, however, who will welcome its candour and see it as part of building support for the change of culture that they want to see.

This book is written for two overlapping audiences. There is obviously the Welsh polity which is interested in what we have done, achieved and botched. The book is meant to be a short account of where we are, how we got here, and where we need to go next. But I have also wanted to write an introduction to the Welsh education system for outsiders. I hope that educationalists across the world will find the analysis of the 'Welsh Way' helpful in forming their own opinions about policy. Wales has a lot to teach about narratives, curriculum and assessment, qualifications and the like, albeit that some of the lessons are of the 'don't do it like this' sort.

National Assembly elections come and go and so do education ministers and civil servants, but at present there is a brooding presence filling the horizon, which looks set to dominate the educational experience of at least one, and possibly two, generations. The Donaldson review of the curriculum took place in 2013 and 2014. It is examined in Chapter 4. We are now on the starting blocks with implementation. We are also confronted with a timetable for implementation which seems wildly unrealistic. This book is a salutary lesson to those tasked with implementation, about the perils of poor delivery and a warning that change of this magnitude is financially costly, time consuming, and far from easy. I hope that those concerned will have the humility to listen to practitioners about the potential pitfalls on the way.

The Learning Country, examined in depth in Chapter 2, for all its strengths, was not focussed sufficiently on outcomes. The story of Wales' decline in the opening decade of the new millennium is relative, not absolute. As Chapter 6 shows, in terms of GCSE results Wales did not go backwards: it simply did not improve as fast as the English system across the border. I'm far from saying that exams are the only value to be placed on a system or the only way in which it can be judged. But they are important, in fact vitally important – they impact on the life chances of a young person. We therefore have a duty to ensure that they are as successful as possible. There are those who see Donaldson as a return to the *status quo ante*, to a place before Andrews' wake-up call, to a new era of touchy-feely education in which results are relegated in importance. The real trick will be to implement the vision of Donaldson without losing the gains of the last few years – and without losing the momentum to improve still further.

There has never been a golden age in education, and never will be. But that doesn't relieve us of the duty to minimise the negatives and accentuate the positives. If what follows pushes even a little in that direction, then this book will have achieved its aim.

Notes

1   Andrews, Leighton *Ministering to Education: A Reformer Reports* (Cardigan; Parthian, 2014).

2   Evans, Gareth *A Class Apart: Learning the Lessons of Education in Post-Devolution Wales* (Cardiff; Welsh Academic Press, 2015).

3   Throughout the book, the terms Department of Education and Education Department are used for the Welsh Government's education department, which has undergone several changes of name.

1

Welsh Education Pre- and Post-devolution

Distinctive Welsh educational policy did not start with the establishment of the National Assembly. For over three decades before 1999 the existence of the Welsh Office, with its own Secretary of State, had meant that policies made in Westminster could be *interpreted* for Wales. Even before the setting up of the Welsh Office in 1964, Welsh education had never been exactly the same as its English counterpart. The establishment of a specific education department at the Welsh Office in 1970 was an acknowledgement of that fact, and not its creator. The distinctive nature of Welsh education had a pedigree which long predated any of these late-twentieth century administrative changes. This chapter will look at some of the most important aspects of that pedigree, their origins and legacy. It will also touch on the immediate establishment of the National Assembly and its first few months of operation, to give a context for all that follows. Towards the end I will present some thumbnail sketches of ministers and the most senior civil servants to root the narrative of the book still further.

The growth of elementary schooling in Wales in the eighteenth and nineteenth centuries was led by the Churches. This development contributed not just physical structures in the form of schools but also a culture and ethos which fed into a Welsh way of doing education. The Nonconformist bodies had greater influence in Wales than elsewhere, but the contribution of the Church of England has been unjustly neglected. Although education was provided along religious lines it would be a mistake to swallow the myth that Wales was a homogenous, Nonconformist society in this period. The National Society, established in 1811, was Anglican in its aim and origin. Its rival, and that is the *mot juste* in this context, was the British and Foreign Society, sponsored by the Nonconformists. Despite being the minor player in terms of adherents, the Church of England always had the majority of schools and majority of pupils.

All these developments and the ones that follow are surveyed in *A History of Education in Wales*, by Gareth Elwyn Jones and Gordon Wynne Roderick.[1]

The narrative of Jones and Roderick's book ends at the dawn of devolution. This book will concentrate on the years since.

The growth of state involvement

Anxiety about British performance on the international scene is not new. Throughout the nineteenth century, concern was growing about the state of education, especially compared to that of commercial rivals, such as the newly reunited Germany. As early as 1858 the Duke of Newcastle had chaired a Royal Commission 'to inquire into the state of public education in England and to consider and report what measures, if any, are required for the extension of sound and cheap elementary instruction to all classes of the people'.[2]

After much wrangling, essentially about what role if any that the state should play in education, the 1870 Elementary Education Act made provision for the elementary education of all children aged 5–13, established school boards to oversee and complete the network of schools, and sought to bring them all under some form of supervision. It is salutary to note that nearly one hundred years before, both France and the Austro-Hungarian Empire had developed state education systems. The Act, often referred to as 'the Forster Act', was framed so that such provision would be both affordable but also acceptable to the many sectional religious interests. Despite the fact that by 1870 the British Society had 300 schools and the National Society over a thousand, competition had meant that while some areas of Wales were oversupplied there were still large areas where provision was extremely patchy.

In the last decades of the nineteenth century, secondary education was becoming increasingly common both in Europe and in the rapidly developing United States. Moreover, in many of these countries, science and engineering subjects were being prioritised. It was felt by many, in words that would echo down the twentieth century, that Britain was 'lagging behind'. The author of the Balfour Act of 1902 warned that 'England is behind all continental rivals in education'.

The 1902 Act replaced school boards with local education authorities (LEAs), based on the county councils and county borough councils established by the 1888 Local Government Act. It also laid the basis for a national system of secondary education into which the higher grade elementary schools and the fee-paying secondary schools were integrated. There were now effectively two types of state-aided secondary school: endowed grammar schools, which received grant-aid from LEAs, and the municipal or county secondary schools, maintained by LEAs. As a result of the Act there was a massive expansion in the building of secondary schools in the years up to 1914.[3]

Ironically the sticking point was not so much cost, though that was a concern, but religion. With all too typical myopia, the 1902 Education Act was bitterly resented by Nonconformists in Wales. They were unhappy about grants to Church of England schools, but incandescent about public money being made to Catholic ones. With the catchy slogan of 'Rome on the Rates', the Nonconformists rode into battle. The 1902 Act was effectively neutralised by the change of government in 1905. Although regarded as a great victory at the time, it was hardly one for the children of Wales. Many of them continued to rely on inadequately-funded church schools for even basic education.

Legislation for Wales

The most significant landmark of the nineteenth century for Wales occurred with the passing of the Welsh Intermediate Education Act of 1889. It was introduced as a private members bill by Stuart Rendell, Liberal Member of Parliament for Montgomeryshire between 1880 and 1894. It made provision for public money to be spent on intermediate education in Wales. This was the first specific, Wales-only piece of legislation since the Act of Union in 1536. As John Davies, doyen of Welsh historians, has commented, this was 'almost revolutionary'.[4]

It was certainly effective. It meant that post-elementary education was more widely available in Wales than in England. The Act was a response to the Aberdare Committee of 1881 which had inquired into the state of Welsh education in general. In hindsight it is possible to criticise the heavily anglicised curriculum and ethos the Act generated, but it was a powerful indicator of the value that was placed on education in Wales. Responsibility for maintaining standards in these intermediate schools was given to a Central Welsh Board (CWB) which was established in 1896 to oversee examinations and inspections.

Just over a decade later, in 1907, a Welsh Department was set up in the Board of Education. The Board of Education had been set up in 1899 by the Tory government at Westminster in an attempt to assert central control over education and undermine the authority of local school boards, who were often pursuing agendas considered far too radical. This Welsh Department encouraged local authorities to set up municipal secondary schools. Headed by the formidable O.M. Edwards, the famous Welsh historian, it was given responsibility for overseeing the administration of education in Wales and the inspection of municipal schools too. Relationships between the Central Welsh Board and the Welsh Department of the Board of Education were at best frosty. Schools complained that they were subject to two different inspection regimes, a state of affairs that was not to be fully resolved until

1925. The CWB examinations were narrowly focussed and had an undue influence over the curriculum. Edwards fulminated that the CWB drove any reasoning and intelligence out of the children who sat their exams. He also feared that the CWB was exerting a malign, anglicising influence over the children of Wales.[5]

Twentieth-Century Developments

The Board of Education established a Consultative Committee which was to advise it on various educational matters. It was responsible for commissioning one from the eminent musicologist Sir Henry Hadow, Vice Chancellor of the University of Sheffield from 1919 to 1930. The Hadow Report of 1926 still seems startlingly modern in many respects. It recommended that in primary schools activity and experience should take primacy over the accumulation of facts. It also broke ranks with the rather prevalent patrician view of society and recommended that every child should receive a secondary education. Although its recommendations would take another twenty years to be fulfilled, the number of children in Wales receiving more than the basics increased dramatically from 24,000 in 1918 to over 40,000 by 1940. Hadow argued that secondary schooling should be split into two strands at eleven with one serving the more academic pupils and the other offering a more vocational curriculum in 'Central Schools'. In Wales, the depression, geography and Labour suspicion meant that very few of the new 'Central Schools' were ever formed.

The Butler Education Act of 1944 ensured that the vast majority of children in Wales and England received a secondary education free of charge. One of its basic assumptions was that the majority of these children would need a more vocational than academic approach. The Act removed some of the distinctive educational topography that had existed in Wales since Rendell's Act of 1889. In 1947 the Central Welsh Board was abolished and its functions given to the newly constructed Welsh Joint Education Committee. The WJEC was established as a consortium of Welsh Local Education Authorities. Half its trustees were drawn from the local authorities in Wales, and half were independent trustees from both England and Wales. Even then the WJEC had a substantial commercial presence within the English qualifications market.

After the war the distinctive ethos of Welsh education was shown in the relative speed with which certain governmental policy was implemented. The alacrity with which grammar schools were abolished and comprehensive schools established in most parts of Wales was a vivid testimony to a more collaborative approach to education. The speed was partly due to Labour's dominance, but cannot be explained completely by that fact. Some of it undoubtedly stemmed from ideological commitment, but some was the result of hard finance. It is significant that in 1957, highly rural Anglesey was the first authority in the United Kingdom to abolish the 11+.

Whether the grammar schools were universally the great divisive evils portrayed by some is surely open to question, given the fact that in some parts of the south Wales valleys, the percentage of grammar places was running at over 50%, exceeded only by some rural areas, where it was well over 60%. In 1951 just over 47% of places in Wales were in secondary modern schools and 45 % in grammars. A decade later secondary moderns claimed 52% of places while grammars had dropped to 34%, with comprehensives offering 11%. By 1965, the year of the notorious Circular 10/65, 28% of Welsh pupils were already in comprehensive schools. All this needs to be seen against the backdrop of England. In 1951 for instance, while 45% of Welsh children attended a grammar school, barely 18% of places in England were in grammars, a proportion which hardly varied until the almost universal abandonment of grammar schools in England.

The comprehensivisation of Welsh schools met with little organised resistance – though there was some in the capital city – and was mostly welcomed. There were to be no Kents in Wales and, by 1988, all grammar schools had, on paper, gone. However, many argued that their ethos still lived on in the new structures.

The Education Act of 1988

A similar reaction can be seen in responses to the Baker Act of 1988. The Grant Maintained Schools of the Act were to be ones that had opted out of local authority control. They would be run by a Board of Governors, could set their own admission policies (and frequently did, to ensure selection), and could apply to central government for capital projects. A decade later, when they were abolished by the incoming Labour Government in 1997, nearly 20% of secondary schools in England were Grant Maintained. By contrast, in Wales in 1995 less than 1% of schools enjoyed this status. The reasons were complex. Undoubtedly some of them were ideological, but heads and governors in Wales also seemed to enjoy a better relationship with their local authorities. Those few schools that did convert did so largely because of local disputes with their local education authority. As a result of such low levels of uptake, the Schools Funding Council did not operate in Wales or beget a Welsh quango.

The Grant Maintained saga is illuminating. The market driven ideology that developed firstly Grant Maintained status and more recently the full-blown Academy programme in England seems to have found little fertile ground in

Wales. The oft-cited attachment to community comprehensive schooling was clear. Indeed, researchers from the Joseph Rowntree Foundation, reviewing the Grant Maintained experiment claimed, with a certain amount of prescience, that 'Welsh LEAs feel the market is not an appropriate mechanism to improve quality in education. They prefer to see schools acting in partnership to improve provision rather than competing'.[6] More and more demand side drivers were being introduced in England under New Labour. They found little parallel in Wales.

It is important to realise that this apparent vote of confidence in local authorities was long before the effects of the reorganisation of 1996 started to bite. After 1996, the original eight counties were broken down into twenty-two smaller units, all much smaller than the authorities in England. This reorganisation was to have profound effects for the Welsh education system, and to lead to the situation in which none were really adequate for their statutory support and intervention functions.

Anxieties about Welsh performance

Wales was not completely subsumed into the English debates about education. Current anxieties about the relative underperformance of Welsh children in regard to the rest of the UK are not purely a product of recent PISA frenzy. In a December edition of the TES in 1981, a Young Turk by the name of David Reynolds caused uproar with an article entitled 'Schooled to Fail' in which he argued that Welsh children were lagging behind their English counterparts. Reynolds' analysis was subtle. He argued that the comprehensivisation of Welsh schools had often been just a change of title with little substantial change. The retention of the old grammar school ethos meant that while those at the top did well, those in the middle and at the bottom left school with little or nothing to show. This was certainly my own experience, attending the Upper Rhondda Comprehensive School, later to be known by the more friendly title of Treorchy Comprehensive School, in the later 1970s. We wore blazers with a phoenix badge and Latin motto, and were rigidly streamed. As well as those who wanted to defend such an ethos, others argued that Reynolds had not taken enough account of socio-economic factors. They argued that, in reality, once these were allowed, Welsh schools were actually outperforming English ones.[7]

In 1981, the Wales Office commissioned the Loosemore Report, which concluded that 25% of Welsh pupils left school without an O-level to their name. According to Jones and Roderick: 'The conclusion drawn was that, while Welsh comprehensives seemed to be serving more able pupils well, they were not as effective with lower-ability pupils and were less successful in the examination stakes than their English counterparts, having yielded an advantage associated with the former grammar schools.' The quest for greater equity in education in Wales had begun. Jones and Roderick also noted that the Loosemore report, and the previous furore, had placed Wales centre stage in the debate over school effectiveness, not necessarily to the country's advantage.[8]

Welsh medium schools

Significantly, with its insistence that parental choice be respected in matters of religion, the 1944 Act also paved the way for the growth of another peculiarly Welsh phenomenon, the Welsh medium school. Perhaps the most distinctive feature of schooling in Wales in the decades before devolution had been the presence and slow but growing prominence of Welsh medium education. This should not be confused with the existence of schools which were 'naturally' Welsh speaking in the heartlands of the language itself. As far back as 1890 the Privy Council had agreed money to be paid to schools that taught Welsh grammar. As John Davies bravely stated, the myth of the 'Welsh Not' has been overplayed.

Welsh medium schools often aimed at protecting the language or at providing education in the language in areas where Welsh was no longer the mother tongue of the majority. Ironically, the rise of the Welsh medium sector coincided with the seemingly terminal decline of those schools which were 'naturally' Welsh speaking.

The first Welsh medium primary school of the modern era, Ysgol Cymraeg, was opened in Aberystwyth in 1939 by Ifan ab Owen Edwards as a means of maintaining educational provision in Welsh against the perception of threat from English speaking incomers. At first it was a fee paying school and regarded by many as somewhat eccentric. A more 'standard' school was opened in Llanelli in 1947. By the time that the National Assembly for Wales appeared on the scene, fifty years later, there were 445 primary schools which claimed to have classes where Welsh was the sole or main medium of instruction, out of a total of 1,666 schools. These schools catered for 51,600 pupils out of a total of 291,687.

The first Welsh medium secondary school, Ysgol Glan Clwyd, opened in Rhyl in 1956. Six years later Ysgol Rhydfelen opened in the south. By the mid-1980s there were fourteen Welsh medium secondary schools in existence, and by 1999 there were fifty-two secondary schools which claimed to be Welsh medium or bilingual, out of a total of 229. These catered for 36,289 pupils out of a total of 204,158.

By 2012 there were to be 62,446 pupils receiving their primary education through the medium of Welsh, 23.82% of the total cohort and a slightly lower number, 41,262, 20.84% of the cohort, receiving their secondary education in this way.[9] Another indicator of success was shown in the fact that between 1995 and 2005 the number of pupils in Years 7–11 taught Welsh as a first language rose from 21,658 (12.2%) to 27,895 (14.8%) of the cohort.

Y Cwricwlwm Cymreig

The growth of Welsh medium education should not be seen in isolation. Whatever the political 'setup' the distinctive nature of Wales was something well on some radar screens before the end of the nineteenth century. The Privy Council had made provision for teaching which also took account of Welsh history and geography, when it agreed monies to pay for the teaching of Welsh grammar in 1890. In 1927 the Wales Department in the Board of Education published a report entitled *'Welsh in Education and Life'*, which realised the unique role of the language, but also its history and culture. In the wake of the report *Curriculum and Community in Wales* of 1952, some Welsh dimension of the curriculum was envisaged as necessary. The Gittins Report of 1967, mirroring the Plowden Report in England, sought to examine the vexed question of transition from primary to secondary schools, and argued that all schoolchildren in Wales should study the language either as a first or second language.

The distinctive nature of Welsh education was thus well established by the time that the National Curriculum arrived on the scene in 1988. The Secretary of State's role in the curriculum was explicitly recognised in the Act, and responsibility for the implementation of the curriculum lay with the Welsh Office. Given the frustration that many now feel with the National Curriculum, it is salutary to recall that many teachers welcomed its development. The curriculum was meant to provide a broad entitlement. Children were no longer to be at the whim of what individual schools would provide. Some have even seen the National Curriculum as the acme of the comprehensive ideal, ensuring that every child is treated equally.

The curriculum had two aims: firstly, it should aim to provide opportunities for all pupils to learn and to achieve; secondly, the school curriculum should aim to promote pupils' spiritual, moral, social and cultural development and prepare all pupils for the opportunities, responsibilities and experiences of life. The curriculum had four avowed purposes: to establish an entitlement; to establish standards; to promote continuity and coherence; to promote public understanding. Over the ensuing decades, in England, the second purpose overtook all others. With a National Curriculum stretching across all schools and with a common exam framework stretching across all children, it now became far easier to compare school performance. The data explosion was under way.

The curriculum was applicable to all 5 to 16-year-olds in England, Wales, and Northern Ireland. It was divided into 'core' subjects of English, mathematics and science, and 'foundation' subjects of art, geography, history, music, physical education and technology, with modern foreign languages studied from age 11. It all looked deceptively simple, and so it proved to be. Governments of every political hue and in all three jurisdictions have tampered with it ever since.

The National Curriculum for Wales differed from that of England. It obviously included the Welsh language, but other subjects, such as history, geography and music, were also modified to take account of the nation's heritage and culture.

The 1988 Act established the Curriculum Council for Wales, which had far greater input than its English counterpart. In 1994 the CCW was supplanted by ACAC (Awdurdod Cwricwlwm ac Asesu Cymru/Curriculum and Assessment Authority for Wales) which was to be responsible for ensuring quality and standards in external, general and vocational qualifications; keeping under review all aspects of the school curriculum and statutory arrangements for maintained schools; and commissioning Welsh bilingual classroom materials to support the teaching of Welsh, and other subjects. For the first time there was a single organisation in Wales responsible for overseeing and advising on both academic and vocational qualifications and the school curriculum.[10] In many ways, ACAC functioned as the Welsh equivalent of England's Qualifications and Curriculum Authority. ACCAC[11] was absorbed into the Department of Education on April Fool's Day 2006, in a specious 'bonfire of the quangos' which also saw the demise of the Welsh Development Agency. As we shall see, as with many other decisions of the mid-noughties this was to have far reaching consequences for Welsh education.

Referendum rejection, but growing identity

The divergence of policy in Wales, coupled with a desire to make it even more divergent, had led to calls for some sort of democratic accountability in the form of devolution. As far back as 1968 the Wilson government had appointed a Royal Commission on the Constitution to look into these matters. The Kilbrandon Commission finally reported in 1973.

The subsequent Wales Act provided for a Welsh Assembly which would exercise executive devolution. It would be able to pass secondary legislation in various designated areas including health, social services and education.

We needn't go into the political shenanigans, led by Neil Kinnock, which ensured that this, one of the dying acts of the Callaghan government, was doomed to failure from the start. The referendum question was: 'Do you want the provisions of the Wales Act 1978 to be put into effect?' The result was a devastating and definite No of nearly four to one. (Yes: 20.3% and No: 79.7%.)

The growth of devolution

Although the '79 referendum was a bitter blow to those who sought political devolution, the trend towards growing distinctiveness in educational policy and approach was not reversed. We have already noted the tepid response to grant maintained schools and the development of a Welsh understanding of the National Curriculum. But in other spheres too, devolution was happening in practice.

Most of the education unions, for instance, had some sort of devolved structure which predated the establishment of the Senedd by quite a number of years. Perhaps the most interesting development was the formation of UCAC, which was established nearly sixty years before, in 1940. Although not as sizeable as the other unions, it was formed by a group of teachers who explicitly wanted a union with aims, policies and services that would correspond to the specific needs of teachers living and working in Wales. The venture had the blessing of the high priest of Welsh nationalism, Saunders Lewis himself. Rhodri Llwyd Morgan (in an article to mark the establishment of UCAC's archive) claimed: 'At the time of its establishment, UCAC was a pioneering organisation. UCAC was the first professional trade union to be established in Wales by Welsh people for Wales. It represented a body that insisted on concentrating minds on the educational and cultural needs of Wales'.[12]

Although other unions maintained their ties with UK bodies, throughout the eighties and nineties they became increasingly aware of the need to allow for devolution-in-practice. Today most, if not all, the education unions operate on a broadly federal structure with responsibility for policy devolved to Wales. All now have some sort of staffing structure which reflects the need for policy development in the Welsh context.

The school inspectorate too was effectively a devolved organisation before devolution. Estyn, (from the Welsh 'to extend') was established under the Education Act 1992 and responsible to the Secretary of State for Education. It was, however, to be an independent entity and not a branch of Ofsted, with its own Chief Inspector producing its own published annual report.

The arrival of the National Assembly

The landslide won by the Blair government in 1997 seemed to indicate that a Welsh Assembly and a Scottish Parliament would now be inevitable, as they were both contained within Labour's manifesto. For various reasons, not least the incoming premier's complete lack of sensitivity towards Welsh and Scottish identities, it was decided a referendum would be necessary to establish their acceptability. Opinion polls consistently suggested that this would be a formal ratification. In the event, the phrase 'too close to call' barely describes the agony for those of us who stayed up on the night of 18th September 1998 to watch the results come in. By barely 0.6%, the people of Wales voted to establish a Welsh Assembly. It was quite an achievement to reverse the hammer blow of 1979, but the narrowness of the majority meant that the new body was, from the start, desperate to prove its legitimacy and the difference it could make. Education policy was clearly one area where that could be shown.

This desire to show the difference it could make sometimes overshadowed the desire to show that Wales could do it better.

Faltering first steps

To many in 1999, it seemed as if Welsh education was poised, Moses-like, about to enter the promised land. That land would be one that was not subject to Tory governments, market forces and competition. It would give Wales the opportunity to develop its own policies and initiatives and to plough a different furrow. It would make schools and schooling more responsive to the needs of Wales and more accountable to its people. In the words of New Labour's 1997 election song, 'Things could only get better'.

Ron Davies, appointed to the cabinet by Tony Blair as Secretary of State for Wales, narrowly defeated Rhodri Morgan for the Labour leadership in Wales in September 1998 and was thus on course to become, in the rather Stalinist phrase, 'First Secretary' of the Welsh Assembly. Most pundits thought that Labour would easily secure an overall majority. But politics is frustratingly human and, after what he called a 'moment of madness' on Clapham Common, Ron Davies resigned from the cabinet and two days later was pushed out as Labour's leader in Wales. Despite Rhodri Morgan's manifest popularity within the Labour Party, he was passed over in favour of Alun Michael as the new Secretary of State for Wales. Michael was also Blair's choice for the Labour leadership in Wales. In the leadership election, Rhodri won 64% of the party vote, but was defeated by the block votes of some of the unions.

The poll for what was billed as 'the first Welsh General Election' was held on 6th May in the following year. Labour did not achieve an overall majority. In the new sixty-member chamber, Labour had twenty-eight seats, Plaid Cymru seventeen, the Tories just nine and the Liberal Democrats six. Labour was heavily punished in some of its traditional heartlands. Plaid unexpectedly won Islwyn, Neil Kinnock's former stomping ground, but the upset of the election was the supposedly rock solid seat of the Rhondda. Here Plaid's Geraint Davies won with a majority of over 2,000.

On 12th May 1999, the new Assembly sat for the very first time and Alun Michael became the first First Secretary of the new legislature.

In his opening speech Alun Michael acknowledged that 'We need improvement in the health service and in education and training'.[13] He named his cabinet. Initially, the education brief was split into two component parts. Tom Middlehurst, the Assembly Member for Alyn and Deeside, was to be in charge of post-16 education and training, while Rosemary Butler, AM for Newport West, undertook the role of Children and Young People's Minister. Both lasted barely a year in the post. The only contentious issue that day was whether or not there should be a debate over lifting the ban on the sale of beef on the bone.

A week later the Assembly's new scrutiny committee structure was announced. Plaid's Cynog Dafis was to chair the Post-16 Education and Lifelong Learning committee, and the Tories' William Graham Pre-16 Education, Schools and Early Learning. The first question posed to the First Secretary was from Plaid's Cynog Dafis: 'What plan does the First Secretary have to review teachers' salaries?' In the subsequent exchange, Michael agreed with the Lib Dem Jenny Randerson that 'Golden Hellos' were needed to attract the brightest and best into the workforce.

Later sessions of the Assembly that term saw questions asked about early years provision and also a statement by Michael, in a 'state of the nation' debate, that 'Demanding targets have been set to raise educational standards, and specific measures have been undertaken to improve literacy and numeracy.'

Jane Davidson, soon to be Education Minister, asked about a proposed PFI initiative in relation to Ysgol Gyfun Rhydfelen. She quoted the Director of Environmental Services, who had written that the 'conditions of the school were detrimental to the health and safety of the teachers and pupils, and that the situation could not be allowed to continue. This is the most dilapidated school in Rhondda Cynon Taff and this is the view of the local authority'. Under Davidson, Wales was to fall further and further behind in its transformation of school buildings.

The question of differential school performance was raised by the Tory AM for Monmouth, David Davies. In response, Butler noted that 'There should be no disparities in the delivery of education across Wales. For example, children living in a rural community should receive the same standard of education as those living in Rhondda Cynon Taff'.

I have included these exchanges from debates now long-forgotten because they are a rather sad proof of the old French axiom *plus ça change, plus c'est la même chose*. The big issues are still with us: school buildings, differences in performance, teachers' pay and conditions and, above all, the need to improve literacy and numeracy.

Michael falls on his sword

Michael had tried to run a minority government, but the project was doomed from the outset. By the turn of the year it was clear that the opposition parties had only to find the right issue and they would unite to defeat him. Money from Europe provided that opportunity.

On February 9th 2000 Plaid Cymru, supported by the other opposition parties, tabled a motion of 'no confidence' in the First Secretary, citing Michael's alleged failures over Objective One money as a reason. Nick Bourne, the Tory leader, took obvious relish in reminding his listeners that Michael 'is where he is because he is Tony Blair's man. Tony Blair wanted him appointed because he would not cause trouble … He was put here because he would do London's bidding'.

Michael realised that the voting odds were against him. He also realised that the loyalty of the Labour group was being strained to breaking point. In the chamber he concluded 'that is why I have decided to put the choice back with the Labour Party, by resigning as First Secretary with immediate effect', handing a written letter to the Presiding Officer, Lord Dafydd Elis-Thomas. There were hilarious scenes in the House of Commons as Tory MPs, who had just been informed of the resignation, taunted Blair, who obviously had not.

Even then Michael's humiliation was not over. The Presiding Officer noted that the motion had not been withdrawn and, despite protests from Labour members, proceeded to call the vote. The motion was carried by thirty-one votes to twenty-seven. After an hour's intermission, the Assembly reconvened to hear that the cabinet had unanimously asked Rhodri Morgan to chair its meetings and to take over responsibilities of the First Secretary overnight. The next week he was unanimously affirmed in post by the Assembly.

In his opening address as First Minister, Morgan noted the narrowness of the referendum victory and acknowledged that the new institution was on shaky ground. He stated that 'if people are cynical about an institution that is only eight months old, then we have a problem. All of us need to bend our efforts to try to solve that problem'. In many ways his time in office can be seen as an effort to confront that cynicism and to curry favour with a lukewarm electorate. Popular policies were to be the name of game. Education was no exception.

The Ministers

This book wants to focus on policy rather than personalities, but they do not occur in a vacuum. Those who have held office, and those who have served them at the highest levels of the civil service, have had a key role in shaping the education landscape as we know it today in Wales. Their strengths and their weaknesses have had a big influence on what the education system has done and what it has sought to achieve.

Davidson

Tom Middlehurst and Rosemary Butler have left no trace of their time in office. In October 2000, Labour formed a coalition with the Liberal Democrats to form a majority administration. The initial cabinet of eight was increased to nine, with the appointment for the first time of a Culture Minister. The education brief was given to the woman whose long shadow can still be felt across the Welsh educational landscape, Jane Davidson. Privately educated at the exclusive and expensive Malvern College, she attended Birmingham University and the University of Wales. She taught PE and drama at Ysgol Uwchradd Aberteifi in Cardigan, and Coedylan School, Pontypridd.

Davidson's overly dramatic demeanour and *modus operandi* hinted at her chosen teaching training subject option. She was not a politician that many warmed to and her patrician attitude meant that any criticism was construed as an act of *lèse majesté*. Davidson was Education Minister for nearly seven years. Firstly in the Labour-Lib Dem coalition of 2000 to 2003 and then in the Labour majority government that followed from 2003 to 2007.

I first met Davidson in 2005, but never found her congenial. By this stage she had been in power for over five years and clearly felt she had little left to learn. *The Learning Country* suite, of which more in the next chapter, was well under way. Wales had just opted to enter the international competition of PISA, and she was clearly of the opinion that this would demonstrate what a world class system she had promoted. She had abolished League Tables and SATs and made much of the difference between Wales and England in this regard.

Much of her time at this stage was spent in the ministerial limousine, being driven around the Schools of Wales. The dilapidation of the building stock must have been clear to see but it was nothing to the dilapidation of the education system that was by this stage well under way. Any attempt to raise underfunding and its effects were stonewalled. The truth was that her deep unpopularity with her cabinet colleagues (she was disparagingly referred to as 'Lady Jane' by more than one of them) was costing the education budget dear, with catastrophic results.

All in all, far from being a progressive and positive time for Welsh education, her overly long tenure of the education portfolio has left what can only be described a 'toxic legacy' of underfunding and wrong focus.[14] Some might feel that judgment too harsh. I hope this book will give them pause for thought. The writing of history is important if its mistakes are not to be repeated. A fact not lost on Davidson, who was caught editing her Wikipedia entry long after leaving office![15]

Hutt

Her successor, Jane Hutt, was much easier to work with. In fact, if anything, Hutt took too much notice of the difficulties and problems that were raised by those who sought to lobby her. Hutt had graduated from the University of Kent, Canterbury and obtained a Certificate of Qualification in Social Work after that. She was profoundly committed to equality, and was one of the founding members of Welsh Women's Aid, which campaigns against domestic violence. Before entering politics she had been Director of Chwarae Teg, an organisation that sought to promote women in Welsh public life.

On her election to the Assembly in 1999, Hutt had been appointed as Health Minister. During her time there, the Leader of the Welsh Tories, Rod Richards, had unkindly labelled her 'Calamity Jane' and the label had stuck. Another confidante of Rhodri Morgan, Hutt was incredibly hardworking and a born consensualist. These positive properties came at the cost of decision making: one senior official told me of a meeting during which twenty-five key priorities were identified for the work of the department. Unlike Davidson, she was prepared to listen and it is to her credit that the Foundation Phase, which we will examine in Chapter 3, was saved from the brink of collapse because of inadequate funding. Her background in equalities coloured her whole approach to education, and she rarely manifested any real concern about what has been labelled the 'standards agenda'. In many ways, Hutt was simply handed the baton by Davidson and no major changes of policy were detectable in her two year tenure of the education brief.

Andrews

The contrast between Hutt and her successor, Leighton Andrews, could not have been sharper. Andrews was, and remained to the very end of his time as an AM, a very divisive figure. He became Education Minister in late 2009. He did not tolerate fools gladly and made that plain. He quickly attempted to stamp his authority and personality on the department. He had arrived with a reputation given by other civil servants elsewhere in the government for having, as one put it, 'an extremely low 'bullshit' threshold'. Those who ignored that did so at their peril, as they soon found out. But for all his acerbic manner, Andrews' intelligence enabled him to grasp facts quickly, and to see through those who did not know what they were talking about.

Andrews was responsible for a complete *volte face* in terms of policy. There was an abrupt screech on the brakes in terms of *The Learning Country* agenda and a completely different course of action, similar to the English 'standards agenda', was put in its place. Andrews summed up his programme as one that focussed on 'literacy, numeracy and narrowing the gap'.

In the end, Andrews' own temper did for him. In the summer of 2013 Andrews was photographed campaigning against the closure of Pentre primary school in his own constituency. The opposition parties went to town on an alleged conflict of interests. The local authority, Rhondda Cynon Taff, was after all only applying guidelines which the Welsh Government had issued. Carwyn Jones, the First Minister, pointedly refused to back Andrews in the Senedd chamber, probably frustrated because this was the second instance of Andrews trying to run with the hare and the hounds. Apparently a shouting match took place in the First Minister's office afterwards, with Andrews storming out to Tweet his resignation. It was certainly unexpected, taking even his Special Advisor by surprise. A few days later I met Andrews at a party to bid farewell to Chris Tweedale, who had been his right hand man in the department. He looked quite sheepish.

Andrews' unexpected crushing defeat at the hands of the Plaid leader, Leanne Wood, in the election of May 2016 has robbed Welsh politics of one of its more colourful characters and one of its most effective ministers to date.

Lewis

Andrews was succeeded by Huw Lewis, AM for Merthyr Tydfil and Rhymney, who had twice before been Deputy Education Minister, including a stint with Andrews. Lewis was born and raised in the constituency he represents. After attending the University of Edinburgh, which seems to have left him with a soft spot for Scotland, Lewis taught chemistry at Afon Taf High School for two years. From his mid-20s onwards, Lewis became a Welsh Labour apparatchik, and was elected to the Assembly in 1999.

Lewis was frank about his shock at finding himself in charge of such a large brief, and even Labour's most partisan supporters would have to concede that he found it difficult to master. The Labour benches often sported glum faces as the minister was trounced in the debates in the Senedd chamber.

Lewis' passionate commitment to social equality led him to nuance some of Andrews' flagship initiatives. School categorisation is now more focussed on the gap between Free School Meals children and their better-off counterparts. He was keen to stress the 'narrowing the gap' aspect of Andrews' overall strategy. Lewis' big idea has been to inaugurate a great debate about the curriculum. He commissioned the Scot, Graham Donaldson, to prepare a report aiming at a complete overhaul of the curriculum. The proposals are examined in Chapter 5.

Lewis' main problem was the reliance he put on the civil servants. Andrews was rightly sceptical of some of their briefings and was prepared to seek advice elsewhere. Lewis lacked the confidence to do so. On January 15th 2016, Lewis announced his intention of quitting politics altogether, and that he would be standing down at the National Assembly elections in May. So even if Labour scraped back to power and continued to hold the education brief, it was clear that there would be another set of hands on the tiller.

The election night of May 5th 2015 was one of the more exciting in the history of Wales. The crushing defeat of Leighton Andrews at the hands of Plaid's Leanne Wood was probably the 'Portillo' moment of devolution so far. But the aftermath had its fair share of drama. Despite losing just one seat Labour found themselves in a minority. The first vote, for the post of First Minister, which saw the Carwyn Jones and Leanne Wood and equal number of votes, left them in no doubt about their vulnerability. Future policy will clearly not now be a Labour-only affair. In education this was doubly the case as Kirsty Williams, the one and only Lib Dem returned to the Assembly, was invited to be the new Cabinet Secretary. The first non-Labour minister to hold that brief Williams will have to show considerable mettle in dealing with the challenges ahead. Tuition fees, which proved so toxic an issue for her London-based colleagues will have to be addressed once the Diamond report is published in the autumn. The devolution of Teachers Pay and Conditions will also almost inevitably take place before 2020 and over her first few months will brood the spectre of the latest PISA results due in December. Labour's minority and Williams' appointment mean that the next five years will certainly not be 'more of the same'.

The Director Generals

In this book I have avoided identifying my sources within the corridors of power or naming those who have been in charge of some of the biggest debacles. However, as the role of Director General is such an important one, I think that names and dates are appropriate. The importance of the role has varied inversely with the strength of the Minister in charge.

In 2006, towards the end of the Davidson era, the Welsh Government secured quite a *coup* in attracting the internationally renowned educational reformer, Steve Marshall, to head up its Education Department. An Australian by birth and upbringing, Marshall was a born educator. He began his career as a primary teacher, rising rapidly to become chief executive of the South Australian Department of Education, where he started to gain an international reputation for innovations that improved literacy and retention levels. Marshall did not think that blaming schools was the answer. He tried to initiate a process of tri-level reform with the government, local authorities and schools, working together in what was labelled the 'School Effectiveness Framework'. In public this new approach was hailed as the way forward and pushed with vigour.

In private, however, he was growing increasingly frustrated by a number of issues. He regarded the Welsh language as an unnecessary distraction to the school improvement agenda, the unions as too numerous and too reactionary to take a strategic role in effecting change, and the local government settlement as the perfect foil for any reform. These, coupled with growing lack of funding, saw Marshall decamping to Ontario after less than two years in the job. His early death at the age of fifty-six robbed education of one of its more moral characters.

Marshall was succeeded by a man who had also had a key role to play in the Australian educational scene. Dr Dennis Gunning began his career as a chemistry teacher in Ayrshire in 1971. He then worked as a researcher with the Scottish Examination Board and held a number of positions in the Scottish Qualifications Authority. In 2001, he became the inaugural director of the Victoria State Qualifications Authority in Melbourne. A wily Scot, secure in his own academic background, Gunning had been instrumental in enhancing the vocational offer for youngsters in Victoria. In 2007 he had taken up the post of Director of Skills, Higher Education and Lifelong Learning in the Education Department. Gunning's natural charm meant that he was well placed to sell some of the government's more difficult decisions. The initiatives around the Learning Pathways, examined in Chapter 4, were largely his initiative. Gunning had a key role in ensuring that the Foundation Phase flagship was not fatally holed.

Gunning was only prepared to do the job on a temporary basis. Marshall's full time successor came from closer to home. David Hawker had begun his career as modern languages teacher in a secondary modern in the Midlands in the 1970s. A key player at one stage in the Jesus Army, the experience had left him with a certain evangelical air. After a stint at the Qualifications and Curriculum Authority, Hawker had become Director of Children's Services in Brighton and Hove in 2001, followed by Westminster in 2007. In 2008 he became Director General for Children, Education, Lifelong Learning and Skills at the Welsh Government. A skilled linguist, Hawker became sufficiently proficient in Welsh to be able to deliver addresses competently in the language. As Director General for Jane Hutt, Hawker thrived. Hutt was more than happy to let him take a lead on education policy. The arrival of Andrews proved a rude awakening.

The two men were very different in approach, and Andrews had no time for those who tried to excuse the poor performance of the department. There were rumours of difficult meetings and rows.[16] Officials found themselves summoned to the Minister without the Director General knowing. It was only a question of time before one of them had to go, and it was not going to be Andrews. Hawker announced his departure, having served less than two years.

This meant that in the space of four years the department had had four Director Generals. The instability of such a situation was becoming more and more apparent and was having a deleterious effect on the department.[17] It was also getting a reputation in the UK civil service as a place not to be. I referred to the post as a 'revolving door'.

Hawker's replacement was meant to steady the nerves. He had an impressively Welsh pedigree. Hailing from Anglesey, Dr Emyr Roberts had completed his PhD at Aberystwyth. After early work with the National Farmers' Union, he joined the then Welsh Office in 1991, rising to become the Director General, Public Services and Local Government Delivery. Although he was candid about his lack of knowledge in regard to education, he was a career civil servant through and through. Leaving educational policy to his Deputy, Chris Tweedale, he set about sorting out a department that the Minister, Andrews, had publicly labelled 'dysfunctional'. In Andrews' words, he gave it a more 'logical' structure.[18] But again, after just two years in the job, Roberts was off to head up Natural Resources Wales.

The choice of his successor baffled many. Before Roberts, Director Generals had had a clear background in education and government bureaucracy. While Roberts lacked the former, his successor, Owen Evans, lacked both. Evans had barely been in the civil service two years when he landed the top job at the Education Department. He had been Director of Skills, Higher Education and Lifelong Learning (SHELL) since 2010. That appointment had surprised some too, as Evans had hitherto had little to do with either education or the work of the department.

In his book Andrews praises Evans as 'a shrewd and calm problem solver' who 'had the great advantage of having worked outside the civil service, and brought with him a powerful network of contacts across industry and civil society in Wales'.[19] Immediately before landing the second top job in the Education Department, Evans had headed up the Welsh wing of Business in the Community, a renowned organisation supporting businesses in making a positive impact on communities. Before that he had been Head of Government Relations, Devolved and Local Government at BT Global Services.

A frantic networker and PR performer, Evans brought some polish to the public image of the department, but his lack of in-depth knowledge of education or the civil service took its toll in terms of coherence and strategic direction. Evans was promoted to be Deputy Permanent Secretary in the summer of 2015, keeping just the schools part of the education brief in his portfolio. The post of Director General was then abolished and the the the door stopped revolving.

The thumbnail sketches hopefully outline something of the personalities of the men and women who have formed the Welsh education scene over the devolution years. But personalities are only part of the story. The rest of this book looks at the policies they pursued, the crises they made and faced, and the solutions they tried to devise.

Notes

1   Jones, Gareth Elwyn and Roderick, Gordon Wynne, *A History of Education in Wales* (Cardiff; University of Wales Press, 2003).
2   Gillard D (2011) Education in England: a brief history www.educationengland.org.uk/history.
3   http://www.parliament.uk/about/living-heritage/transformingsociety/livinglearning/school/overview/reform1902-14/
4   Davies, John *A History of Wales* (London; Penguin, 1993) p. 458.
5   Jones and Roderick, p. 112.
6   Joseph Rowntree Foundation, Educational accountability in Wales (1995).
7   https://www.tes.com/article.aspx?storycode=84984
8   P. 198.
9   http://www.mercator-research.eu/fileadmin/mercator/dossiers_pdf/welsh_in_uk.pdf
10   http://researchdevelopment.academiwales.org.uk/uploads/attachments/9My7jExL7.pdf
11   In 1997 ACAC acquired another C (Cymwysterau/Qualifications) to become ACCAC.
12   Amser Egwyl, Issue 1, December 2000.
13   This and other quotes can be found in the Record of Proceedings.
14   http://www.walesonline.co.uk/news/wales-news/two-wales-most-respected-schools-2036117
15   http://www.walesonline.co.uk/news/wales-news/wikipedia-former-minister-jane-davidson-2495943
16   https://www.tes.com/article.aspx?storycode=6052504
17   See footnote 3.
18   Andrews, p. 40.
19   Andrews, p. 48.

2

The Grand Narrative

From *The Learning Country* to *Qualified for Life*

Paved with good intentions?

In 2014 the Organisation for Economic Cooperation and Development (OECD) published a damning report on the state of Welsh education. It provided a sharp critique and focussed remedies for a system that, by several indicators, was performing noticeably below the OECD average. Among them was the recommendation that 'the Welsh Government should define and implement a national education vision'.[1] The OECD clearly thought that such a vision was lacking at that time. It was also clear that without one, Wales would continue to languish. A national vision would help focus resources and give a clear indication of purpose.

However, the root of the problem was not the piecemeal reforms then under way in the wake of a string of poor results in the OECD's Programme for International Student Assessment (PISA) but rather the failure of an earlier vision which had not delivered. For almost the entire opening decade of devolution, the Welsh Government's vision and implementation for education had been determined by the overarching framework of *The Learning Country*.

In 2001 the then Welsh Assembly Government launched *The Learning Country: A Paving Document*, which claimed to be 'A Comprehensive Education and Lifelong Learning Programme to 2010 in Wales'. In her introduction, Jane Davidson, the recently appointed education minister, set out her vision and ambition: 'Wales should become internationally renowned as a Learning Country: a place which puts learners' interests first; offers wider access and opportunities for all; aspires to excellence across the board; and which will not settle for second best in making lifelong learning a reality'. She claimed that the document itself was the 'first comprehensive, strategic statement on education and lifelong learning in Wales'.[2]

With chapters on 'Comprehensive Education and Lifelong Learning in Wales' and 'Learning and Equality of Opportunity', it certainly had a different flavour to the policy agenda being pursued by New Labour in England. It also showed how the legacy of previous thinking on education in Wales, examined in Chapter 2, was now flowering in devolution.

The introductory chapter of *The Learning Country* noted that Wales had much to boast about, though the examples given were rather thin. In a reference to the restructure of funding arrangements for post-16 education, it was stated that 'Wales has led the field in a distinctive strategy towards school improvement – evidence-based; locally managed; and professionally valid'. In another statement that was to come back and haunt the document's authors as the decade progressed, it was claimed that 'Pupil attainment at both primary and secondary levels has improved faster than ever before, and by comparison with England too'. However, the document was candid that economic activity was unacceptably low in Wales, in part due to the poor level of qualifications and the number of disengaged youngsters. The synergy between the economy, education and society needed to be captured far more effectively: 'The plain fact is that training and education are equally and intimately related to successful community development, social inclusion, wealth creation and personal fulfilment'.[3]

In its second chapter, *The Learning Country* sought to lay 'Solid Foundations' which would give 'every child a flying start'. These rather cheesy slogans, of course, became the tags for the fully developed programmes that would emerge later in the decade. Already it was noted that more well qualified and trained practitioners would need to be secured, and that upgrading the system to ensure that over 75% of children aged three were at least in part time school settings would be costly. Provision for SEN (Special Educational Needs) children was also to be a priority. The document noted the patchy and varied provision across Wales and promised a more strategic approach to the integration of services.

The section on primary schools was more detailed. Estyn had recently reported on the sector and found that 94% of classes were satisfactory with 48% being classed as good or very good. Girls outperformed boys on the whole. Estyn noted that 14% of primary schools had fifty or less pupils compared with just 4% in England, while 33% of primary schools had less than 100 pupils compared with less than half of that (15%) in England. No comment was provided on these statistics. There was to be a consultation on the abolition of national tests for seven-year-olds, and the idea of a 'Foundation Phase' for children aged between 3 and 7 was floated. There was also to be a more strategic approach to raising the standards of literacy and numeracy. Finally, there was a concrete pledge to cut junior class sizes to thirty and primary class sizes to twenty-five by 2003. No rationale was given for this pledge, and no evidence cited as to the educational benefits it would provide.

The Learning Country noted the alleged dip in performance between exit from primary and entrance to secondary schools but did not probe the assumptions that lay behind the data. Instead it proposed a variety of measures to ensure a smoother transition, including requiring primary and secondary schools to form 'families or consortia', the introduction of a unique learner identifier number and, in rural areas, one leadership team.

In hindsight, the document's boasting about the funding given to schools was possibly one of the biggest hostages to fortune in the history of devolution. Average budgeted spending per pupil was £2,870, which the reader was told was above every region of England except London and the Metropolitan Authorities of the Midlands and the North West. It seemed as if Education Department officials were already trying out their smoke and mirrors toolkit in regard to funding. The chapter closed with a pledge to establish school councils.

With more than a nod towards the emerging Academy agenda in England, Chapter 3 stated that what Labour in Cardiff Bay wanted was 'a confident, characterful and comprehensive school system in Wales'. It would avoid unnecessary competition, being based rather on mutually beneficial collaboration. In this it echoed the alleged long tradition of Welsh educationalists. While the document noted 'serious problems of variation in performance and attainment between the best and least well performing schools and local education authorities', it was also keen to stress that 'investment in education alone is not the key determinant of successful outcomes'. Someone was starting to think seriously about justifying the underspend.[4]

In another nod towards the tightening agenda emerging in England, *The Learning Country* took a more liberal approach: 'We see secondary schools, in particular, progressively moving away from rigid timetables, and even classroom-based teaching, to very much more flexible modes of provision, tailored to the needs of the individual learner and supported by ever-strengthening distance learning and ICT'. A little later, advice was explicitly sought about proposed developments in England including the awarding of earned autonomy, deregulation of governors and options to secure school improvement.[5]

The most telling departure from the English agenda was in relation to the alleged plateauing of core subject attainment at Key Stage 3 and elsewhere. Whereas England was quickly developing and implementing national strategies to address deficiencies in the teaching of literacy and numeracy, *The Learning Country* stated that: 'we do not consider that a common or mandatory approach to literacy, numeracy, and standards in other subjects more generally is appropriate in Wales'. Instead the Welsh way, as ever, was to have a committee of the great and the good: 'We intend that a team of experienced practitioners should be brought together with colleagues from Estyn and the Qualifications, Curriculum and Assessment Authority for Wales (ACCAC) to develop suitable guidance for the different settings in Wales'.[6]

Pupils were to be offered 'a significant degree of subject choice and within an overall curriculum entitlement, strong vocational pathways complementing the academic ones'. They would also be able to mix the two strands, thereby achieving the longed-for 'parity of esteem'. To this end the qualifications framework was to be made more 'flexible and adaptable'. A newly floated Welsh Baccalaureate was to be pivotal in delivering this Holy Grail.[7]

In another telling departure from the English agenda, Wales-wide performance tables would be abandoned: 'Performance tables featuring information on individual schools were introduced at a time when there was relatively little information available to practitioners, or indeed to parents, about achievement. Ten years on the situation is very different. There is much more data available'. Moreover, *The Learning Country* made the bold claim that 'Parents are interested in the performance of the school to which their child is going, or is already placed. The publication of booklets featuring schools across the whole of Wales is of little relevance to them'. No evidence was produced to support this claim, and the fact that some parents might have made their judgment based on comparative evidence was simply not entertained.[8]

The gap between boys' and girls' performance was addressed in Chapter 4 which dealt with equality of opportunity, along with Black and Minority Ethnic issues and other matters around the equality agenda. Curiously, the Welsh language was also addressed in this section. Later on, ICT was proposed as a solution to many problems in a way that portrayed it as an almost universal panacea. (I have lost count of the number of government initiatives which think that improved IT will deliver vast improvements. The OECD is quite right when it said in September 2015 that 'too many false hopes' had been raised by such agendas.)[9]

Chapter 5 was largely devoted to practitioners. It promised, predictably, a 'Made in Wales' framework of continuous development for teachers which would be 'evidence-based, locally supported and capable of commanding international recognition'. There would be a National Headship Development Programme and a similar principalship qualification for FE. The newly established ELWa (a joint branding of the National Council for Education and Training and HEFCW) was tasked with raising standards among staff and governors in FE institutions. The form and content of Initial Teacher Training would be scrutinised, and particular concern paid to developing the links between CPD and the Communities First areas of noted deprivation.[10]

Chapter 6 was entitled 'Beyond Compulsory Education' and dealt largely with skills and training in the FE sector. The document noted that there was already a Modern Skills Diploma for Adults, and Modern Apprenticeships would be extended beyond the age of 25. The key priority would be 'Extending Entitlement' which sought to generate a synergy between providers in the sector. ELWa was to provide advice about the accreditation of informal learning and ACCAC to do the same for external qualifications.

The entitlement theme was similarly present in the following chapter on Higher Education, which opened with a subsection entitled 'Opening Doors'. While Welsh HE provision was no worse for disadvantaged groups than it was in England, it was certainly nowhere nearing matching that of Scotland and Northern Ireland. It was noted that 'there is no future in a parochial model for Welsh HE'. The sector needed to attract more research and development funding which was not helped by there being 'thirteen relatively small institutions'. However, *The Learning Country* did not want to pre-empt the findings of the Assembly's Education and Lifelong Learning Committee, which was by now undertaking an investigation into the sustainability of funding of the HE sector in Wales.

The final chapter set out a comprehensive list of outcomes by which the success of *The Learning Country* could be judged. It is worth quoting these at length, as any estimation of the vision will need to be assessed in the cold light of day by the available data. The document, in its own words, described 'a range of measures which aim at nothing less than transforming the life chances of people in Wales for the better. It is designed to enable Wales to vault the barriers to social progress and prosperity through lifelong learning'. The outcomes had a qualitative dimension, but the quantitative could provide a powerful expression of success:

- Level 2 Qualifications. The percentage of 15-year-olds achieving 5 GCSEs A* to C grades or equivalent to increase from 44 per cent in 1997, to 54 per cent by 2002; to 58 per cent by 2004; to 64 per cent by 2007; and over 75 per cent to finish compulsory education achieving at least 5 GCSE A* to C grades or equivalent by 2010.
- The percentage of 15-year-olds achieving 5 GCSEs A* to G grades or equivalent should be lifted from 80 per cent in 1997, to 91 per cent by 2002 and to 95 per cent … All to remain in education or go on to training in employment by 2010, and none to leave school unqualified.
- No schools having fewer than 25 per cent of 15-year-olds achieving at least 5 GCSE A* to C grades by 2002; none having less than 30 per cent by 2004; and none having less than 35 per cent by 2007 and none having less than 40 per cent by 2010.

- Reduction in absenteeism in secondary schools to below 8 per cent by 2004; below 7 per cent by 2007; and below 5 per cent by 2010.
- Local authorities should work with schools to ensure that 75 per cent of 'looked after children' should leave school with at least two GCSEs or equivalent by 2003; with at least a range of qualifications at Level 2 by 2007; and a range of qualifications at Levels 2 and 3, (and a minimum of 5 GCSEs or equivalent) by 2010.
- No infant classes with over 30 pupils (save for permitted statutory exceptions), by September 2001; cut junior classes to 30 or less pupils by September 2003; (and press ahead with a view to cutting all primary classes) to 25 pupils or less within the second term of the National Assembly.
- Local authorities to have made a significant investment in the repair, renewal and replacement of school buildings and all local authorities to have in place by 2003 asset management plans and programmes of capital investment in school to repair, renew and replace schools – so that by 2010 they are in good physical shape, properly maintained; and enable learners to make fully effective use of IT.[11]

Reception of *The Learning Country*

The Learning Country received an enthusiastic welcome from many in the Welsh education establishment. Jones and Roderick, authors of *A History of Education in Wales*, described it as a 'landmark document for those who hoped that the Welsh Assembly would not just nibble at the edges of educational policy-making but would also conjure up a wider vision of an education system to serve the Welsh nation'. It was 'a major strategic policy statement [that] signalled a radical departure from the English vision'. As well as listing some of its key proposals, Jones and Roderick discerned 'yet another level of ambition in the document, that of providing Wales with an education system based on different social principles, which amounts to a statement about the nature of Welsh society'. They praised Davidson's endorsement of comprehensive schools 'without cavil' and the rejection of the Academy schools getting under way in England. This they noted (in retrospect unfortunately) was due to the 'better performance of Welsh comprehensive schools than their English counterparts'. In gushing praise they claimed that the document was in itself 'a vindication, if such were needed, of the value of a National Assembly'.[12]

Other academic praise was forthcoming too. Professors Daugherty and Jones, leading lights in the world of Welsh education, wrote in the *Journal of Education* that '[n]ot since the end of the nineteenth century has there been a similarly significant publication', citing the Aberdare Report of 1881 and the subsequent Welsh Intermediate Education Act of 1889 as the proper comparisons for *The Learning Country*. They went on to say that the scope of *The Learning Country* was 'impressively wide and its emphases intriguingly distinctive'. Moreover the chapter headings themselves, on learning and equality, signified 'an underlying value system [...] quite different from the English mindset of "New Labour" in Millbank, the Department for Education and Skills, and 10 Downing Street'.[13]

How far this fundamental difference in mind-set would actually benefit the pupils of Wales we will examine later. The proposed Foundation Phase was singled out for special praise, though they noted that this was 'picking up and running with a policy direction that was already in place before 1999'. The difference, other than the increased pace of that direction of travel, would lie in the fact that enabling clauses in the 2002 Education Act would mean that Cardiff rather than Westminster would now have control over curriculum and assessment arrangements. Daugherty and Jones' Research Note was angling for more money to be spent on developing educational research, not an unfair ask given the Minister's repeated insistence on evidence-based policy. In conclusion they expressed their belief that '*The Learning Country* is not a blueprint but rather a series of position statements'. The unkind might have said it was really a wish list with no coherent plan for delivery. But we are jumping ahead of ourselves.

The unions too were fulsome in their praise of the document. The Association of Teachers and Lecturers, for instance, welcomed 'the radical step taken by the National Assembly' and described the document as 'a breath of fresh air from Wales'.[14] Most other unions welcomed the proposed direction of travel in similar vein, though the NASUWT worried about workload implications for teachers. *The Learning Country*, after all, espoused many of the causes that they had been fighting with successive governments, such as the abolition of SATs and better CPD.

The newly established General Teaching Council for Wales broadly welcomed the 'thrust' of the direction outlined in *The Learning Country*, and was particularly pleased to see the commitments to comprehensive education, improved access to CPD for teachers, ICT, and the abolition of SATs for seven-year-olds. Interestingly, it sounded a note of caution though, about the need for a clear strategy of implementation: 'the Council would urge the Assembly to recognise the need for a coherent approach when implementing these proposals. The problems identified in the document such as teacher workload, excessive bureaucracy and pupil behaviour, all impact on recruitment and retention in the profession. Isolated initiatives are unlikely to have much impact and the Council urges the Assembly to develop and implement coordinated strategies to deal with these issues'. The problem of delivery was surfacing. The GTCW was also less warm than many others about the proposed Foundation Phase. In a prescient comment it noted: 'there is a need to ensure that any curriculum changes for pupils aged 3–5 years do not undermine the existing Key Stage 1 programmes of study which provide a firm foundation for future development'.[15]

Analysis of *The Learning Country*

Government policy is a good example of the axiom that hindsight is a wonderful thing. Looking down across the years, realising that certain claims, expectations and courses of action were the wrong ones now seems blindingly obvious. It is therefore important to see *The Learning Country* in context and to note its major strengths before we proceed to analyse some of its weaknesses. The almost universal approval for the document is a sign that things seemed different then. As we have noted above, while certain aspects of *The Learning Country* might have been more cautiously welcomed than others, the overall response was one of acclaim.

The Learning Country obviously provided a coherent vision for education in Wales which replaced the rather fractured approach of previous years. It was also a genuine attempt to make policy fit for Wales rather than make Wales fit a policy. Education, along with Health, was the big area where devolution could make a real difference, and the then Welsh Assembly Government was right to try to shape a vision for education in its opening decade. Much of the content of *The Learning Country* was a distillation of previous, more piecemeal, policy formation. The proposals for a Foundation Phase, for instance, did not spring newly formed but were rather a reflection of the considered opinions of practitioners in the field the world over. Similarly, the move to abolish SATs for seven-year-olds was something that the unions and others had been lobbying for over several years. The scope of *The Learning Country* was also commendable. If not to the grave, it certainly plotted a course for education from the cradle to adulthood. It also realised the importance of trying to join up services around the child.

The major weaknesses of *The Learning Country* are now clear to see. Perhaps the most disastrous was its incorrect analysis of the state of the Welsh education system. As Leighton Andrews, Minister for Education between 2009 and 2013, was later to put it succinctly, this was in reality not a good system aiming to be excellent but a fair system hoping to be good. In fairness, at the time the wealth of data, especially about international comparisons, was simply not available and all systems were to some extent operating in the dark. The available data from GCSE and A-level results also seemed to point to a system that was marginally better than that prevailing in England.

However, Jane Davidson's hubris did create a climate in which the rhetoric of 'world-leading' became the norm. Any attempt to inject any reality into any discussion about any aspect of the Welsh Government's performance was quickly slapped down by the First Minister who accused anyone who highlighted concerns as 'talking Wales down'.

Another major failure was, as the GTCW noted, the lack of a coherent and detailed plan for implementation. It certainly was *not* a blueprint. In retrospect the mechanisms for delivery, which were being finely honed in England under Michael Barber and others, were simply assumed to be fit for purpose in Wales. They were not. As we shall see time and time again, the civil service simply failed to ensure proper deliver of key elements of government policy. Blair and others in the New Labour camp were not afraid to bypass the civil service when necessary. Only Leighton Andrews was to show the same courage in Wales. All other ministers have been too quick to accept the briefings and excuses of their officials.

A major lacuna of the document was its weakness in regard to CPD for school staff. There were some wishes but little substance. Thus the key driver for school improvement was all but ignored. While England was embarking on a major upskilling process, Wales was doing little by comparison. The ambitious targets too became something of an albatross as the years progressed.

The Learning Country 2: delivering the promise

As *The Learning Country* was envisaged as a ten-year process, on 7th April 2006, just over a year before the first PISA results for Wales, the then Welsh Assembly Government issued its midpoint consultation. Jane Davidson noted in her Foreword, 'the halfway point on this journey is a good time to take stock'. She claimed that there had been 'considerable progress' in turning Wales into 'The Learning Country'. She also noted 'further major developments in devolved government in Wales. In April 2006 ACCAC, ELWa, the Wales Youth Agency and Dysg will merge with the current Department for Training and Education, creating a new Department of Lifelong Learning and Skills'.[16] Such deck chair shuffling, as we shall see later, was to have severe consequences for the children of Wales.

The document itself boasted that 'we have achieved an enormous amount'. In its opening chapter it listed the successes to date: Class sizes had been reduced in infant and primary schools; statutory national testing arrangements for pupils aged 7, 11 and 14 had been abolished in 2000, 2004 and 2005 respectively; funding for school buildings had increased; an attendance action plan had been published; the Welsh Baccalaureate was being piloted in thirty-one schools across Wales; teachers had been supported at the start of their career by the introduction of a statutory induction period and Early Professional Development programme; while heads would benefit from the National Headship Programme introduced in 2001; in HE, Wales outperformed the rest of the UK in terms of participating students from low-participation neighbourhoods.

To bolster the claim that 'an enormous amount' had been achieved, the document cited the analysis of Estyn's Chief Inspector of the time, Susan Lewis, who had:

> pointed in recent annual reports to substantial improvements in the following areas: standards achieved by children under five have improved year on year; standards achieved by pupils with special educational needs are now much higher than they were in 1999; there has been a big improvement in the standards that pupils are achieving in primary and secondary schools over the same period; test results have greatly improved in Key Stages 2 and 3; in further education institutions, more students now finish their courses and gain qualifications than did six years ago ... the quality of teaching in schools has improved significantly.[17]

Susan Lewis' successor was to be far less sanguine. But even at this stage it is strange that no one in Estyn or the Welsh Assembly Government seems to have probed the exact causality between the 'greatly improved' test results in Key Stage 2 and 3 and the abandonment of the statutory testing regime. These 'greatly improved' test results were to prove decisive to a future minister all but re-inventing the SATs regime.

The Learning Country 2: Delivering the Promise was candid enough to admit that 'major challenges' still remained. Among others the following concerns were identified:

> Investment to bring all school buildings to a fit standard needs to continue; Secondary schools need to raise standards of attainment at Key Stage 3; The curriculum for 7 to 14-year-olds must be more learner centred and skills focussed so that it builds on the Foundation Phase and links effectively with the 14-19 Learning Pathways programme; More must be done to sustain the rate of improvement in the number of 15-year-olds gaining 5 GCSE grades A*–C and 5*A–G or equivalent; The number of young people who leave school without any qualifications needs to be reduced; We must address the relative underachievement of boys compared to girls.[18]

It appeared as if the magic wand of devolution would require some more rigorous waving if the vision of the entire *Learning Country* project was to become a reality. That magic was to be provided by two developments noted in the opening chapter of the document. Firstly, the White Paper *Better Governance for Wales* would significantly enhance the Assembly's powers over primary legislation with resultant 'greater freedom to take forward our distinctive policy agendas'. Secondly, as alluded to in the Ministerial Foreword to *The Learning Country 2*, the shuffling of chairs would bring a far more efficient Education Department. Ominously, it was claimed that 'The machinery for bringing practical action to bear upon the challenges ahead, and on getting the most from the related national and international opportunities, lies in the new Department for Education, Lifelong Learning and Skills itself. Merging the existing Department for Education and Training with ELWa, ACCAC, the Wales Youth Agency and Dysg will create an organisation with a capacity greater than the sum of its parts'.[19] If only it had proved so simple.

Subsequent chapters elaborated on efforts under way to deliver the vision. The second chapter was entitled 'Empowering Children, Young People, and Adults' and spoke about the promotion of education in the broadest terms and across the broadest age range. The themes were continued in Chapter 3 which was entitled 'Sound Foundations – Early Years and Inclusion'. The Flying Start initiative was mentioned in passing and the Foundation Phase in more detail. The Foundation Phase was intended to 'excite' learning from the earliest school age. Already, the document noted, 'Foundation Phase Pilots are running in forty-one settings or schools' with a roll-out planned for all over the following three years, which would be completed by the end of the 2010/11 school year. It was noted that 'in order to achieve this roll-out and deliver the Foundation Phase to the quality levels that will be required, it is essential that we have in place the appropriate workforce – teachers, teaching assistants and other professionals. This will require new training routes to be in place and the professional development of existing staff.' A workforce development plan was spoken about, which would ensure that the required number of bilingual practitioners would be forthcoming.[20]

As we will be examining the Foundation Phase in greater depth in the next chapter, the only comment worth making now is that yet again the difficulty of implementing such a programme was severely underestimated.

Chapter 4 restated the Assembly Government's longstanding commitment to comprehensive education – all the more necessary, as the Academy experiment was by now really getting under way across the border. Secondary schools were to provide 'a broad and stimulating curriculum' and have 'methods of assessment designed to recognise a wider range of achievement'.[21]

There was a realisation of the link between attainment and deprivation when the document promised 'a more forensic approach to tackling poverty of educational opportunity and low educational outcomes.' This would be addressed, as the Assembly Government would 'enhance the ability of local authorities and others to support these schools, involving any local Communities First Partnerships in discussions'. There would be a focus on 'schools where fewer than 25% of pupils achieve 5 A*–C GCSEs or equivalent; on those schools where the level of pupil attainment (measured by 5 A*–G GCSEs or equivalent) is low compared to schools in similar circumstances; and on those just above this level which are judged to be underperforming and could do better'.[22]

A curriculum review had been undertaken by Professor Richard Daugherty of Aberystwyth University in 2004. His specific brief had been to review the curriculum in regard to assessment arrangements. This review complemented one that the soon to be axed ACCAC had undertaken. *The Learning Country 2* noted that the Minister had wasted no time in putting into practice some of the recommendations of that review: 'In the light of the Daugherty and ACCAC reviews, we have already announced a series of changes during the next four years which will replace the current testing regime with a system which is more geared to the pupil and puts teacher assessment at its heart'. It was hoped that 'The new school curriculum and assessment arrangements will promote an approach that is more learner centred and skills focussed so that it builds on the Foundation Phase and links effectively with the 14–19 Learning Pathways programme'.[23]

As we shall see when we look at assessment in Chapter 4 and accountability in Chapter 6 of this book, the problem was that only part of Daugherty's review had been put into effect. A key element, rigorous moderation, was overlooked – with devastating effect.

In Section 4.18 of *The Learning Country 2* the rash promise was made that 'The Assembly Government is committed to providing resources to enable all school buildings to be brought up to a standard of fitness for delivery of the National Curriculum by 2010'. Writing five years later it is quite clear that this target has been missed by a mile. Children in Wales still have to endure substandard buildings and the learning environment is generally far poorer than across the border.

Chapter 4 ended with some 'Forward Outcome Indicators':

- Free breakfast initiative rolled out to all primary schools that want it by 2007.
- All schools to be fit for purpose by 2010.
- Junior class sizes to be maintained at thirty or less.
- No secondary schools to have fewer than 35% of 15-year-olds

achieving 5 GCSE A*–C or equivalent by 2007 and none to have less than 40% in 2010.

Chapter 5, entitled *14–19 Learning Pathways and Beyond*, opened with some similar ambitious targeting. By 2015, 95% of Welsh youngsters would be ready for high-skilled employment and/or higher education by the age of 25. This would be achieved by Individual Learning Pathways, which would provide bespoke support for all young people. There was a need for richer curriculum options, the document noted, and the stale old chestnut about parity of esteem between vocational and academic routes was trotted out. Higher standards of literacy and numeracy were mentioned in passing but given little other importance. Learning Coaches would be introduced, a new group of professionals who would help young people 'understand and develop their study skills and learning styles, and make choices which reflect their aptitudes and potential'.[24] The unique Welsh Baccalaureate was also to be piloted and then rolled out to all post-16 providers in 2007.

The chapter concluded with the following Forward Outcome Indicators:

- The percentage of 15-year-olds achieving 5 GCSE A*–C or equivalent to reach at least 55% by 2007 and approaching 60% by 2010.
- The percentage of 15-year-olds achieving 5 A*–G or equivalent to reach around 87% by 2007 and approaching 90% in 2010.
- By 2010, no pupil to leave school without a recognised qualification.
- Attendance in secondary schools to be at least 92% by 2007, and at least 93% by 2010.

As is now depressingly obvious, the levers for achieving these high ambitions were not clearly identified. It is now a truism that 'no education system can exceed the quality of its teachers', but the following chapter, entitled 'Supporting Practitioners', was notably thin, at barely just over two pages. The need to develop the skills and capacity of staff was recognised but not addressed. The document was clear that 'more needs to be invested in frontline services. We need to reconfigure training and development for practitioners to meet the needs of the twenty-first century' but beyond a few platitudes about 'sharing experience and best practice' nothing else was nailed down. The National Headship Development Programme was to be 'refreshed'; the GTCW charged with 'exploring' the concept of Chartered Teacher status, and the Basic Skills Strategy *Words Talk, Numbers Count* would strengthen teaching in literacy and numeracy.

Shuffling the chairs

Perhaps the most peculiar aspect of *The Learning Country 2* was Annex 1, which dealt with the creation of the new Department for Education, Lifelong Learning and Skills. In true Fabian fashion, progress was to be secured by reshuffling the bureaucracy.

There were 'New Opportunities' in all this: 'Merging ELWa, ACCAC, the Wales Youth Agency and Dysg with the Assembly Government creates a strong department with greater capacity and reach to deliver results for learners, employers and communities. Part of this involves delivering on the principles of "Making the Connections". The intention is to secure real performance gains across the full range of our activities and to generate savings for reinvestment at the front line for learners. We will use the resources available to deliver more, and better'.[25]

Fine words but no one seems to have remotely considered how these different organisations, with different cultures and different remits, would be blended into one. A sizeable portion of the new mix was to be provided by the ill-fated ELWa which by this stage was already battered, bruised and discredited in the eyes of many stakeholders. More tellingly, the danger of assuming responsibility for the regulation of exams, which the absorption of ACCAC represented, was not properly thought through at all. A few years later the folly of subsuming the regulatory role into government was laid bare before the whole of the UK, as we shall see in Chapter 5 of this book.

The Mission of the new department was to 'drive [a favourite Davidson word] forward improvements in children's services, education and training provision to deliver better outcomes for learners, business and employers'. Among some of the new department's touchy-feely values was to be 'creative, innovative, and respected as an agent of progressive change; effective in delivery and determinedly cross-cutting and cooperative in behaviours externally and internally; actively communicative and outward facing for individuals (including children and young people), business, and communities'.[26] The reality has always felt somewhat different.

Progress would be benchmarked through 'effective engagement with stakeholders – especially children and young people – and the use of feedback surveys; peer review visits to and from other education departments worldwide; joint work with the Organisation for Economic Cooperation and Development (OECD) on comparative performance of education and training departments worldwide'. The last two were badly needed but rarely, if ever, done.

As well as a Ministerial Advisory Group, Stakeholder Groups were to be set up, covering Early Years Education and Care, Additional Needs, 7–14 Schools Standards and Improvement, Skills and Lifelong Learning, 14–19

Education and Training, Higher Education, Children and Young People's Participation, and Curriculum and Qualifications.

A section on Performance Measures set some of the ways in which the new department would measure the productivity and effectiveness of its work. It moved with alacrity to distance itself from a results-based methodology. While it would still use 'established indicators (including qualification attainment levels)', it would 'seek to extend the range of indicators used to embrace wider vocational qualifications and to value the other achievements of learners that are harder to measure. We want to be able to capture a broader range of achievement not solely related to qualifications – for instance, the involvement of young people in community work or out of hours' study activity'.[27]

In a sleight of hand that crudely tried to gloss over the slippage in ambition, it was claimed that 'we have reviewed and rationalised the targets published in *The Learning Country* – reducing the number of targets to manageable proportions with the interests of practitioners in mind'.[28]

The lack of rigour was further emphasised when it was claimed that targets would be treated primarily as 'forward progress indicators, describing a broad direction of travel. We recognise that not all important educational outcomes can be reduced to simple quantitative measures. Performance measures have to be interpreted sensitively. For example, we do not expect that every school will perform at the average level captured by the indicators for Wales as a whole. We stand against crude "naming and shaming" for individual schools and colleges or any other institutional provider'. It seemed as if provider capture and supply side solutions were here to stay. No amount of 'challenging and supporting local authorities and institutions over progressively improving provision for children, and the attainments and qualifications of learners' would make the most entrenched and recalcitrant up their game.

The Learning Country: vision into action

Following hot on the heels of the consultation document, *Delivering the Promise*, came the final chapter in the Learning Country saga. *The Learning Country: Vision into Action* was published in November 2006.[29] This was a glossy document packed full of edifying pictures of children, young people and adults in learning situations. It followed the outline of *Delivering the Promise* with each chapter devoting space to what research revealed, what the Welsh Assembly Government was doing, with objectives and outcomes described. The chapters included ones on 'Strong Foundations – early years and inclusion, Schools and Learning, 14–19 Pathways, Supporting Practitioners, Beyond Compulsory Learning, the Future of Higher Education, and Quality Provision'. There was little new except for the pictures. Davidson, in a characteristic piece of hubris, had both a Foreword and Endword.

In the foreword we were introduced to 'Megan', a child who would now live through the brave new world of *The Learning Country*. She would benefit from Flying Start, the Foundation Phase and free breakfasts. Her primary school curriculum would offer 'a rich range of opportunities and experiences'. She would be assessed by teachers who would 'use that assessment to inform Megan's learning'. We were assured that her 'education will take place in buildings which have been extensively refurbished or even replaced'. She would have to make important choices at age fourteen of high quality courses that 'will take her either along a traditional route to GCSEs and A-levels, or a new vocational learning route that will be well established'. The reader can make their own judgment about Megan's actual experience to date, but what follows will highlight some of the issues that affected Megan since then.

The Endword, printed beneath a particularly cloying photo of Jane Davidson and some children, contained some prophetic words: 'The Assembly Government is a key contributor to the international debate on education reform. Wales is acknowledged on the world stage and our achievements are applauded by other countries.' That November saw the entry of Wales into the world of PISA. There would certainly be acknowledgement, but not of the sort Davidson hoped.

Aftermath

There was no formal evaluation of *The Learning Country*. The following table indicates the actual results against those proposed in *The Learning Country* and *The Learning Country 2*. The revision of the targets in the latter makes the original ones look even more absurd.

Target	TLC 1	TLC 2	Actual in 2010
5 GCSE A* to C grades or equivalent	75%	60%	63.8%
5 GCSEs A* to G grades or equivalent	95%	90%	89.7%[30]
Leaving unqualified	0%	0%	1%[31]
NEET (Not in Education, Employment or Training)	0%	7%	11%[32]
Secondary Absenteeism	Below 5%	Below 7%	8.6%[33]

Figure 1: The Learning Country – Targets and Outcomes

The targets for 'no secondary school to have fewer than 35% of 15-year-olds achieving 5 GCSE A*–C by 2007 and none to have less than 40% in 2010' ring particularly hollow in 2016 as a cursory search of the 'red' category institutions on the Welsh Government's 'My Local School' website will reveal.[34]

Some considerable progress had been made. It is virtually unheard of now for a child to leave compulsory education without any qualifications whatsoever. Also to be noted with approval was the increase in youngsters leaving with 5 GCSE A* to C grades, which had risen from 49.1% to 63.8% between 2000 and 2010.[35] These should not be dismissed. But as even better improvement had been seen in England during this time it would be absurd to claim that Wales' improved success rate stemmed from *The Learning Country* alone. Absenteeism had also seen notable improvement and although the NEET target had been missed it had been quite an achievement to get it to just 11%. In other areas the targets were still far from being met ten years on, even in their revised forms. In a rare show of realism – or should it be despair – the target for Looked After Children, which stood at two GCSEs or equivalents by 2003 and 75% achieving five GCSEs by 2010 in the original *Learning Country* document was dropped altogether in 2007 as part of a reduction in the number of targets 'to manageable proportions'. The Wales Audit Office commented unfavourably on the difference between this approach and that over the border in England where revised targets were incorporated into Public Service Agreements that each local authority was required to develop plans to support achieving.[36]

Teaching makes a difference

Davidson relinquished the education brief in 2007 convinced, if rumours are to be believed, that there was by then little more to be achieved. She was replaced as Education Minister in 2007 by the future First Minister, Carwyn Jones, who held the brief for a few weeks until the formation of a Labour-Plaid Cymru coalition government. Jones was followed by another of Rhodri Morgan's supporters, Jane Hutt. As Hutt had been a particularly ineffective Health Minister earlier in her career, handing her another big portfolio was questionable. As the die had been cast in terms of *The Learning Country* agenda, there were few big policy announcements. Hutt, however, was more open to advice than her predecessor and was genuinely consensual in her approach. As we shall see in the next chapter, she was prepared to be convinced that the flagship Foundation Phase was being underfunded and to her eternal credit persuaded her cabinet colleagues to vote it more money.

After Carwyn Jones won the Labour leadership election in 2009, he set about reshuffling the cabinet he had inherited. Davidson's pleasant but ineffectual successor was replaced by Leighton Andrews, who had retaken the Rhondda for Labour in 2003. Andrews had made no bones about his desire to gain the Education portfolio and many saw his appointment as a reward for masterminding Carwyn's successful leadership bid. Initially, little seemed to change, though insiders spoke of a much tougher line with civil servants and a far more questioning attitude of previous policy. But in quiet he was thinking, consulting and formulating an entirely new approach. Whether it was simply a metaphor or, knowing Andrews, an actual occurrence, it was said that the new minister had thrown *The Learning Country* into the waste-paper bin. Reflecting on his time as Minister I later wrote that:

> From the start it was clear that Leighton was going to be different to his predecessors. Gone were the mumsy muddle of Jane Hutt and the patrician hauteur of Jane Davidson. Instead we were presented with a politician who knew his own mind. He had already done a lot of background research and had his own views about the state of Welsh education. And they weren't very complimentary.
>
> He simply didn't buy the 'Wales is best' line, nor the civil service's Frank Spencer mantra of 'every day in every way it's getting better and better'. He had done some of the statistical analysis and he knew that we were lagging behind. One of his first significant acts was to summon the arch-heretic Professor David Reynolds, who had been a voice crying in the wilderness for some time that all was far from well in the educational world of Wales.[37]

Others too were summoned for their views. I was quite surprised to be one of them and I remember our first meeting well. After breaking the ice we had the freest and frankest exchange that I've ever had with a governing politician. When pressed on the Education Department itself, and urged to 'tell me what you really think', I described it as 'dysfunctional'. I knew that things were going to be different. How different, would be revealed in his first big public statement, delivered in February 2011, when he would publicly label the entire system dysfunctional.

Entitled 'Teaching Makes a Difference', this seminal lecture was delivered in the rather faded grandeur of the Reardon Smith Theatre of the National Museum of Wales. A few weeks previously I had been asked in a meeting I was having having with Andrews and Chris Tweedale, the then director of the schools side of the department, if I would chair the speech. I was both surprised and flattered. My only condition being that I could see a copy of the speech the night before. When I read it I knew what was to come would change the face of Welsh education for ever.

There was a very good turnout of the great and the good of the Welsh education scene: directors of education, CEOs of various quangos, senior civil servants, the media and many others. A few eyebrows were raised as I appeared on the stage with Andrews.

The speech was striking, not just in content but in tone and delivery. Commenting afterwards I said:

> Within months of taking office he set out his stall in a lecture 'Teaching Makes a Difference' ... It was a *tour de force*. The great and the good of Welsh education were gathered and our collective responsibility exposed. PISA showed that we were underperforming and, by extension, failing to give our children the requisite skills for life.
>
> We were lagging behind comparative regions in England in terms of GCSEs. Too many of our youngsters were becoming NEET (Not in Employment, Education or Training). There was far too much inexplicable variation between schools and local authorities. We had developed an overly cosy consensus in which we kidded ourselves that we were a good system. The structure of our education service delivery was far from optimal. And so it went on. The analysis was incontrovertible. Only the head-bangers denied it. The atmosphere was akin to the headteacher telling the sixth form that he was disappointed in their conduct. We left rather sheepishly, realising that we had all played a part in what was labelled 'systemic failure'.
>
> From the lecture emerged twenty points that were to focus the rest of Leighton's time as Minister. There was to be a relentless focus on standards, above all on literacy, numeracy, and narrowing the gap.
>
> One cynic commented that the Ministerial programme boiled down to the aphorism: 'Ditch the Davidson legacy'. Whatever the truth of that, in the words of Professor David Egan, Leighton really did 'make us wake up and smell the coffee'.[38]

The speech contained twenty points that would drive the process of reform over the subsequent two years. The points were concrete proposals and demands, rather than the weaving of some grand narrative as in *The Learning Country*. There was no glossy brochure with cuddly pictures of the minister talking to children to accompany it. Andrews was quite clear that the stakes could not be higher: 'If we believe in the comprehensive model in Wales, then we have to make sure that it delivers for all our children. The evidence of PISA is that it is not. Performance has fallen back.'[39]

He then went on to spell out why it was that PISA mattered both to the education system, but also to Wales as a whole. The evidence of Wales' underperformance was backed up by other indicators such as GCSE and A-level results and more qualitative evidence from employers. Andrews proceeded to outline what was generally thought necessary to drive up performance. Overall there had been system-wide failure. He was not slow to lay blame at the door of what he derided as 'learner choice'.

Equally to blame was the cosy consensus which arose from Wales being 'the land of the pulled punch'. There was to be an end for the search for alibis, whether in terms of social deprivation or government spending, which attempted to get the system off the hook. Compounding all this was the major dysfunction of the Education Department and the fragmentation of local government in twenty-two entitles that were mostly too small to be operationally effective. Commenting obliquely on the abolition of SATs, one of Davidson's much trumpeted reforms, her successor was damning: 'Abandoning SATs was not meant to be a signal for anything goes'. He bemoaned the lack of effective accountability that meant that schools could drift for years before anyone would make any effective intervention.

The Twenty-point Plan

He then outlined what would be done to rectify the situation, in his famous twenty-point plan:

1. Performance will be our driver. We have reorganised our own department to ensure a clearer focus on educational performance and outcomes [...] we will be creating a Standards Unit to lead performance and provide challenge on a national basis.
2. [...] no new initiatives will be approved unless they add value to our demand for higher performance.
3. The Foundation Phase ... will not be allowed to lead to a reduction in literacy.
4. As part of our National Literacy Plan, we will introduce a national reading test which will be consistent across Wales.
5. By the 2012-13 academic year, we will have developed similar plans for numeracy.
6. We will expect all local authorities to ensure that Key Stage 2 teacher assessments are robust and consistent with the nationally defined standards, especially in respect of literacy.
7. We will look to integrate PISA assessments into school assessment at 15. [...]

8. We will ensure that all teachers and headteachers have appropriate levels of literacy and numeracy as part of their professional accreditation.

9. I have asked officials to examine whether we can revise initial teacher training so that it becomes a two-year Masters course, with more classroom practice. [...]. There will be a statutory requirement on all qualifying teachers to be trained in literacy and numeracy. All new ITT entrants will have been required to pass literacy and numeracy skills tests on entry and exit.

10. We will introduce a national system for the grading of schools, which will be operated by all local authorities/consortia.

11. Estyn's new Common Inspection Framework is beginning to bite. Where schools are found by Estyn to be failing, and I regard the situation as irredeemable, I will close them.

12. In the Education Measure [before the Assembly was granted law-making powers its Acts were 'Measures'], we are taking powers to allow local authorities to federate boards of governors of schools.

13. Also in the Education Measure, we are introducing statutory training for governors and effective clerking.

14. Use of data is critical to performance. From next year, no school will pass an Estyn inspection unless it can demonstrate that its governing body has discussed the family of schools data.

15. We will change the performance management provisions for headteacher performance management and teacher performance management to enable closer monitoring of their approach to raising standards, engaging local authorities and consortia in this.

16. We will review teacher induction, alongside our review of the GTCW, following the Framework powers we expect to receive as a result of UK legislation.

17. CPD will in future be focussed on system-wide needs, including literacy and numeracy, linked to the three priorities of the School Effectiveness Framework, and to the application of the Skills Framework.

18. We will produce Statutory Guidance for school improvement, which sets out the best practice currently available in Wales and elsewhere, which we will expect schools to implement through the SEF.

19. We will expect local authorities to participate in consortia arrangements, including shared consortium services, or suffer financial penalties, including the withdrawal of Better Schools Funding.

20. If there is poor behaviour in the classroom, children cannot learn. [...] I feel progress on our Behaving and Attending Action Plan is not going at the pace I want to see. It is now time to revitalise and refocus activity in this area ... I expect zero tolerance of truancy.

Some of the changes were more controversial than others, many were a systematic unpicking of the Davidson legacy. Despite Andrews' linguistic contortions no one seriously believed that the proposed school grading system, which would soon become the notorious School Banding, was anything other than a partial reintroduction of the League Tables, abolished in 2001. Or that the proposed national literacy and numeracy tests were not the reinstatement of some sort of the SATs abolished with such trumpeting from 2003 onwards. What Andrews thought of the teacher assessment regime was clear from Point 6, which promised far more robust moderation – the very point lost sight of when the SATs had been abolished. The promised National Literacy and Numeracy plans were the protégés of Tweedale, then the Director of the school side in the department. They were rehashes of what had been put into place in England a decade before. Davidson had refused to do the same in Wales during her time in office, as we saw in the analysis of *The Learning Country* outlined above.

But there were other more subtle clues that the whole Learning Country project and agenda was over and done with and had been booted into the dustbin of history. The first point of the speech, which focussed on performance, was notably at odds with the vision espoused in *The Learning Country* where, as we have seen, actual outcomes were never paid the attention they deserved. The standards agenda had hardly been present up till now. Andrews' proposed reorganisation of the department was itself an attempt to sort out the confusion and mistrust that had occurred from the less than optimal incorporation of the ill-fated ELWa and ACCAC into the Education Department. The silos were as strong as ever, it seemed. The strictures on the Foundation Phase not leading to a reduction in literacy was in response to Estyn's concern that it was doing just that. If the Foundation Phase was *the* flagship policy of the first three Welsh Governments (the thing that Rhodri Morgan said he was most proud of) then this new minister was making a clear attack on that legacy. Even the last point about behaviour, whilst acknowledging that a good plan was in place, betrayed the minister's frustration with the pace of reform.

It would be facile to suggest that this abrupt about-turn in government policy was simply the desire of a new minister to make his mark. It was absurd to suggest, that Leighton Andrews was simply out of the same mould as Michael Gove, the then Secretary of State in England, who was causing uproar with his proposed reforms. It was far more serious than that. Andrews had, in Egan's words, 'smelt the coffee'. He was clear that he had not inherited the Garden of Eden from Davidson, but something more like Jurassic Park. His driver was not the desire to throw his weight around but rather the realisation that the current system was failing the children of Wales. Little Megan of *The Learning Country* fame was not getting the best start in life, and she and her fellow pupils were not being helped as they should be by the educational establishment. The focus on standards was not a political whim so much as a moral conviction.

Over the next few months the Education Department and local authorities grappled to make the twenty points into a workable programme of reform. A School Standards Unit was established, National Literacy and Numeracy Frameworks developed and imposed, and School Banding introduced. These are investigated in the following chapters, but the point to note here is the pace and urgency with which these reforms took place. For those who were used to a department that at best seemed like a mighty tortoise, the gazelle-like speed of the changes were quite breathtaking.

These reforms were set out in the *Improving Schools* plan issued by the department in October 2012.[40] Unlike *The Learning Country* documents, this was short on glossy photos but replete with hard targets. The Ministerial Foreword was blunt: 'Progress has been made in improving examination results at GCSE and A-level and ensuring fewer young people leave school without a qualification, but there is still more to do to create an education system that is at least good for all learners'. This latter point chimed with the claim that the education system in Wales wasn't a good one aiming for excellence but rather a fair one aiming to be good. Andrews reiterated his lecture theme: 'The Programme for International Student Assessment (PISA) in 2009 was a wake-up call to an education system in Wales that had become complacent … It was time to face up to the harsh truth: the education system in Wales needed reforming'. Andrews claimed that the 'implementation of some of the reforms is well underway and having an impact. For others, further policy development or legislative work is necessary'. The School Improvement plan provided the 'details the "how" and "when" of implementing the reforms… Setting this course will give clarity, provide an overview of all the reforms and set clear expectations'.[41]

The introduction set the scene for improvement. Section 1 focussed on learning and teaching. Section 2 addressed school leadership. Section 3 set out how the system would provide support and challenge to schools, and Section 4 clarified the roles and responsibilities of those concerned. Detailed timelines were set for implementation.

The plan, like the speech, contained one major hostage to fortune, which was to come back to haunt Andrews and his successors again and again. Andrews had left his audience in no doubt that day about the importance of PISA in judging the performance of an education system. His ambition in that regard was 'overvaulting' on the scale of Macbeth's. He stated that 'we will create some clear targets. We should aim to be in the top twenty of school systems measured in the PISA scores in 2015. In other words, the PISA scores after next. But we will be aiming for improvements in 2012 over the 2009 results'. In the event the PISA scores of 2012 showed further regression, but the 'top twenty' aspiration was to become the focus of particular ridicule. In private his advisors (not the civil servants) had urged him to be nuanced and at least had managed to change his mind about aiming to be in the top 20%, which would have put Wales in the top thirteen countries in the world. As it was, the 'top twenty' was to be one of those political albatrosses that politicians fashion for themselves.[42]

Qualified for Life

As befits one of Wales' most colourful politicians, Andrews' career as Education Minister came unexpectedly and spectacularly to an end in 2013. The previous chapter has sketched the issues that ensured his downfall. His replacement was Huw Lewis AM, who, after a very brief stint as a teacher, had spent his entire career as a Labour Party apparatchik.

One of the first problems the new regime had to deal with was the devastating report by the OECD on the state of the Welsh Education System, in 2014. In it, the OECD lamented that Wales lacked a vision for education, as noted at the beginning of this chapter.[43] It's easy to see how such a conclusion could have been drawn given the myriad of initiatives and programmes that abounded. What is more puzzling is that the OECD report made no mention of *The Learning Country* suite.

Stung into action, the Department for Education and Skills quickly cobbled together a document that purported to give a clear vision for education for Wales.

The best things that could be said for the resultant *Qualified for Life: An Education Improvement Plan* was that it was very short and contained no new material.[44] In his Foreword the new minister admitted that 'excellence is not widespread, nor is practice consistently good ... *Qualified for Life* is the Welsh Government's plan for ensuring that all learners benefit from excellent teaching and learning'. He reaffirmed the three priorities that Andrews had set out at the start of his tenure: 'Strengthening literacy and numeracy and breaking the link between disadvantage and educational attainment remain our priorities'. After enumerating some of the successes since 2012, though curiously none that might have stemmed from *The Learning Country*, he went on to warn that 'The PISA results in 2013 are a stark reminder, however, that we cannot be complacent, and there is still some way to go to ensure that our reforms impact on outcomes for our learners. So *Qualified for Life* sets out our reform programme to 2020'. As an obvious response to the damning criticism levelled by the OECD he claimed that: '*Qualified for Life* sets out our vision that learners in Wales will enjoy teaching and learning that inspires them to succeed, in an education community that works cooperatively and aspires to be great, where the potential of every child and young person is actively developed'.[45] The fundamental opposition to market-driven, demand-led reform was clear.

Lewis was less sanguine and very articulate in telling union colleagues in one of his first meetings, that unless we showed that comprehensive education worked at least as well as the models being developed in England, we would not be able to 'withstand the winds that would blow in favour of more radical reforms'.

The document was rather dull, even the glossy format, with its corny pictures and silly emoticons could not enliven it. There were six short sections, which rehashed much of the analysis of Andrews and his plan of action. These were entitled: The Vision; Improving Education the Welsh Way; A Better Wales; The Improvement Challenge; Our Strategic Objectives and Commitment for Action; and Realising the Benefits.

The Vision was iterated as: 'Learners in Wales will enjoy teaching and learning that inspires them to succeed, in an education community that works cooperatively and aspires to be great, where the potential of every child and young person is actively developed'. It set out clearly the aim of the education system and four key objectives. The aim was uncontroversial: 'Every child and young person to benefit from excellent teaching and learning'. The objectives:

- An excellent professional workforce with strong pedagogy based on an understanding of what works.
- A curriculum which is engaging and attractive to children and young people and which develops within them an independent ability to apply knowledge and skills.
- The qualifications young people achieve are nationally and internationally respected and act as a credible passport to their future learning and employment.
- Leaders of education at every level working together in a self-improving system, providing mutual support and challenge to raise standards in all schools.[46]

The section on 'Improving Education the Welsh Way' steered an uneasy course between criticism and celebration of the alleged 'Welsh Way'. It noted the Welsh commitment to collaboration, but also the unacceptable variability within the system. The vision 'captured' the six key principles on which Welsh education was built. 'Confidence and pride in Wales as a bilingual nation with the strength and assurance to nurture both languages' was top of the list. Next was the truism that 'Learners are at the heart of all we do'. It was then claimed that 'Every child and young person benefits from personalised learning', though obviously the compositing civil servant seemed unaware of the debates in England a decade before which attempted to give some substance to the rather nebulous concept of 'personalised learning'. The commitment to comprehensive education was restated by insisting that 'The success of our education system depends upon the success of all children', which in turn demanded 'Collective responsibility, supported by cooperative values.' The last two points dealt with 'Developing the capacity for a self-improving system' and a call to 'Celebrate success, recognise excellence and share both'.[47]

The section on 'A Better Wales' was an attempt to justify the importance of education to the wider polity. A successful education system would *inter alia* mean 'a stronger economy, greater innovation, improved productivity'. It would also be a way of 'ensuring the Welsh language thrives', provide 'greater community cohesion...greater creativity...greater care for the vulnerable... [and] a more equitable and successful society'.[48]

'The Improvement Challenge' was a candid assessment of the strengths and weaknesses (coyly referred to as challenges) of the Welsh education system. It drew largely on the damning OECD report, the work of the former Blair policy advisor Robert Hill, and the annual reports of the Chief Inspector, Ann Keane.[49] In what must be considered one of the grossest understatements of the decade it was also noted that Wales' '2012 PISA results tell us we are not performing well'. Of note was the acceptance, quoting Hill, of the same judgment that Andrews had made a few years before: Wales was 'a fair system moving to good'. The final nails were being driven into the coffin of *The Learning Country*.

The section on action noted that to 'deliver our vision we need to be clear about the actions that we will take in the years ahead, building on the strong foundations provided by the reforms that have been implemented to date and the improvements that have already been made. At the same time we must be bold and honest in facing up to and tackling the areas that need to improve'.[50]

What then followed was an expansion of the four strategic objectives identified earlier in the document.

Strategic Objective One was concerned with forming 'An excellent professional workforce with strong pedagogy based on an understanding of what works'. It nodded at the chronic problems connected with Initial Teacher Training, noting that some moves had already been made to improve the quality of entrants by both raising the bar of required qualifications but also providing incentives to make the profession more attractive. Belatedly it was noted that 'We have more to do to create a culture of continuous improvement across the entire workforce'. But help was already at hand:

'The implementation of the new professional learning model that underpins the New Deal for the workforce will see practitioners have wider access to high-quality development activities to support their practice'.[51] (The 'New Deal' was Huw Lewis' own idea, it seemed. The problem was that there was little behind the slogan. For months after, officials at the department strove to find a way to clothe the barest of outlines with some substance. Things were not helped by the lead official saying on several occasions 'OK, it's not new and it's not much of a deal'.)

Other support was to be forthcoming in the form of a relaunch of Andrews' Masters in Educational Practice and some inchoate support from the newly established Education Workforce Council. The damning OECD report of 2014 had noted that there was insufficient differentiation in teaching strategies, which seemed to impact most on those who were most in need of tailored approaches to learning. The concept of 'personalised' learning was again advanced, with the introduction of Individual Learning Plans for ALN children. The section concluded with the obligatory mention of the advantages promised by digital learning.[52]

Strategic Objective Two was the establishment of 'A curriculum which is engaging and attractive to children and young people and which develops within them an independent ability to apply knowledge and skills'. It praised the work undertaken by the Foundation Phase. It claimed that the situation in regard to literacy and numeracy was improving, thanks to the introduction of the Literacy and Numeracy Framework and national testing. The National Support Programme was also highlighted as a key action in raising standards. A few months later, the NSP was unexpectedly pulled, a year ahead of time. *Qualified for Life* accepted the OECD criticism that there was not enough 'assessment for learning' taking place in schools. It pinned its hopes of the review of the curriculum then under way by the Scot, Graham Donaldson.

Given the bruising encounters in the previous years over GCSE results, which we shall examine later, it was perhaps not surprising that Strategic Objective Three was to ensure that 'The qualifications young people achieve are nationally and internationally respected and act as a credible passport to their future learning and employment'. The decision to take the regulatory function into government had almost resulted in catastrophe for Welsh children. The Review of Qualifications in 2011/12 had argued strongly for the retention of the GCSE brand. It had also called for a strengthening, in effect a rebranding and reworking, of the Welsh Baccalaureate, to make it far more rigorous. The establishment of Qualifications Wales to be an independent regulator was simply a restoration of the *status quo ante* and a tacit acknowledgement of the perils of too close government involvement.[53]

The final Strategic Objective was that 'Leaders of education at every level working together in a self-improving system, providing mutual support and challenge to raise standards in all schools'. It was a bit of a ragbag section. The importance of leadership as second only to teaching in raising standards was noted. The criteria for the NPQH had been redeveloped and a National Leadership Development Board put in place. The last was but a poor substitute for the National College which had existed in England since 2000. This was also the section that dealt with the role of Consortia and Local Government. It was claimed that the National Model for Consortia was delivering both support and challenge, though many detected little of the former. The local authority role in school improvement was relegated to commissioning, not providing support. The importance of Schools Challenge Cymru, again an initiative arriving a decade late in Wales, was highlighted. There was a promise that the controversial banding system would be revised.

So far, so dull. There had been little if anything controversial in *Qualified for Life*. It was merely a cut and paste exercise bringing into a more formal order the raft of remedial initiatives launched in the Leighton years. It was obviously an attempt to rebut the stinging criticism of the OECD in suggesting that there was no coherent vision for education in Wales. But it was to be the response to the OECD's other judgment on Wales and the world made in terms of PISA that was to provoke the most interest.

In the final section, 'Realising the Benefits', there was promise of a yearly 'Wales Education Report Card'. But also there was a none too subtle attempt to wriggle out of Andrews' aim to be in the PISA top twenty. The new ambition was for Wales 'to achieve scores of 500 in each of reading, mathematics and science in the PISA tests of 2021'.[54]

Apart from the ridiculously long timeframe which would mean ministers and senior civil servants would be long gone when this new target was missed, it also meant that Wales was aiming to be, in 2021, where Scotland had been in 2006. It was also not lost on most informed commentators that this new ambition was for Wales to achieve the OECD average. Because of this, *Qualified for Life* quickly became known as 'Aiming for Average'. The ludicrous attempts by the senior civil servant responsible to justify this craven collapse of ambition was greeted with guffaws and laughter by the journalists present at the press briefing. Cross-examined at another meeting, the official had to retort that the ambition was still demanding, as it was by no means clear that Wales would achieve the coveted 500 Club in seven years. To include the revised PISA target in this document was not so much an exercise in burying bad news as trumpeting it far and wide.

And so *The Learning Country*'s bold, confident vision of Wales being hailed as an example of a world-class education system had come to this: a desperate hope that Wales could at least scrape in to being average on the world stage.

Notes

1   OECD, *Improving Schools in Wales: An OECD Perspective* (OECD, 2014), p. 115. http://www.oecd.org/edu/Improving-schools-in-Wales.pdf

2   The quotes that follow are located in the relevant chapters of *The Learning Country* (TLC).

3   TLC, p. 7.

4   TLC, p. 25.

5   TLC, p. 25.

6   TLC, p. 27.

7   TLC, p. 32.

8   TLC, p. 35.

9   http://www.bbc.co.uk/news/business-34174796.

10   TLC, pp. 44–45.

11   TLC, pp. 61–65.

12   Jones, GE and Rodderick, GW *A History of Education in Wales* (University of Wales Press; Cardiff, 2003), pp. 124 and 125.

13   Richard Daugherty and Gareth Elwyn Jones, Research Note The Learning Country, University of Wales Journal of Education, vol II, Number 1, 2002 pp. 107–113.

14   Internal document in the author's possession.

15   Hard copy document in the author's possession.

16   TLC2, Foreword.

17   TLC2, p. 5.

18   TLC2, p. 6.

19   TLC2, p. 10.

20   TLC2, p. 20.

21   TLC2, p. 24.

22   TLC2, p. 25.

23   TLC2, p. 27.

24   TLC2, p. 35.

25   TLC2, p. 55.

26   TLC2, p. 55.

27   TLC2, p. 58.

28   TLC2, p. 58.

29   http://gov.wales/topics/educationandskills/publications/guidance/learningcountry/?lang=en

30   https://statswales.wales.gov.uk/Catalogue/Education-and-Skills/Schools-and-Teachers/Examinations-and-Assessments/Key-Stage-4/ExaminationAchievementsOfPupilsAged15-by-Year.

31   https://statswales.wales.gov.uk/Catalogue/Education-and-Skills/Schools-and-Teachers/School-Leavers-Without-Qualifications/SchoolLeaversWithoutQualifications-by-Year.

32   http://www.assembly.wales/Research%20Documents/Young%20People%20not%20in%20Education,%20Employment%20or%20Training%20-%20Research%20paper-05092011-223764/11-051-English.pdf

33   See https://statswales.wales.gov.uk/Catalogue/Education-and-Skills/Schools-and-Teachers/Absenteeism/absenteeismbypupilsofcompulsoryschoolageinsecondaryschools-by-schooltype-year (though in fairness unauthorised absence accounted for but 1.5%).

34   http://mylocalschool.wales.gov.uk/

35   https://statswales.wales.gov.uk/Catalogue/Education-and-Skills/Schools-and-Teachers/Examinations-and-Assessments/Key-Stage-4/ExaminationAchievementsOfPupilsAged15-by-Year (These figures refer to those achieving the Level 2 Threshold, equivalent

to 5A* to C GCSE grades, but not necessarily including English or Welsh and Maths. This latter figure was not measured in 2001 and stood at 54% in 2010.)

36   See pages 11 to 14 of The educational attainment of looked after children and young people (Wales Audit Office, 2012).
http://www.audit.wales/system/files/publications/The_educational_attainment_of_looked_after_children_and_young_people_English_2012.pdf

37   Philip Dixon, Click on Wales, June 28th 2013 http://www.clickonwales.org/2013/06/leighton-andrews-assault-on-systemic-failure/

38   Ibid.

39   Leighton Andrews, Teaching Makes a Difference, p. 2. http://gov.wales/docs/dcells/publications/110202teachingmakesadifferenceen.pdf

40   http://learning.gov.wales/news/sitenews/improvingschools/?lang=en

41   Department for Education and Skills, *Improving Schools* (2012), pp. 2–3.

42   Ibid.

43   OECD Improving Schools in Wales: An OECD Perspective (2014) pp. 116–118 http://www.oecd.org/edu/Improving-schools-in-Wales.pdf

44   Welsh Government, *Qualified for Life: An education improvement plan for 3 to 19-year-olds in Wales* (2014) http://gov.wales/docs/dcells/publications/141001-qualified-for-life-en.pdf

45   *Qualified for Life*, p. 4.

46   *Qualified for Life*, p. 5.

47   *Qualified for Life*, p. 7.

48   *Qualified for Life*, p. 8.

49   Robert Hill Consulting 'The future delivery of education services in Wales' (2013) http://gov.wales/consultations/education/future-delivery-of-education-services-in-wales/?lang=en

50   *Qualified for Life*, p. 12.

51   *Qualified for Life*, p. 12.

52   *Qualified for Life*, pp. 12 and 13.

53   This will be examined in greater detail in Chapter 6.

54   *Qualified for Life*, p. 25.

3

A Child's Journey in Wales

Laying the Foundations and Building the Pathways

So, according to *Qualified for Life*, the highest hope the Welsh education system can have is that it just about scrapes in to being average. A vision that is far from inspiring. Governments come and go, policies appear and vanish, but children have to be educated and schools are entrusted with that task. In this chapter we look at how the devolution journey has impacted on the ground. You will remember Megan, the mythical child of the ill-fated *Learning Country 2*. What has been the actual journey of her and her siblings? How have the abrupt and radical shifts in the 'grand narrative' stemming from central government actually affected her? We will examine her progress through the Foundation Phase, her transition from 8 to 14, and then onwards along the 14–19 Learning Pathways.

The Foundation Phase: Learning through Play or Playing with Learning?

Policy divergence in the early years

Rhodri Morgan, the man who supplanted the jinxed Alun Michael as Welsh Labour leader in 2000, once said that the Foundation Phase was his proudest achievement, and the 'most momentous change to education in Wales since devolution'.[1] Unlike many of the other policies from his period in office, when Jane Davidson was Minister for Education for nearly seven years, the Foundation Phase is still with us. Much was made at the time of its introduction of the significance of its labelling: it would not be a rigid state but a much more fluid phase, taking account of the different development rates of young children.

According to the Welsh Government website, the Foundation Phase is 'The statutory curriculum for all 3 to 7-year-olds in Wales, in both maintained and non-maintained settings. It encourages children to be creative, imaginative and makes learning more enjoyable and more effective'.[2] By contrast, the English Early Years Foundation Stage (EYFS), which replaced the original Foundation Stage, covers children from birth to five years old. But the differences are not simply chronological. The EYFS 'sets standards for the learning, development and care of children from birth to 5 years old. All schools and Ofsted-registered early years providers must follow the EYFS, including childminders, preschools, nurseries and school reception classes'.[3] Already one can see the deep-seated 'standards agenda' of England being emphasised.

The overarching statement of the purpose of the Welsh curriculum seems, at least on first sight, to be far more child-centred than its English counterpart. Throughout, the proposed Welsh experience is couched in far more child friendly language:

> Children will be given opportunities to explore the world around them and understand how things work by taking part in practical activities relevant to their developmental stage. They will be challenged through practical activities and develop their thinking with open-ended questions. Children will be encouraged to explore concepts and share ideas for solving problems.[4]

The Foundation Phase celebrates seven 'Areas of Learning' to be delivered through practical activities and active learning experiences, both indoors and outdoors. This last emphasis was one that caught the imagination of parents as well as children from its very first pilots. The seven Areas of Learning are arranged around: personal and social development, wellbeing and cultural diversity; language, literacy and communication skills; mathematical development; Welsh language development; knowledge and understanding of the world; physical development; and creative development. While the English early years curriculum covers much the same territory – communication and language; physical development; personal, social and emotional development; literacy; mathematics; understanding the world; and expressive arts and design – a closer examination reveals that the headline differences continue beneath the surface. Obviously one would not expect the English curriculum to be concerned with Welsh language development but it is telling that, whereas in Wales literacy is lumped together with 'language, literacy and communication skills', it stands alone in England.

Origins of the Foundation Phase

By the time New Labour came to power in Westminster in 1997, many early years practitioners across the UK had been unhappy for some time with the diet provided for children at the pre-school and Key Stage 1 level. It seemed overly prescriptive, too linear, and did not take account of more recent development in child psychology, which threw light on how young children actually learned about the world around them. In many ways the debates had been around for centuries. One could take the Augustinian view that young children were essentially savages who needed to be tamed, or Rousseau's line that they were innocents who were corrupted by the world. Schooling in Britain had tended to the former view, though there had been ground-breaking reports such as Plowden in 1967, which suggested a more nuanced approach.[5]

One of the first acts of the new Blair government, in 1997, was to announce its general approach to early years by requiring that each local authority constructed an Early Years Development Partnership which, as it said on the tin, brought together all early years interests. In July of the same year a white paper was published, *Education in Wales, Building Excellent Schools Together*, (inevitably known thereafter as BEST), which outlined a commitment to securing high quality provision for the under-5s. Guidance from the Welsh Office followed. Almost a year later a green paper appeared, entitled *The National Childcare Strategy in Wales*.

After the establishment of the National Assembly for Wales, the nascent Welsh Government was keen to promote a more positive celebration of the early years and quickly announced its intentions of developing a more suitable introduction to children's schooling. According to the folklore surrounding the Foundation Phase, the globe was scoured for the best examples of early years learning. These, it transpired, were to be found in some of the Scandinavian countries, notably Sweden and Denmark, with New Zealand, Spain and the Italian region of Reggio Emilia providing some more ingredients. If any other common educational attribute exists between these it has yet to be found. It's also doubtful that in the light of their PISA scores some of these contenders would make it into the mix today.

The Learning Country: Foundation Phase, 3 to 7 years

The Learning Country had announced a thorough overhaul of early years education, but it wasn't until 2003 that more formal proposals were made, when a consultation document, *The Learning Country: Foundation Phase*

3 to 7 years was published.[6] (The accompanying review was to be led by the respected educationalist Shan Richards). It sought to develop a new Foundation Phase that would extend from 3 until 7, build on the advice of Estyn, the Early Years Advisory Panel, the Education and Lifelong Learning Committee's Policy Review *Laying the Foundations: Early Years provision for all 3-year-olds*, and, importantly, ACCAC's *Desirable Outcomes for Children's Learning Before Compulsory School Age*, which had been knocking around since the turn of the millennium. Davidson was gushing in her foreword to the consultation: 'I believe that the proposals contained in this document represent one of the most important and exciting developments that we have initiated for Wales under the Learning Country banner'.[7]

The first chapter examined the current situation, comparing the 'Desirable Outcomes' identified by ACCAC and the current curriculum of Key Stage 1, which took children into the first years of compulsory education. One of the major changes advocated by the consultation, apart from the promise of developing a more child-centred curriculum, was that there should be a 'learning continuum from 0 to 7'.

Chapter 2 outlined why it was felt that changes were needed. There were good features of the current setup: achievement was broadly good in the early years which dealt with pre-compulsory education, about 80%, and this continued, with some decline, in Key Stage 1. But there were major common shortcomings too. In early years it was felt that 'children spend too much time doing tasks while sitting at tables, rather than learning through well-designed opportunities to play'. It was also felt that they did not have 'enough opportunity to develop their language'. Somewhat startlingly, but probably accurately, the document noted that 'almost half the settings do not plan or assess effectively and do not keep records that are easily understood'. In Key Stage 1 nearly 40% of teaching had some weakness and teaching in Year 1 was of poorer quality to that of Year 2 on the whole.[8]

Change was necessary in order to spread good practice, but also to focus on the growth and development of children. The main aims of the Foundation Phase would be to: 'raise children's standards of achievement; enhance their positive attitudes to learning; address their developing needs; enable them to benefit from educational opportunities later in their lives; and help them become active citizens within their communities'.[9]

In words that were to become something of a millstone round the neck, it was then claimed that 'For young children – when they play – it is their work. Through working in this way, children learn to: make sense of the world around them; develop a better understanding of themselves; and form relationships with others. Well planned play gives children opportunities to be actively involved in learning and to investigate and discover for themselves'.[10]

A framework was proposed which, drawing on the best in the Desirable

Outcomes and the curriculum at Key Stage 1, would 'provide a list of experiences and objectives for children's learning. The new areas of learning will form a rich, exciting curriculum for young learners'. The seven proposed learning areas were then outlined:

- Personal and Social Development and Well-being;
- Language, Literacy and Communication Skills;
- Mathematical Development;
- Bilingual and Multi-cultural Understanding;
- Knowledge and Understanding of the World;
- Physical Development; and
- Creative Development.[11]

These were to remain constant areas throughout the development of the learning phase though the proposed area of bilingualism was modified to 'Welsh Language Development'. This was an acknowledgement both of the Welsh Government's intensifying commitment to sustain the language but also because societal changes meant that an increasing number of Welsh children were bilingual, it was just that, for some, one of their two languages wasn't Welsh. Perhaps it was felt that explicit trilingualism was a step too far for small children, though some advocated it.

The document noted the obvious fact that children learn best when involved in planning and reviewing their work. 'Practice in Denmark, Germany, Reggio Emilia in Italy and New Zealand, for example, shows how children can be encouraged to make decisions about their learning, to be independent and physically active in doing so.'[12]

Also cited, though not by name, was the fact that 'Recent research also suggests that an over-emphasis on making children read and write, before they are ready to do so, can be counterproductive. Indeed, in countries such as Australia, Sweden, Denmark, Finland and Norway, there is little or no formal teaching of literacy and numeracy until the children are older'. An analysis of the vastly different societal make up and social provision of Scandinavian countries might have given some more subtle insights into why children in those countries seem to catch up so rapidly.

One of the big features of the proposed Foundation Phase was to be the facilitation and emphasis on the outdoor environment. We have already seen how it was felt that young children were tied to their desks too early. The proposals went further, to claim that:

The use of the outdoor environment is regarded as an important element for effective early years education. Currently it is not a strong feature of early years provision in Wales and is even less evident in Key

Stage 1. Yet the outdoors features strongly in the experiences offered to young children in many countries, including those with climates similar to or more variable than our own. The outdoor environment is an appropriate space to use large toys and equipment and is also an excellent resource to develop children's understanding of mathematics, science, geography, art and technology. Placing a greater emphasis on the use of the outdoor environment as a resource for learning in Wales, would provide children with opportunities for first hand, experiential learning and real life problem solving. It should also enable children to learn about, to enjoy, and care for their environment and begin to understand issues such as conservation and sustainability so central to their long term futures.[13]

Whatever the eventual outcomes of the Foundation Phase in terms of attainment, achievement and overall education, it certainly has transformed young children's first encounter with the world of education and the physical school setup itself. There is no longer simply an asphalt yard for children to run around in or a playing field if they were lucky, but a whole range of equipment and terrain. This kit has often had to be funded by Parent Teacher Associations and other sources of income.

The authors of the document were acutely aware, though, that like Jackie in 'Puff the Magic Dragon', children move on. They were concerned about transition and saw it as vital that 'Children should be progressively introduced to more formal ways of working during the last year of the proposed Foundation Phase, or earlier, for those who show readiness and have acquired the necessary early skills.'[14] The Foundation Phase was not meant to be a retarding experience. Considerations such as these inevitably led to questions about the relationship between the Foundation Phase and the increasingly prescriptive National Curriculum, introduced in 1988. It recommended that 'The Foundation Phase should best be regarded as a distinct curricular stage within the overall National Curriculum for Wales – a Phase with its own separate character'. It was hoped that a more informal approach to learning could help to 'prevent underachievement and raise overall standards' and, tellingly, it might also 'prevent some children from being labelled too early as having special educational needs'.[15]

Chapter 4 was a consideration of the issues that would surround implementation. Fronting all these was the vexed issue of assessment. The document was candid that many centres were finding it difficult to get a handle on this complex area and urged streamlining, but also guidance, to ensure more standardisation to make certain that everyone was clear about 'what constitutes good assessment practice in early years'. The generally expected 'Desirable Outcomes' was to be replaced by 'a list of experiences and descriptions about what children should learn during the Foundation Phase'. It also promised that this 'assessment record' would be 'rigorously trialled during the pilot phase'. The goal was to achieve an assessment continuum to seven, focussing on all seven areas of learning. The way in which a seamless transition between the Foundation Phase and Key Stage 2 was to be achieved was outlined in a flow diagram in the appendix to the document.[16]

The next issue to be addressed was staffing. Unsurprisingly the training of staff was key: 'Teachers who work in the Foundation Phase should have studied to degree level child development and the way children learn between the ages of 3 and 7 years of age'.[17] The number of staff should also be increased dramatically and be based on the standards set by the Care Standards Inspectorate for Wales, one adult to eight children. The document was keen to emphasise that this should be examined further and not moved to immediately. The next brief chapter of the document counselled that there should be a rolling programme of implementation. Part of this would be the development of a suitable training and development plan. This was still being worked on ten years later.

The provision of suitable 'bright, stimulating play and activity areas' was the next consideration, followed quickly by quality assurance which would be provided for by Estyn. A table was provided, laying down the stages for full implementation by 2008. The need for an indepth longitudinal study was also flagged up.

A class reception for the Foundation Phase

As is obvious from the language surrounding the Foundation Phase, the entire project was to be child-centred, characterising children more as exploratory learners than empty vessels to be filled with knowledge. In headline terms this whole approach became known by the rather troublesome slogan of 'Learning Through Play'. The BBC announced the whole exercise as 'More play, less "work" for the early years'. There was far more to the philosophy and pedagogy of the Foundation Phase than that rather glib soundbite, but it stuck and, as subsequent evaluations were to prove, it gained a certain amount of traction in schools themselves. Even the announcement of possible changes to the early years curriculum had inspired one headteacher, Phil Rowlands of Pentre Primary in the Rhondda (now closed) to tell the BBC that 'All the education research tells us that this is the way we should be going ... The bottom line is learning should be fun'. Mr Rowlands also advocated the scrapping of the KS2 tests.[18]

The official consultation received 644 responses, a very high level of engagement, signalling the interest that the proposals had generated. A massive 96% were in favour of introducing them (even some of those opposed did so on the grounds of reform fatigue rather than ideological objection). The proposal received 100% backing from the unions.[19]

Those who opposed had largely predictable axes to grind, fearing that it would lead to a dumbing down of learning and simply retard children's progress into formal learning. But the objectors were not simply right-wing bigots. As late as 2010 a book review in *Planet: the Welsh Internationalist* was warning that 'The authors instead prefer to laud the Foundation Phase (another of Davidson's pet projects), a much more dubious reform. While its emphasis on play in early years is laudable, unfortunately the Foundation Phase means that many pupils will be taught by assistants. Standards of literacy and numeracy will go down, so this policy will have to be altered: a combination of play and formal learning is needed'.[20]

However, the overwhelming number of respondents and commentators were keenly in favour of the proposed changes. It was believed that the whole philosophy would lay firm foundations for lifelong learning, tackle disengagement and, interestingly, narrow the gender and deprivation gaps too easily seen in children's measurable performance. It is hard to think of a government initiative that has been so welcomed as the Foundation Phase. There wasn't quite dancing in the streets, but it was in that league.

Clouds on the horizon: funding

It was clear from the start that such a bold project would involve considerable expenditure. It wasn't the sandpits and climbing frames that were the biggest cost but, as always, the people. The ratios governing child to adult were very low, as little as eight to one in the earliest stages, and required the recruitment of an army of teaching assistants. Although no one could remotely consider the remuneration that many of these are paid a king's ransom, their sheer number meant considerable recurrent expenditure. By 2014 there were well over 20,000 teaching assistants, the highest number relative to teachers in the world, a fact that did not go unnoticed by the OECD in its damning report of 2014.[21]

It was one thing to pump-prime a pilot, but quite another to fund whole system change, and as the project scaled up so too did the demands for extra money. As early as October 2004, informed stakeholders were worrying in public that, not for the first time, the department had got its sums seriously wrong. The *TES* found that some of the forty-one pilot schools were having difficulty in recruiting suitable staff while others, more disturbingly, were still waiting for the disbursement of funds from the government. These delays were fuelling concerns that the original funding envelope would not be enough to sustain a country-wide roll-out. The notorious funding fog of Wales was bedevilling the whole process. Moelwen Gwyndaf, General Secretary of UCAC, demanded 'more transparency in how money will be allocated for the long term'. The budget for early years at that stage was £25 million, with the promise of an extra £67 million over the following three years. Anna Brychan, Director of the National Association of Head Teachers in Wales (NAHT), worried about the longer term plans and proposed that 'every school should be looked at in terms of staffing, space and facilities, and there needs to be dedicated funding so that every school can offer the same thing'. A government spokesman promised detailed monitoring and evaluation of the pilots, adding somewhat worryingly that 'As a result, we will be able to firm up detailed costings'. One hopes he did not have the same blasé approach to his personal finances.[22]

The funding issue rolled on and on, and greatly soured the relationship between the NAHT, whose membership was drawn largely from primary heads, and the Welsh Government. Jane Davidson resolutely refused, as usual, to examine the legitimate concerns of those who had given the new initiative enthusiastic backing. Her successor, Jane Hutt, was more amenable. In January 2008 an extra £32 million was added to the £75 million allocated in the budget the previous November, to be followed by a further injection of £62 million the following autumn.

Behind the scenes the sudden departure of Steve Marshall as Director General of the Department of Education had brought a wily old timer to watch over it. Dennis Gunning, acting DG, had quickly realised that the NAHT concerns were real, not fabricated, and the 'detailed costings' were finally firmed up – just in time. This was just another instance when neither the politicians nor the civil servants could discern the help that was being offered to them from those who really knew what was happening until it was almost too late. Gunning's experience had been almost exclusively post-16 but he deserves the thanks of the youngest children of Wales in ensuring that the Foundation Phase didn't keel over and die.

Clouds on the horizon: the debacle over measurement

Assessment was to become another civil service-fabricated thorn in the flesh for Andrews, who succeeded Hutt as Minister for Education in 2009. Obviously any evaluation of the Foundation Phase as a whole and, more importantly, any part it could play in making sure that children progressed through their vital early years, would need to show how such progression could be measured. As with all assessments there needed to be a baseline which could show the skills and knowledge that children possessed at the start of the phase, and those that they had hopefully gained at the end. It was manifestly ludicrous that children should – or even could – be formally tested on entry, so over the years various 'desirable outcomes' had been developed, which chartered reasonable expectations. These had been imported into the Foundation Phase, but a more rigorous, systematic and nationally consistent measure needed to be put into place. Estyn had constantly harped on about variation in practice in early years settings and here was an opportunity to put it right once and for all.

What happened was another classic piece of civil service mis-delivery, and a clear and comic example of the lack of overview that bedevils the department. The Child Development Assessment Profile (CDAP) was an attempt to provide a robust benchmark measure. It was developed by the department with a planned roll-out date of September 2011. The profession had been consulted sporadically and a piecemeal manner, the resultant pieces had been cobbled together but trialled separately. When the whole was put together and roll-out attempted, there was uproar. The civil servants had produced a Behemoth that was completely inoperable in practice. Practitioners were expected to identify and assess up to 114 behaviours of children within their first six weeks at school. The unions were damning. Rebecca Williams of UCAC was to speak for many when she said that 'it is neither fish nor fowl – and of absolutely no use to anyone'. I warned that 'Civil service "cut and paste" is a grossly inadequate substitute for the wisdom of practitioners in the classroom'.[23]

The debacle did, however, show the difference a strong and intelligent minister like Andrews could make. Concerns about the CDAP had risen almost from the start, with quite a number of stakeholders warning that it was not fit for purpose. Andrews was adept at discerning real concern from the fabricated ones that greet many new initiatives or requirements. In private he consulted some of the unions and others. He grew increasingly convinced, just as Gunning had done over the funding, that here was another area where the whole Foundation Phase could be derailed. Knowing the real value of the civil servants' counter-briefings – that all was going well, and that there were just a few local teething problems – Andrews acted swiftly. Within a few weeks of the roll-out of the CDAP, he ordered a rapid review to be undertaken by the doyenne of early years, Professor Iram Siraj-Blatchford. It was absolutely damning.

The review took place between December 2011 and January 2012. Siraj-Blatchford found that the CDAP was far too detailed and time consuming in its application for what should be an on-entry assessment. It contained 'too many descriptions of behaviour and, in some cases, they are not the right ones'. This last comment highlighted the perils of leaving bureaucrats with little or no recent experience of the chalk face in sole charge of developing policy. In any case, the CDAP just added another layer of confusion and inconsistency to the whole process. Considering that the CDAP was meant to be an example of formative assessment, it was appalling that Siraj-Blatchford could state bluntly that it was 'not useful as an on-going tracker to monitor and measure progress. The information generated does not support school improvement or tracking, in part due to the lack of clarity of guidance and inconsistency of practice'. Moreover the 'lack of clear links to the Foundation Phase Outcomes and statutory assessment at the end of Year 2 reduces the value of the assessment'. Overall 'the lack of clarity of core purpose makes it difficult to judge CDAP's suitability. In particular, core purpose would have considerable influence on consideration of whether a "best-fit" approach is appropriate, on language of assessment and timing'.[24]

Siraj-Blatchford's report could only be kept under wraps for so long. In February the minister issued a written statement. It could not have been clearer: 'I have been listening to the representations made to me by teachers and headteachers and Professor Siraj-Blatchford's early findings that there are significant problems with the Child Development Assessment Profile (CDAP). I have therefore decided to withdraw the statutory requirement to use the Child Development Assessment Profile (CDAP) in all education settings ... Work is already in hand to ensure that we move quickly to replace the CDAP with a tool that better supports children's early learning and development'.[25]

There was almost universal relief at the announcement. The *Western Mail* described the minister's decision as a U-turn. ATL labelled it as a courageous decision of a listening minister. The other unions piled in to commend Andrews and to take credit. Chris Keats of the NASUWT claimed that the decision had been made because of her union's ongoing industrial action. Beth Davies of the NUT spoke for many when she said: 'The minister stated that he remains committed to a single assessment tool for children in the Foundation Phase. We would welcome the opportunity to work with him on that to ensure that any future initiatives are developed alongside the profession and so offer teachers, parents and pupils something positive'. Aled Roberts, the Lib Dem education spokesman, was also voicing the reaction of many when he said: 'I find it astonishing that the system could have been introduced last September only to be withdrawn and replaced just five months later. Quite clearly, there were major concerns at the outset'. The education correspondent of the *Western Mail*, Gareth Evans, hit the nail bang on the head when he commented that the 'scrapping of CDAPs just a few months after their introduction raises fresh questions over the Welsh Department of Education's ability to see through major policy initiatives'.[26] Those questions have never gone away.

The mistakes over funding had been costly to rectify and would have long-term implications for budgets in other parts of the education system. The errors surrounding the CDAP debacle confirmed the impression of a department that was clueless about scale-up and implementation. Without Andrews it is doubtful that the bold and brave decision to pull the CDAP would have been taken. The resultant damage to the Foundation Phase doesn't bear thinking about. Yet again the profession had had to scream at the top of its voice that the system was on the wrong course. It is perhaps another salutary lesson that the *Foundation Phase Final Report*, which we will examine soon, found that even in 2014/5 '11% of schools were still using CDAP in full and 36% were using some elements of it. Only 36% say they are using some other on-entry assessment tool. The remaining 17% were unsure what on-entry assessment they are using'.[27]

It wasn't until July 2015 that some of the confusion was dissipated when Huw Lewis, Andrews' successor, announced the new Foundation Phase Profile. This would be part of the promised Early Years Development Plan, to become statutory for Reception Year children from the start of the coming school year. Painful lessons had obviously been learned, as Lewis noted that there was a 'need to ensure that the Profile is manageable for teachers and other early years practitioners'. So much so that 'officials have worked closely with teachers and practitioners in developing the Profile, through a Practitioners' Task and Finish Group and undertaking a robust trial on a draft profile with around 150 schools and nurseries from January to March 2015'.[28]

If the same officials had listened a few years before, the CDAP debacle could have been prevented. The new profile would also now take account of the Literacy and Numeracy Framework and, in the longer term, be adapted as the Donaldson Review of the curriculum was rolled out. It had taken ten years to get to the stage where there was a usable way for practitioners to assess what impact the Foundation Phase was making to their children.

Evaluations of the Foundation Phase: how good is it really?

Estyn

From the start it was obvious that Estyn, the inspectorate in Wales, would need to be closely involved in evaluating how the whole project was going. In 2007 it produced an evaluation of the Foundation Phase pilots, which summarised its findings to date. It found that: 'Almost all practitioners in the pilot schools and settings are enthusiastic about the Foundation Phase, and they have worked extremely hard to integrate it into their current practices'.

However, despite this enthusiasm, there were concerns about the balance of child-led and adult-led activities in a significant minority of settings. Also there seemed to be general confusion about assessment and recording. Ominously this meant that there was 'a lack of common criteria for recording assessment, which means that transition between schools and settings does not always build well enough on children's prior learning'. These transitionary problems have bedevilled the continuity of the Foundation Phase and the rest of the curriculum up until the present day.[29]

By 2011, three years after the implementation of the Foundation Phase in full, Estyn was echoing the concerns of several commentators about its patchy implementation. Estyn found that while 'the impact of the Foundation Phase on the wellbeing of children has been positive ... in a minority of schools, this is not the case, often because leaders and practitioners do not understand the principles and practice of the Foundation Phase'. Worryingly, it reported that 'in a number of schools the fundamentals were still not being grasped by the professionals in charge'. It went on to express concern that 'Leaders and practitioners generally have not evaluated the Foundation Phase robustly enough to identify where it is working well and what needs to be improved'. The concerns that some, including Andrews, were having by now about the impact that the Foundation Phase was having on literacy were fuelled by the inspectorate's conclusion that while 'in the majority of schools where leaders and practitioners have implemented the Foundation Phase well, there is a focus on raising standards, particularly in literacy', it was the case that for 'a significant minority of schools, there is not enough direct teaching of reading and appropriate opportunities for children to practise and use their reading skills are not always provided', adding for good measure that 'the range and quality of children's written work in many schools are often limited because writing tasks are formulaic and undemanding'.[30]

Estyn was more positive about the implementation of the keynote feature of outdoor learning. 'In two-thirds of the sessions observed as part of the survey, learning experiences in the outdoors were good or better. The provision for outdoor learning has been more successful in schools than in nonmaintained settings... In most cases, children's enjoyment, wellbeing, behaviour, knowledge and understanding of the world, and their physical development improve as a result of using the outdoors'. But even here the inspectors found that drawing out the implications of these experiences for learning was patchy at best: 'the outdoors is not used enough to develop children's reading and writing, Welsh language, creativity, or their ability to use information and communication technology'.

There were also the now seemingly perennial problems with assessment: 'Practitioners tend to assess children's learning less often and less well outdoors than indoors. They do not track the progress children make in developing their skills outdoors well enough. With children spending more time outdoors, this means that important milestones in their development may be missed'. Tellingly, the inspectors went on to highlight deficiencies in implementation: 'Senior leaders and managers have not always received enough training on the Foundation Phase to identify good practice, challenge less effective practice, or make cost-effective decisions on improving outdoor provision and facilities'. It wasn't just the funding or the CDAP that had not been thought through fully.

Stocktakes

But funding and CDAP apart, behind the scenes the Welsh Government was also getting increasingly concerned about the Foundation Phase, its pet education project. A three year rolling evaluation was being undertaken by WISERD (Wales Institute of Social and Economic Research, Data and Methods) led by the respected academic Chris Taylor. This was in many ways a response to the original proposal that there should be an indepth longitudinal study of the project.

Interim reports from WISERD were throwing up some interesting facts about the Foundation Phase but this wasn't enough to calm government fears. In July 2013, out of the blue, Andrews ordered an independent stocktake to examine, *inter alia*, the implementation of the Foundation Phase, its impact on literacy and numeracy skills, and whether or not it was having any effect on narrowing the gap caused by socio-economic deprivation. There was particular concern about 'how the innovative early years programme is being implemented on the ground', a sure sign that at last the department was starting to realise that idea and reality might be somewhat discrepant. The aim of the stocktake was 'about improving quality and reducing variability', a further indication that the best might not be telling what was going on with the rest. Andrews was clear: 'Getting it right in the early years is imperative if our young people are able to reach their full potential … Conducting a stocktake will ensure that we are ahead of the game in terms of identifying and addressing issues that could impact on quality'. For once, something had penetrated the murky corridors of Cathays Park before it was too late.[31]

The stocktake ran for six months and was chaired by Professor Iram Siraj-Blatchford, who had done the rapid review of the CDAP some months before. It was published in March 2014. Her report noted that the Foundation Phase had already received some strong support from previous investigations which had shown that 'the underpinning pedagogy and practice within the Foundation Phase are known to have a positive impact on teachers' and practitioners' practice and lead to improvements in the quality of provision for children and their families'. She also noted that 'the focus on improving the lives of children and families in poverty through supporting the learning and teaching of young children is also well evidenced and is particularly important for Wales'. (The actual impact of this focus would be dealt a body blow by a report the following year.) But she also noted, in a nod towards the funding problems and wobbles of the Welsh Government, that 'for the implementation of the Foundation Phase to be effective in Wales, it requires a fundamental change in culture within many of the maintained schools and funded non-maintained settings engaged with it, which will take time to embed'. Moreover 'UNESCO (2004) considered quality improvements of this type across the world and concluded that they not only require a strong lead from government with a robust long-term vision, but also require sufficiently motivated and well supported staff'.[32]

The report was largely concerned with the demands of implementation and raising the standard of staff in particular. Although it was undeniable that 'there appears to be a general move in the right direction', care needed to be exercised to ensure that the variability in implementation on the ground was kept to a minimum. The report produced twenty-three recommendations which fell under three broad headings. The first was that there should be a ten-year strategic plan to support the improvement process. The second batch concerned training and support for teachers and other staff, and the third concentrated on short-term priorities. The introduction of the National Literacy and Numeracy Frameworks by Andrews had meant that the linkages between the Foundation Phase and other parts of the curriculum needed to be rendered far more explicit. Nine of the recommendations explicitly dealt with training needs, but a number of the others reflected the need for better CPD for staff engaged in delivery.[33] There were no fireworks in this report, unlike the one on the CDAP, and the overall impression was given of a ship that was now well on course to deliver.

WISERD

The most important evaluation of the Foundation Phase by far has been the longitudinal study conducted on behalf of the Welsh Government by WISERD (the Wales Institute of Social and Economic Research, Data and Methods). The original 'title deeds' of the Foundation Phase had suggested that such a study should be undertaken. In April 2011, the Welsh Government invited tenders for an independent evaluation with four main aims: the process evaluation, which would concentrate on implementation and highlight improvements; the outcome evaluation, which would assess the Foundation

Phase's impact to date; the economic evaluation, which would judge its value for money and finally provide a framework to track the future outputs and outcomes. During the three years of research, WISERD provided eighteen interim reports on the state of play in several of these key areas.

The final report was impressively comprehensive.[34] Relying on a variety of quantitative and qualitative data, it provided some well needed reassurance to government and practitioners alike that they were on the right track. The Executive Summary provided some key findings. It would come as no surprise that 'pupils who attended schools with greater use of the Foundation Phase pedagogies were more likely to achieve the Foundation Phase Indicator'. It was also pleasing to note that 'Schools with greater use of Foundation Phase pedagogies have greater levels of observed pupil involvement and pupil wellbeing during learning'. Also very encouraging, and relieving to the government and Foundation Phase advocates, was the conclusion that the Foundation Phase was actually raising standards: 'Pupils in the Foundation Phase are more likely to achieve Level 4 or above in Key Stage 2 English (based on the first three cohorts of over 1,500 pupils in pilot schools who have since reached the end of Key Stage 2)'. Similarly, absenteeism was in decline as a result of the Foundation Phase. Enduring practitioner enthusiasm was confirmed by the fact that 'The majority of practitioners and key stakeholders interviewed and surveyed think that the Foundation Phase is having a positive impact on children and learning (behaviour, wellbeing and attitudes to learning)'. Similarly, 'The majority of practitioners believe that the Foundation Phase has led to improvements in literacy (both English and Welsh) and numeracy'. The following table shows how practitioners were viewing the Foundation Phase at the time.

Table 8. Perceived Impact of the Foundation Phase on Different Groups of Pupils (by School Foundation Phase Lead Practitioners) % of respondents[35]

	Disadvantaged	No change	Benefitted
Boys	6	9	85
SEN	6	16	78
First language not English/Welsh	4	34	62
Summer-born	3	35	62
Not being educated in first language	4	38	58
More able and talented	13	31	56

	Disadvantaged	No change	Benefitted
Girls	5	42	53
Living in poverty	2	45	53
BME (black minority ethnic)	2	59	39
Advantaged backgrounds	3	58	39

The report was not, however, afraid to pull its punches. Commenting on the final report, Huw Lewis said: 'It's truthful, it's challenging, it's not afraid to point to inconsistencies and insufficiencies within what we have, and it gives us a platform, I think, for some really focused work over the next few years'. Truth be told the report had calmed fears about regression in terms of literacy and numeracy, and there were clear signs that standards were improving, but it had contained a bombshell which presented the Welsh Government with an unexpected headache.

It was almost universally assumed that the Foundation Phase was a key part of 'narrowing the gap' between the attainment of girls and boys and also in reducing the socio-economic impacts on attainment. The popular narrative was that its less formal pedagogy and (literally) more hands on learning would engage boys and the disadvantaged more effectively than its predecessors.

The Welsh Government had explicitly made this narrowing of the gap one of the key targets in its plans to tackle the effects of poverty, in its document *Building Resilient Communities*:

Target: To narrow the gap in attainment levels between learners aged 7 eligible for free school meals and those that are not eligible for free school meals, who achieve the expected levels at the end of the Foundation Phase, as measured by the Foundation Phase Indicator, by 10 per cent by 2017.

The difference between e-FSM (ie eligible for Free School Meals) and non-FSM (ie non-eligible for Free School Meals) attainment in 2012 was 18.3 per cent.[36]

The WISERD research, however, told a starkly different story. The executive summary stated that while 'The Foundation Phase is associated with improved attainment for pupils eligible for free school meals ... the evaluation has found *no evidence to suggest it has made any observable impact so far on reducing inequalities in attainment* at the end of Key Stage 2'(my emphasis).[37] The report had been delivered on time but was apparently sat on by the department to enable the requisite media spin to be devised. Although the Foundation Phase was delivering, what the final report showed was that the great beneficiaries of the Foundation Phase were not impoverished boys, as many had hoped, but non-FSM girls! The Foundation Phase was really helping the *Learning Country's* little Megan from leafy Llandaff, whereas little Dean from deprived Dowlais was improving at a much slower rate and falling further and further behind.

In the detail of the report the problem was laid bare: 'Analysis of the National Pupil Database (NPD) shows that the introduction of the Foundation Phase is not, to date, associated with any significant changes in the differences in educational outcomes between pupils at the end of Key Stage 2 based on their gender, their ethnicity or their eligibility for free school meals (an indicator of socio-economic disadvantage)'.[38]

It piled on the agony: 'For example, the evaluation estimates that girls were over 40% more likely than boys to achieve Level 4 or above in KS2 English before the Foundation Phase. But after the introduction of the Foundation Phase they are now nearly 75% more likely to achieve Level 4 or above compared to boys'.[39] So the gender gap had not narrowed, not even reduced or slightly increased, it had almost doubled.

There was little comfort in terms of the gap that existed between children in poverty and their more affluent peers: 'For pupils eligible for free school meals, the evaluation estimates that they are nearly 30% less likely to achieve Level 4 or above in KS2 English than other pupils. After the introduction of the Foundation Phase this differential remains the same'.[40]

The report threw a few crumbs of comfort by noting that the 'analysis is limited to a relatively small number of children who attended Foundation Phase pilot schools early in its implementation and who have reached the end of Key Stage 2 [and did not] take into account variations in the implementation of the Foundation Phase between schools.' However, it concluded sombrely that despite these caveats 'it is worth noting that observed child involvement and wellbeing ratings in case study schools are generally higher for girls than for boys, even for schools with a high degree of Foundation Phase implementation. This would suggest that there is still a long way to go before the Foundation Phase can fully address differences in the educational experiences of boys and girls'.

The final report laid to rest some of the more extreme scare stories about children being allowed to play to the detriment of any learning, and the spectre that we were raising a cohort of seven-year-olds who were way behind their peers in the rest of the UK. While the *Western Mail* rightly highlighted that the poverty 'silver bullet' had proved to be counterfeit, I felt it was important to note that the report painted a 'very encouraging picture' overall and the Foundation Phase was 'highly valued' by children, parents and school staff. 'It justifies the general assumption that the Foundation Phase has been one of the more successful Welsh Government policies to date'.[41]

We must wait a few more years before we can make a definitive judgment on the true value of the Foundation Phase. By the end of the decade we will have a clearer picture if our children are happier, better behaved and more independent learners. Their GCSE results will be pored over for signs of the Foundation Phase effect and they are also the cohort which will secure the Welsh Government's 'aiming for average' PISA target in 2020. We shall see.

The in-betweeners

If FE has often been called the 'Cinderella Sector', then the Key Stages 2 and 3 can lay a good claim to the title 'the Wilderness Years'. Enclosed by 'sexier' phases it has often been difficult to detect any clear programme or strategy for the years a child spends in school between 8 and 13. The Foundation Phase rightly received enormous interest, focus and funding. As we shall see the post-14 landscape was to change significantly over the period of devolution, but the purpose for the time in between was far more inchoate. Obviously, it should build on what the Foundation Phase had laid but there are still issues surrounding the dovetailing of that phase in Key Stage 2, nearly ten years on. Should Key Stage 3 be merely an ante-chamber to the exam factory of Key Stage 4? More disturbingly, the continual pressure on schools to perform well in GCSEs is pushing that preparation further and further down the years.

Concern about the fate of children between the ages of 8 and 14 was not new, and had been examined in *The Learning Country*. But as the Foundation Phase was being put in place for early years and the Welsh Government's strategy for 14 to 19 pathways being developed at the same time, the 'in-between' years were receiving less attention. Professor David Egan, former Special Adviser to Jane Davidson, and a seemingly permanent fixture of the Welsh educational scene, summed up the concerns well. At a conference organised by the Institute of Welsh Affairs in February 2010, Egan said: 'Some form of systemic reform is required. It's unlikely that the objectives of the Foundation Phase and 14–19 Learning Pathways can be fully achieved, unless changes are made to the 8-14 experience. There's a significant financial concern: we would be throwing money away unless we make changes'.[42]

Egan was speaking with some anxiety. The previous year the outgoing minister, Jane Hutt, had accepted all the recommendations of a report produced by him as chairman of a Task and Finish group convened specifically to look at the what he called 'the bit in the middle'. However, a spokesperson for the incoming minister, Leighton Andrews, had engaged in a classic piece of civil service stalling: 'The minister is keenly aware of the importance of this phase of education. In particular, he wishes to see major improvements in boys' literacy and is currently considering his whole portfolio before announcing decisions on his priorities and the way forward'.[43]

The Task and Finish Group on 8–14 Education Provision in Wales had grown out of concerns from the Webb Review of Further Education, published in December 2007. That review had recommended that the Welsh Government commission a complementary review of 11–16 education. For various reasons, not least the ones outlined by Professor Egan, it was decided to morph this suggestion into a review of the educational experience of 8 to 14-year-olds.

The group began its work in March 2009, and reported the following September. Its remit, as befitted such a group, was quite narrowly drawn:

- To consider the impact and effectiveness of each current DCELLS (Department for Children, Education, Lifelong Learning and Skills) initiative, together with an assessment of the likely impact and effectiveness of initiatives in their early stages of implementation.
- To consider whether the combined effect of the initiatives and approaches looks set to deliver the step change which DCELLS wishes to see in preparing 8 to 14-year-old learners to get the best out of further learning opportunities.
- To identify any gaps, overlaps, issues of fitness for purpose and effectiveness in the combined policy/programme agenda.
- To recommend how DCELLS can make any improvements in educational provision for and wellbeing for 8 to 14-year-olds in Wales.[44]

The report was essentially a desk top exercise with the group members contributing from their own experience. The group itself was noticeable for its dominance of headteachers, to the exclusion of other professionals. Evidence too was limited to that provided by DCELLS (the then DfES) officials. In fairness these should not be considered deficiencies if the report had meant to be 'a starter for ten' to kick off a more wide-ranging debate about the whole 'middle years' problem. It could not be the last word in reviewing 'the underpinning philosophy and structure of the educational experience of 8 to 14-year-olds.' It focussed on the then current initiatives of the Education Department in place, designed to improve the learning and wellbeing of 8 to 14-year-olds in Wales, above all the Schools Effectiveness Framework, which had been introduced in 2008. It was clear simply from the listing of initiatives that there was already a plethora of different directives and demands abroad.

The Task and Finish Group was very concerned by data provided by Estyn that seemed to show a downward trajectory for children's achievement from 8 to 14. The first PISA results were also cited as giving corroboration for these concerns.[45] It was felt that the allegedly low aspirations of the more economically deprived sections of the cohort were exasperated during this period. And while it was clear that 'some individual teachers and schools are able to overcome the effects and associations [of poverty] ... this is not a system-wide feature of the education system in Wales between the ages of 8 and 14'.[46]

The report was candid about the 'data darkness' in this area: 'there is much more that we need to know and understand about the experience and achievement of young people as they pass through 8–14 education... We lack a rigorous body of educational research, other than inspection evidence and specific to Wales on these issues'.[47] The group was genuinely puzzled by the alleged performance dip, especially between the ages of 11 and 14. It wondered 'Why, for example, in relative terms, do eleven-year-olds in Wales appear to do so well in comparison to 14-year-olds?'

No one seems to have suggested that it was the teacher assessments that needed examination, before hypothecating about the causes of the gap they *seemed* to show. The closest they came was when the report pondered the data in regard to the decliners: 'What is not clear, however, is the extent to which the performance of these students was already problematic in the latter years of their primary schooling. For some this would have been evident in their teacher assessment scores at age 11. For others, whilst their teacher assessment scores may have been at the expected levels at age 11, this might mask declining performance'.[48]

With hindsight it is clear that it was the teacher assessments themselves that should have been scrutinised much more closely. But this was in the period before the seismic PISA shocks, the GCSE data and Leighton Andrews' clarion call had alerted the educational establishment to the fact that the way in which the SATs had been abolished had left the system dangerously open to inflated estimations of the performance of students and schools alike.

The Task and Finish Group attempted to provide some answers. But first they ruled out those who wanted no change or total revolution. Those in the first camp, who argued that initiative overload and fatigue should preclude any change, were reminded, rightly, that the welfare and attainment of children should outweigh all other considerations. In the second camp those who were arguing for a system of middle schools had seriously underestimated both the organisational upheaval involved, but also its prohibitive cost.[49] The report wisely tacked to the middle ground and recommended that the government 'designate the educational experience of 8 to 14-year-olds in Wales as being within an "8–14 Phase" that is underpinned by a distinct and coherent educational philosophy... [not] expressed as a single stage, but that rather it be seen as a discrete phase in the same way as the Foundation Phase and 14–19 Learning Pathways'. This recommendation had several implications. There would be a need to develop a stronger 8–14 learning and teaching pedagogy; to develop leadership programmes where primary and secondary leaders worked more collaboratively; to make Year 6 and 7 more coherent in both its delivery and its assessment. The report ended with a plea that the department commission some 'rigorous educational research ... to clearly establish at quantitative and qualitative level the extent to which and the reasons why, the expected educational performance of 8-year-olds in Wales is relatively higher than that of 14-year-olds'.[50]

The Conservatives kept the debate alive. Their manifesto for the 2011 elections urged the formation of a distinct middle phase. A document published by them two years later, the Welsh Conservatives' Alternative Programme for Government, which outlined what they would have done in office, was explicit once more: 'Our policy to introduce a middle phase of 8–13 to ensure the school system is integrated and the gap between the Foundation Phase and 14–19 phase is bridged [sic]'.[51]

That this was no mere flash in the pan was made clear in a Senedd debate in October 2013 when the feisty shadow Minister, Angela Burns, said:

> 'We believe there is a significant gap in the lack of a clear, robust and discrete strategy for the children within our schools who are aged 8 to 14...Of course, students are being educated throughout these years, but unlike the Foundation Phase, with its distinct ethos and pedagogy, and unlike the 14–19 Pathways, with their emphasis on getting to grips with developing appropriate skills for the future, the years between 8 and 14 appear to lack sufficient focus...The Welsh Conservatives have long advocated a middle-phase strategy that recognises the difficult transitions that face pupils as they leave primary school and move to secondary school.'[52]

There followed a rather compelling analysis of all that youngsters faced as they proceeded from childhood into adolescence, and also a restatement of the apparent decline in attainment.

It was interesting to note the interjection of Andrews, by then on the back benches once more: 'The reason that we did not go forward on the 8–14 proposals of Professor Egan was because we were just completing the move to the Foundation Phase and its full roll-out. We wanted to see how that bedded down first. The important thing was to get that right, which is what I think we have done. I do not think that it would have been sensible to have immediately proceeded to a move on the 8–14 agenda.'[53]

In his book, *Ministering to Education*, which came out a year later, Andrews was more forthright. While acknowledging the concerns he had about curriculum change overload that he had expressed in the debate, he also boasted that 'I deliberately kicked into the long grass a review of the 8–13 curriculum, undertaken by a group chaired by Professor David Egan. I read the group's work and concluded that it would require further and deeper work'.[54] Considering that this is the only reference to Egan in the whole of the book it is quite a put-down and indicates the animosity that many believe exists between them.

Lewis, Andrews' replacement, was not going to deviate from that line: 'I note again that the Conservative Party has called for a robust and discrete 8–14 education strategy. My response to this is that I agree that there is an issue, for instance, with Key Stage 3. We will be revisiting what that is delivering for our young people. I have also announced that we will be looking at change at Key Stage 2. However, I do not accept that we need an 8–14 education strategy per se'. And there the matter rested until the Donaldson Review, which we shall examine shortly, suggested a radical reform to the entire curriculum.[55]

14–19 Pathways. Up the garden path?

We saw in Chapter 1 that anxiety about Britain's educational performance in the latter years of schooling was nothing new, and not peculiar to Wales. In his foreword to the seminal report of Professor Alison Wolf on Vocational Education, the then Secretary of State for Education, Michael Gove, had noted in his own laconic manner that 'Since Prince Albert established the Royal Commission in 1851, policy-makers have struggled with our failure to provide young people with a proper technical and practical education of a kind that other nations can boast. A hundred and sixty years later the same problems remain'.[56]

Learning Pathways

No amount of legislation or public moralising could convince some parents that the best routes for their children lay along the non-academic trajectory. In more recent years a different tack has been tried, by blurring the distinction between vocational and academic. This has some merit. After all, into which category would a law degree fall, or even medicine for that matter? The more pressing practical problem, however, has been to ensure that youngsters are informed about choices and then making a raft of choices available. It was to address both these issues that the Welsh Government introduced the whole concept of Learning Pathways, to cover the years from 14 to 19.

Learning Country: Learning Pathways 14–19 was put out to consultation in October 2002. In her foreword, Davidson was gushing as usual and introduced the main policy contours :

> The proposals break new ground. They aspire to widen choice and
> opportunity through local networks. They identify four distinctive

routes, providing access for all young people to appropriate learning past the age of 16. They incorporate the Welsh Baccalaureate as an overarching award. They establish the concept of a continuum of learning for all young people from 14–19. They create a framework for individual Learning Pathways which will ensure exciting and extended experiences and opportunities for all young people, whilst allowing a tailored, flexible curriculum for each of them.

Most importantly, the proposals focus on the wider needs of all young people. Without a wide range of skills essential to modern life, young people cannot make best use of their knowledge, aptitudes or talents. Nor can they develop the degree of self-motivation essential for employability and personal success. These skills are best developed through experience and practical application in community groups, voluntary activities, sports or cultural activity, or in the workplace, as well as in day-to-day learning environments.[57]

The document celebrated the work that was already being done in many parts of Wales and inevitably urged the spread of such best practice. Its proposals had quite specific aims: 'to increase the participation rates for 16 to 18-year-olds in education, training or employment from the present 88 per cent to at least 95 per cent; ensure that every student leaves school with qualifications; increase the percentage of 16-year-olds who achieve 5 A* – Cs [interestingly no target was set for these, even though one had been explicit in the foundation *Learning Country* document – another indication of the silo mentality of the civil service].[58]

This increase in participation and results was to be accomplished by achieving a balance of three overarching demands: 'knowledge – subject knowledge, technical and occupational knowledge (hard skills); opportunities to apply this capacity in real life contexts, to deepen knowledge and understanding and to develop as a learner; opportunities to develop wider personal and interpersonal skills (soft skills) through practical experience'.[59] The quest for this balance was to occupy practitioners for the next decade.

The overriding desire was to embed 'flexibility', and the key to the approach was to be 'choice'. This would lead away from standard understandings of success as comprising a clutch of good GCSEs. Each student would have their own personal, tailored 'approved learning pathway', which could challenge traditional assumptions of suitable qualifications mix. The document was also clear that youngsters should develop the 'soft skills' such as initiative, communication and team working, that employers had been lamenting the absence of for decades. Interestingly, in the light of future debates, it urged that 'the age of 16 is a progress check rather than an exit point', as it was hoped most youngsters would continue in education and training beyond this point. The highly radical approach, subsequently adopted by the CBI, that national examinations at this point were therefore otiose was not canvassed. The ill-fated ELWa was to be entrusted with ensuring that work experience was more relevant and fruitful than before. The doomed ACCAC was tasked with the not insubstantial undertaking of removing prejudices about the academic and vocational divide.

The document refreshingly also realised that the youngsters themselves had a great deal to contribute to the ongoing debate. This axiomatic realisation has not always been so evident. The seven core aims of the UN Convention of the Rights of the Child were to underpin all such engagement. Nationally, voices could be canvassed through Funky Dragon – the Children and Young People's Assembly for Wales – but more locally there should be forums in all local authorities and each school should have its own council. In colleges, student councils and the National Union of Students were considered as vital to the symbiotic process which characterises the best education.[60]

An entire chapter was devoted to 'Advice, support, and guidance', a clear acknowledgement that far more needed to be done in this area. The idea of an 'individual learning coach' was first floated here. It was realised that such support would need to intensify post-14 and would also require skills which took account of the youngster's life as extended beyond the school gate. There were also proposals for online guidance and an online 'Progress File'.

Returning to earlier musings on GCSE, the document made something of an impassioned plea about those who achieved under the bar. 'Despite the intentions of its design and the value placed on the achievement at grades D–G in *The Learning Country*, the perception of too many learners, teachers, parents and employers is that grades A*–C constitute the only worthwhile achievement at GCSE'. The main elephant in the room at this point, the government's own performance measure of schools, was not mentioned. It was proposed that those achieving grades D–G should be seen as having 'succeeded at foundation level, rather than having effectively fallen short'.[61] Modular and online assessment should become the norm rather than the exception. The document looked forward to the report back from the Welsh Baccalaureate which it hoped would boost its take-up in schools.

Delivery of the whole package was to be the responsibility of emerging 14–19 networks. The funding streams were to remain unchanged, with schools being funded via the Local Education Authority and colleges via ELWa.

The Webb Review

However, the making of policy was not itself the magic wand that would transform the educational landscape. *The Learning Country* had promised a root and branch review of Further Education provision in Wales. That belatedly got off the ground towards the end of 2006. Wales was the last part of the UK to conduct a review of Further Education. The Webb Review, or to give it its full title, *PROMISE AND PERFORMANCE: The Report of the Independent Review of the Mission and Purpose of Further Education in Wales in the context of the Learning Country: Vision into Action*, was thorough, wide reaching and damning. Chaired by the somewhat flamboyant former Vice Chancellor of the University of Glamorgan, Sir Adrian Webb, the report did not fail to tell it as it was. Although the remit was only FE, very early on he and his fellow experts, Sheila Drury and Gary Griffiths, decided that they should look at 14–19 provision in the round. While this expansion was welcome, the lack of a voice from the school sector was evident.[62]

The Webb Report was keen to note the economic benefits that upskilling could bring both for the individual, and for the country as a whole. The lack of achievement exhibited by many youngsters could have lifelong consequences. It noted that significant progress had been made since the advent of devolution, especially in regard to the development of innovative policies focussed on the learner and the achievements of the learners themselves. It was full of praise for the 14–19 Pathways policy, which it praised as 'one of the most significant educational developments for many years [which] entrenches the principle of learner entitlement by guaranteeing a variety of learning routes, from academic to practical, and imaginatively recognising the importance of non-formal and informal learning alongside traditional learning methods'.[63] The authors were critical of the 'long shadow' cast over school education by the assumption that university was the finishing post to which all should be aiming.

But the report went on to claim that there had been a lack of substantial achievements in key areas: the promised expansion of choice for 14–19 learners had failed to materialise; employers were still complaining about the products of the system; and the number of NEETs (Not in Education, Employment or Training) was still unacceptably high. The report wanted to see several outcomes, among which were the virtual elimination of the basic skills gap and of NEETS; the virtual eradication of disengagement among school age learners; and ensuring that all learners left compulsory education with meaningful qualifications or accredited skills.

The report did not want to point the finger of blame at 'the many in the education system and in government who strive to achieve what is needed. It is to recognise reality ... Nonetheless, the education system itself is a factor in the equation and historically it has been least good at developing and engaging those learners who seek or who need vocational and practically-based learning opportunities'. It warned that 'Learner entitlement will be a chimera if these issues are not tackled'.[64] It was clear that the report's authors were quite critical of the status quo, especially in regard to schools, noting that there was too much unauthorised absence and disengagement in schools, too many empty places that were exacerbated by falling rolls, and 'too many providers in unhelpful competition'. It was not surprising therefore that the report, noting the Leitch report of the previous year about the need for the UK to become more competitive, urged 'further radical change; marginal adjustments will not suffice'.[65]

Fundamental to any real progress in rolling out the 14–19 Pathways programme, the report's authors believed, was the embedding of the principle of choice: 'The first challenge is the provision of a real choice to learners. To embed more personalised learning we need to offer each learner a choice of a wide range of subjects, pathways and modes of learning to suit as many interests, capabilities, learning styles and career opportunities as possible. Choice should apply equally to all learners, whether they are academically or practically orientated'.[66] There were naturally concerns about the curriculum offer, especially about 'bogus' vocational courses that were taught so traditionally that the distinctive flavour of proper vocational education was lost. The authors believed, however, that the Welsh Baccalaureate could become 'a unique philosophy of post-14 holistic personal development, which unites excellence with breadth and celebrates a rich combination of academic and vocational education, knowledge and skills, technical and social competencies'.[67] But they were equally clear that the Welsh Bacc as it stood was 'not the finished article' and needed a great deal more work. The importance of apprenticeships was also highlighted, but employer frustration with schools' lack of engagement was palpable. And as was to be expected for a report in the wake of Leitch, concern was expressed about the comparative decline in the numbers studying the so-called STEM subjects and the quality and reliability of the qualifications gained.

If choice was to be the watchword of the new regime, then the provision of information about the actual choices available was key. But here the report was full of warnings that this was not the case in many parts of Wales. Although ostensibly not wanting to point the finger of blame it was clear that the authors felt that schools were the worst culprits. It lamented that 'some teachers and headteachers still view vocational routes as an easy option for those who cannot succeed in GCSEs and A-levels' and also that they had been given 'a number of examples of institutions preventing learners from gaining information about opportunities provided by other local providers'. They were adamant: 'Such restrictions on the information available about choices must cease'.[68] What was not commented on was the Welsh Government's funding regime, which made schools desperate to cling on to pupils.

Taking no prisoners, the report realised the major challenge of implementation was always the government's Achilles heel: '14–19 Learning

Pathways is an excellent policy. It is the implementation of this policy which now challenges the Department'. They had been upfront from the start about this, noting in the opening chapter that while their 'recommendations are designed to improve policy ... we emphasise that in large measure it is the speed, determination and effectiveness with which policies are implemented on the ground that will determine success. To develop good policies is difficult, but to implement them effectively is the bigger task'. The obstacles to good implementation were several but chief among them were resources and the proliferation of institutions, especially very small sixth forms. Estyn had found the year before that the relationship between institutions was best described as 'competitive' in nearly two thirds of Wales.[69]

Voluntary cooperation and moral exhortation were not enough. Structural change was needed, and the report mooted the formation of nine managed consortia to deliver across a geographic area. Several pages outlined the governance arrangements for this proposal. The consortia would be responsible for commissioning learning from the institutions within it, to provide a broad and wide offer and facilitate real choice. The level of opposition from schools and local authorities was not factored in.

By the end of the report it was becoming increasingly obvious that its authors were quietly pointing the finger at what they considered the weakest link – schools. Urging that there should be a renewed 'determination to place the interests of learners and Wales as a nation above those of providers' they called for a complementary independent review of 11–16 schooling, aimed at providing a transformation of provision, practice and pedagogy. The goal would be to develop highly personalised Individual Learning Plans which would be tailored to meet the needs of each child and enhance his or her journey.

Towards its end the report presciently drew attention to the emerging funding gap both for programmes and for capital expenditure in Wales. It was quite clear that whereas England was spending more on the 14 to 19 cohort, Wales was comparatively spending less and less. The inefficiencies in the system – the proliferation of institutions, geographical costs, the myriad of grants and funding streams – served only to make the matter worse. For policy makers, the data was disturbing, especially when coupled with the ever widening per pupil funding gap between Wales and England, which was opening up at an alarming rate from 2005 onwards. In 2004/5 it stood at £241; by 2008/9 it had more than doubled to £532.

But funding was only one of the Welsh Government's key roles. The report was clear that the Department needed to 'establish outcome-focussed departmental strategies, set priorities, determine the allocation of funding, drive efficiency and performance, and create productive links between all aspects of delivery from centre to localities'. Many would say that we are still waiting. One of the report's many barbs still rings true, almost ten years on: 'small countries can slip into a cosiness that limits ambition'.[70]

The Report made 136 recommendations in all. The response of the Welsh Government was interesting. In recent years we have grown used to 'independent' reports being accepted in their entirety which, depending on your point of view, is either a reflection of the overwhelming consensus or a matter of reporting 'behind the chair'. The Webb Review was different. While accepting the vast majority of its recommendations, especially those connected with more nuts and bolts issues such as basic skills, the government was not prepared to take on the schools and local authorities. The proposals for more mandatory collaboration were rejected: 'We do not intend to prescribe a specific model for collaborative arrangements. We are developing a policy and framework to assist stakeholders to make improvements to the delivery of post-16 education and training provision across all sectors'.[71] Similarly, there were to be no changes to the funding mechanism.

The Terracotta Document

The policy referred to became known as 'the Terracotta Document' from the colour of its cover. Published in September 2008 and entitled *Transforming Education and Training Provision in Wales: Delivering Skills That Work for Wales*, this became the Welsh Government's blueprint for transforming provision for the cohort.[72]

The *Skills that Work for Wales* strategy was an attempt to address the well-documented skills deficit, and arose out of the *One Wales* agreement of the Labour-Plaid Cymru coalition government of 2007 to 2011.[73] The thrust of it was threefold: to widen the options available for students at 14–19, to reduce unnecessary duplication, and to do so by building excellent networks of providers. There would be a National Framework but local delivery, though the funding mechanism would be used to ensure compliance with the broad thrust of the policy. While the document blustered about cooperation and collaboration, it was clear that the vested interests in the system would not be forced into line. The strategy's developers, most of whom sat in the FE/HE silo of the department, might have thought that this, coupled with the clear rejection of the more outré of the recommendations of the Webb Review, would have been sufficient to establish buy-in from the school sector. They were sadly mistaken. In fact, phrases such as 'notwithstanding the improvements to provider delivery, there is substantial evidence to show that there are too many small school sixth forms and, in a few areas, too many secondary schools' were hardly likely to win friends.[74] The establishment of the geographic and sectoral Learning Partnerships between providers could do little to allay initial suspicions.

And so began the long and tortuous process of 'transformation'. As the department had ducked the whole question of tertiary versus sixth forms, the resultant map was patchy in the extreme and bore more relation to the power of vested interests than it did to actual student need. A full and proper debate about the best way of providing for post-16 education and the institutional form that should embody it would have provided an overall narrative for its purpose. It would also have meant that youngsters in Wales would not be penalised by another post code lottery. If one looks at the present configuration of post-16 provision, what is most striking is that those in leafy suburbs have greatest choice while those who live in the most deprived areas of Wales, such as Merthyr Tydfil and Blaenau Gwent, have no choice but to continue their education in the local FE college. That is not to suggest that the education provided by the colleges is worse than that provided in school sixth forms – comparisons are virtually impossible to make and there is some evidence that in a number of areas the college provision is better – but it does mean that a key component of 'choice' set out in the original Learning Country document is denied to those who live in the poorer areas of Wales.

Choice in action

As well as the transformation of providers, there was also to be a directed transformation of the provision. The Learning and Skills Measure (before changes in constitutional arrangements, the Assembly passed Measures rather than Acts) was passed in 2009. Its key provision was the formation of a local curriculum which would guarantee a minimum choice for learners and, importantly, dictated some of the composition of that choice. Students henceforth would need to be presented with a menu of at least thirty courses of study options, five of which had to be of a vocational nature.[75]

The Guidance which accompanied the measure was telling. 'Information should be given in an impartial manner and advice should be tendered which is considered to promote the best interest of the young person and does not seek to promote the interests or aspirations of any school, institution or other person or body against the best interests of the young person concerned'.[76] But again it was one thing to make policy and another to enforce it. Complaints continued that schools were not making a full list of options available to their students, and there were several eyebrows raised about the quality of some of the 'vocational' courses on offer.

With the advent of Leighton Andrews and the explicit rejection of the mantra of choice, 'the thirty options' menu became more contested. Not that he was alone. An investigation by the Children, Young People and Education Committee of the National Assembly was blunt. Its first recommendation was: 'The Minister for Education and Skills should review the decision to set thirty courses (including five vocational courses) as the minimum number of courses of study necessary to form a local curriculum at Key Stage 4'.[77]

Andrews accepted the committee's recommendation and also set up a Task and Finish Group to look into this and other recommendations. Chaired by Claire Armitstead, Headteacher of Rhyl High School, the group met for six months between February and September 2013. The Foreword to their report spoke volumes: 'It is our belief that the quality of the choices rather than quantity of courses available is what counts. By reducing the size of the curriculum offer at KS4, we want to make the offer real, deliverable and fair. By including in this offer the need for a minimum of three vocational courses we show our respect for vocational learning and our understanding that skills are taught and shown in more than one way'.[78]

The tide was obviously turning and despite the protestations of Colegau Cymru, the FE principals' lobbying organisation, who believed 'a minimum of five vocational courses to be about right for 14–19 learners', the regulations were amended so that 'the minimum number of courses that a local authority must include in its local curriculum are twenty-five, of which three must be vocational'.[79] Much time, energy and anger had been expended in the meantime. The Welsh medium lobby had been particularly incensed by the insensitive way the original proposals had flip flopped back and fore in confusion over Welsh medium provision and bilingual provision. Schools had feared a grab on their sixth forms, and colleges had the prize snatched from them. At present there are still loud rumblings over insufficient vocational provision, provider capture, and inaccurate advice. The long shadow of the vocational-academic divide does not seem to be shortening.

So Megan's journey continues. She has had the benefit of the Foundation Phase and has, hopefully, acquired the habit of lifelong learning. As a girl from the right side of the tracks, her achievement has soared; Dean from deprived Dowlais has continued to languish. The cost of their education has weighed heavily on the education budget. They are now in the 'middle phase', which still lacks coherence. When she gets to 14 she will have subject option choices to make but not from as wide a menu as was once promised. Megan can choose to stay on at school and attend the sixth form or go to the local FE college as she wishes. Dean, however, will have no choice but to go to the latter.

Notes

1   http://www.walesonline.co.uk/news/wales-news/flagship-foundation-phase-requires-10-year-7142602
2   http://gov.wales/topics/educationandskills/earlyyearshome/foundation-phase/?lang=en

3   http://www.foundationyears.org.uk/eyfs-statutory-framework/
4   http://gov.wales/topics/educationandskills/earlyyearshome/foundation-phase/?lang=en
5   http://gov.wales/docs/dcells/publications/120419fpconsultationen.pdfp://www.educationengland.org.uk/documents/plowden/plowden1967-1.html
6   The Learning Country: The Foundation Phase 3–7 years http://gov.wales/docs/dcells/publications/120419fpconsultationen.pdf
7   Ministerial Foreword.
8   P. 5.
9   P. 6.
10 P. 9.
11 P. 10.
12 P. 10.
13 P. 13.
14 P. 13.
15 P. 14.
16 P. 26.
17 P. 18.
18 http://news.bbc.co.uk/1/hi/wales/2752895.stm
19 Summary of Consultation Reponses to the Learning Country Foundation Phase (2003) http://gov.wales/docs/dcells/publications/120419fpsummaryen.pdf
20 Planet 200, (2010)http://www.francisboutle.co.uk/pages.php?cID=6&pID=115
21 OECD, *Improving Schools in Wales: An OECD Perspective* (2014), p. 54.
22 https://www.tes.co.uk/article.aspx?storycode=2043640
23 http://www.walesonline.co.uk/news/wales-news/welsh-government-pupil-assessment-tool-2026756
24 Siraj-Blatchford Iram, An Independent (Unfunded) Rapid Review of the Child Development Assessment Profile (CDAP) on entry to the Foundation Phase in Wales (Institute of Education, University of London) p. 9. http://gov.wales/docs/dcells/publications/120430cdapreviewen.pdf
25 http://gov.wales/about/cabinet/cabinetstatements/2012/childdevelopmentprofile/?lang=en
26 http://www.walesonline.co.uk/news/wales-news/leighton-andrews-u-turn-key-early-education-2036518
27 Final Report, p. 81.
28 http://gov.wales/about/cabinet/cabinetstatements/2015/foundationphase/?lang=en
29 The Foundation Phase Pilots August 2007 http://www.estyn.gov.uk/english/docViewer/175566.3/the-foundation-phase-pilots-august-2007/?navmap=30,163,
30 Summaries of Estyn Remit Surveys 2011, http://www.google.co.uk/url?sa=t&rct=j&q=&esrc=s&source=web&cd=5&ved=0CDkQFjAEahUKEwiN2pr8_InGAhXFhSwKHSkqAJg&url=http%3A%2F%2Fwww.estyn.gov.uk%2Fdownload%2Fpublication%2F234015.6%2Fsummaries-of-estyn-remit-surveys%2F&ei=Wrh6VY3FLcWLsgGp1IDACQ&usg=AFQjCNEQpTjr0kuDphx-0slQ1XgY5S4igA
31 http://learning.gov.wales/news/pressreleases/prof-iram-siraj-blatchford-stocktake/?lang=en
32 http://gov.wales/docs/dcells/publications/140519-independent-stocktake-of-the-foundation-phase-in-wales-en.pdf, p3
33 Pages 7–10. Training helpfully italicised.
34 Chris Taylor et al., *Evaluating the Foundation Phase: Final Report* (2015), http://gov.wales/docs/caecd/research/2015/150514-foundation-phase-final-en.pdf
35 *Evaluating the Foundation Phase: Final Report*, p. 94.
36 *Building Resilient Communities*, p. 14, http://gov.wales/docs/dsjlg/publications/socialjustice/130703takeforpovactplanen.pdf
37 WISERD *Evaluating the Foundation Phase: Final Report* p. 3.

38   P. 95.
39   P. 95.
40   P. 3.
41   http://www.walesonline.co.uk/news/wales-news/flagship-education-policy-raising-performance-9251215
42   Reform middle years now, urges Assembly adviser https://www.tes.co.uk/article.aspx?storycode=6036465
43   Ibid.
44   TASK AND FINISH GROUP ON 8-14 EDUCATION PROVISION IN WALES FIRST STAGE REPORT September 2010, http://gov.wales/topics/educationandskills/publications/reports/taskandfinishgroupfirststagerpt/?lang=en
45   P. 18.
46   P. 19.
47   P. 21.
48   Pp. 20 and 21.
49   P. 22.
50   P. 24.
51   Welsh Conservatives' Alternative Programme for Government (2013). No page number but under section on education. http://www.welshconservatives.com/sites/www.welshconservatives.com/files/welsh_conservative_programme_for_government.pdf
52   http://www.yoursenedd.com/debates/2013-10-23-welsh-conservatives-debate-8-14-education
53   Ibid.
54   Andrews, *Ministering to Education*, p. 231.
55   Same debate.
56   https://www.gov.uk/government/publications/review-of-vocational-education-the-wolf-report p. 4.
57   http://gov.wales/dcells/publications/publications/circularsindex/04/learningpathways/learningcountry-e.pdf?lang=en, p. 3.
58   P. 5.
59   P. 5.
60   P. 22.
61   P. 27.
62   http://gov.wales/dcells/publications/policy_strategy_and_planning/furtherandhighereducation/fehereviews/webbreview/promiseperformance-e.pdf?lang=en
63   P. 12.
64   P. 6.
65   P. 7.
66   P. 28.
67   P. 29.
68   P. 39.
69   P. 68, figure 7.
70   P. 107.
71   Welsh Assembly Government, Department for Children, Education, Lifelong Learning and Skills Response to the Recommendations Contained in 'Promise and Performance' – (The Webb Report). R64
72   http://gov.wales/docs/dcells/publications/100301transformationpolicyen.pdf
73   'One Wales: A progressive agenda for the government of Wales' http://gov.wales/strategy/strategies/onewales/onewalese.pdf?lang=en
74   P. 22.
75   http://www.legislation.gov.uk/mwa/2009/1/pdfs/mwa_20090001_en.pdf

76   http://gov.wales/docs/dcells/publications/140514-learning-and-skills-measure-2009-local-curriculum-for-students-16-18-en.pdf p.17

77   CYPC Inquiry into the Implementation of the Learning and Skills Measure (Wales) 2009. May 2012 http://www.senedd.assembly.wales/documents/s7574/Inquiry%20into%20the%20Implementation%20of%20the%20Learning%20and%20Skills%20Wales%20Measure%202009%20-%20Report%20-%20May%202012.pdf p. 5.

78   The Review of Local of Collaborative Provision at Key Stage 4 Task and Finish Group Report http://gov.wales/docs/dcells/report/131008-review-collaborative-provision-en.pdf p. 1.

79   The Education (Local Curriculum for Pupils in Key Stage 4) (Wales) (Amendment) Regulations 2014 http://www.legislation.gov.uk/wsi/2014/42/note/made?view=plain

4

Teaching and Learning
From the National Curriculum to the Donaldson Review

So as little Megan makes her way through the Welsh school system, what will she be taught and how will we know what progress she is making? As she approaches the end of her period of compulsory education, what qualifications will she take and what value will they have?

The triumvirate of curriculum, assessment and qualifications has been one of the most dominating concerns of education in the UK for decades. Since devolution their importance has, if anything , increased in Wales. While some issues come and others go these are seemingly perennial. In this chapter and the next we will examine the debates and decisions around them, the cul-de-sacs entered, and some of the progress made. In the seventeen years since devolution there have been numerous large and small reviews of all three areas, and a plethora of recommendations made. Ministers have constantly proclaimed that things are getting better and that we have learned from the past. During those seventeen years no child in Wales will have been left unscathed by changes to the curriculum, assessment and qualifications regimes. Some changes have been for the better, others are far more questionable. One thing is certain – stability remains elusive.

Curriculum

Politicians love tinkering with educational structures. One has only to look across the border at the '57 varieties' of schools now on offer, to see the importance attached to structural arrangements. We have been spared that in Wales, by and large, but the desire to tinker with structures is as nothing to their deep seated desire to interfere in the curriculum. In that regard, politicians in Wales share the frenzied desire to shape the curriculum, and it shows no sign of abating.

The frenzy is so prevalent that we can wrongly take it as the norm. It is not. In many other countries, curriculum reform has been kept to an absolute minimum, Finland being a good instance. But the mania for curriculum reform was not typical of the British system until fairly recently. One has only to look over the number of Parliamentary Acts to see the truth of this claim.[1]

There are a number of reasons why curriculum has come to preoccupy politicians. One is the decades' long fear that our commercial rivals are overtaking us. Anxiety in this area tends to focus especially on youngsters' mathematical ability and, more recently, on their command of computer technology, especially programming. Another is the perception that curriculum is one of the main transmitters of culture. Here anxieties tend to be fixated on the content of the History and English curriculum. None has been a more articulate advocate of this approach than Michael Gove, Westminster Secretary of State for Education from 2010 to 2014. In Wales, as well as the anxieties outlined above, another main cultural driver has been the preservation and promotion of the Welsh language. Suffice to say that the curriculum looks set to be a contested area in education in Wales and England for some time to come.

Part of the problem lies in the framing of the fundamentals of the debate. Is the fundamental question 'What should the curriculum contain?' or 'What should the curriculum do?' The first inevitably leads to frenzied debate, on the right, about kings, queens and wars, and on the left, about leading women, ethnic history and peace studies. The second question produces answers which focus on skills and employability, which are more nebulous.

The link between curriculum, assessment and qualifications is not denied but is similarly contested. Obviously assessment needs to take place so a child's progress can be monitored and enhanced, but should this be a tool of the professional alone or should national assessment be imposed? Qualifications link with the curriculum in an intimate way and should be determined by it, but all too often qualifications reform has been used to drive curriculum reform. In many ways what is not tested is not valued. Once performance measures for schools include qualifications achieved by pupils, the stakes become much higher again.

The National Curriculum

Although the 1988 National Curriculum was devised on an England, Wales and Northern Ireland basis, provision was made for the different characteristics of each. In Wales this recognition of difference was well over a century old. As we saw in Chapter 1, as early as 1890 the Privy Council had made provision for teaching which took account of Welsh history and geography when it agreed monies to pay for the teaching of Welsh grammar. In 1927 the Wales Department in the Board of Education had published a report entitled 'Welsh in Education and Life', which realised the unique role of the language but also history and culture. After the Second World War the report *Curriculum and Community in Wales* of 1952 had argued that at least some Welsh dimension was necessary. I re-emphasise these little footnotes of history because they show that the distinctive nature of Welsh education was well established by the time that the most homogenising of ventures – the creation of the National Curriculum – arrived on the scene in 1988. From the start the National Curriculum for Wales differed from that of England. It obviously included the Welsh language, but other subjects, such as history, geography and music were also modified to take account of the nation's heritage and culture.

These differences were not dependent on ministerial whim. The 1988 Act established the Curriculum Council for Wales, a body which was to have far greater input into its deliberations than its English counterpart. In 1994 the CCW was supplanted by ACCAC (Awdurdod Cymwysterau Cwricwlwm ac Asesu Cymru/the Qualifications, Curriculum and Assessment Authority for Wales) which was to be responsible for: ensuring quality and standards in external, general and vocational qualifications; keeping under review all aspects of the school curriculum and statutory arrangements for maintained schools; and commissioning Welsh bilingual classroom materials to support the teaching of Welsh and other subjects. For the first time, there was a single organisation in Wales, responsible for overseeing and advising on both academic and vocational qualifications and the school curriculum. In many ways ACCAC functioned as the Welsh equivalent of England's Qualifications and Curriculum Authority. So, well before the advent of the National Assembly, there was a significant element of devolution in regard to the curriculum to be delivered in Welsh schools. There was also a lively debate about several of its aspects – the Gittens Report of 1967, for instance, had made several radical proposals in regard to the early teaching of the Welsh language. And crucially there was a body of expertise and knowledge on which the fledgling Assembly could draw.

The Foundation Phase, which we examined in depth in the last chapter, was a case in point. The debate about early provision was not one that started in 1999. The fundamental changes to the curriculum in the earliest years were the product of a debate which had commenced some decades before. With hindsight, the debate about the Foundation Phase was too narrowly focussed on the early years which, though important, is only, after all, part of a child's educational experience. It would have been better to have held a national debate on the nature and purpose of the curriculum as a whole – but that was to be another fifteen years in the coming.

The debate about the Foundation Phase had at least shown some coherence: it covered a specific phase, it advocated a specific pedagogy and approach, and it was reasonably clear about its purpose. Beyond the age of seven, the 1988 curriculum was to be subjected to a plethora of reviews, amendments and tweaks which at best provided sticking plasters in place of more fundamental reforms. At the time of writing, the curriculum to be followed by 3 to 19-year-olds is comprised of the following: the Foundation Phase; skills development; the National Curriculum; personal and social education; sex education; careers and the world of work; religious education. The National Curriculum also incorporates the *Cwricwlwm Cymreig*. Each of those areas has been subject to continual scrutiny and we have already examined the Foundation Phase in detail. We shall now consider the *Cwricwlwm Cymreig* and the attempts to make the whole system more skills focussed. (Obviously the acceptance of the Donaldson Review of the curriculum means this current regime is on the way out. It will be beneficial, however, to examine it in depth. Not least to learn the lessons it teaches, and to avoid repeating some of the mistakes made.)

Y Cwricwlwm Cymreig[2]

The development of a specifically Welsh curriculum had been the quest of many in the Welsh education establishment for decades. Largely this was dictated by the desire to preserve Welsh language and culture, but after 1988 it was also driven by the desire to create a more modern curriculum. In 1989 the Curriculum Council for Wales (precursor to ACCAC) had issued a consultation document *A Framework for the Whole Curriculum 5–16 in Wales: A Discussion Paper*. In 1991 it published its response in the form of *The Whole Curriculum in Wales 5–16* which used the phrase *Y Cwricwlwm Cymreig* for the first time.[3]

The Curriculum Council for Wales had identified three key characteristics as contributing to the *Cwricwlwm Cymreig*: the Welsh language as a subject and as a medium of teaching and learning; aspects of curriculum content which are distinctive to Wales; and the general 'Welshness' of pupils' learning experiences. Two years later they published further guidance which highlighted five elements to be developed in pupils: 'a sense of belonging; a sense of place and heritage; an awareness of the importance of language and literature in the history and life of Wales; an understanding of the creative and expressive arts in Wales; and an awareness of the factors that have shaped Welsh religious beliefs and practices'.[4]

But, as ever, policy development was one thing and implementation another. In 2001, an Estyn Report, *Y Cwricwlwm Cymreig, The Welsh dimension of the curriculum in Wales: good practice in teaching and learning* noted that there had been relatively little progress since *Advisory Paper 18*, almost a decade before. Practitioners were broadly supportive of a more distinctive Welsh curriculum but provision varied wildly across the country. Access to good quality resources, which were not overwhelmingly Anglo-centric, was also a key issue.[5] It was also noted in passing that many Heads of Department felt that the new smaller unitary authorities had curtailed practitioners' own ability to develop suitable resources.[6]

Although the inspectors noted almost universal enthusiasm for the concept of a distinctively Welsh curriculum, and reported that nearly three quarters of schools had provision which was good or satisfactory, there was considerable regional variation. While in south-west, mid and north Wales less than 20% of lessons were rated as unsatisfactory in regard to the Cwriculum in south-east Wales twice as many, 41%, were so rated.[7] The report concluded by recommending, *inter alia*, that the Cwriculum should be more central in schools' planning, that its links with other non-traditional subjects be enhanced, and more resources be produced. It also urged the ironing out of regional variations and the use of INSET days to do this.[8]

In 2003 ACCAC published more definitive guidance in the form of *Developing the Curriculum Cymreig* [sic]. This was part of a series of publications to help embed the revised curriculum. The guidance claimed that the *Cwricwlwm Cymreig* 'helps pupils to understand and celebrate the distinctive quality of living and learning in Wales in the twenty-first century, to identify their own sense of Welshness and to feel a heightened sense of belonging to their local community and country'. It would also help 'to foster in pupils an understanding of an outward-looking and international Wales, promoting global citizenship and concern for sustainable development'.[9] This perspective was also being developed in the emerging Welsh Baccalaureate qualification, which was mentioned with approbation. The document was keen to stress that it wanted to see a whole school approach to implementation and a whole curriculum approach. This was not to be another discrete bolt-on to the status quo.

Noting that the Common Requirements of the school curriculum identified five aspects of the *Cwricwlwm Cymreig* – cultural, economic, environmental, historical and linguistic – the guidance went on to provide salient examples of each in turn. The document was refreshingly candid: 'Because Welsh society is very diverse, there can be no single view of what it is to be Welsh'.[10] Later reviews were to be less nuanced. In an almost verbatim quote from the Estyn report of 2001 it warned that 'Schools should be wary, however, of promoting a stereotypical view of Welshness. Wales has never been a homogenous society. The standard images of dolls in Welsh costume, red dragon flags, daffodils, castles and sheep have some value in helping to convey a sense of identity to younger pupils. If their use continues with older pupils, it gives a very false impression of Wales in the modern world'.[11] The bulk of the document then produced a raft of case studies as to how the *Cwricwlwm Cymreig* could be mainstreamed into the statutory and non-statutory subjects, as well as into other aspects of the day to day routine of the school.

A 'Phase 2' report by Estyn in 2006 showed that substantial progress had been made. It found that 'Standards and the quality of teaching are good or better in three-quarters of the survey schools. In these schools, the *Cwricwlwm Cymreig* is often a strong feature and provides purpose, direction and significance to pupils' learning'. However, it noted that 'Few of the teachers who are new to working in Wales have received in-service training or an induction pack on the *Cwricwlwm Cymreig*. They have limited awareness of the distinctive nature of the school curriculum in Wales'. The report went on to say that 'The provision of resources for the *Cwricwlwm Cymreig* is satisfactory overall. It is a continuous challenge for most schools to provide up-to-date materials for the *Cwricwlwm Cymreig'*.[12] Anna Brychan, Director of NAHT Cymru, called on the General Teaching Council for Wales (GTCW) to do more in that regard.[13]

Skilling up the curriculum

One of the major battlegrounds over the curriculum has been the exact nature of the balance between skills and knowledge. Partisans at both extremes can be found. Gove is probably the best known advocate of a curriculum which still majors on the learning, retention and command of knowledge. The curriculum reforms in England have largely gone in that direction. Others have argued, rather facilely, that in the Google age knowledge is there at the swipe of a finger and skills are all that matter. Wales has remained more in the mainstream by emphasising both, at least in policy terms.

The National Curriculum of 1988 had barely had time to bed in before a raft of reviews was unleashed upon it. In 1993 and 1994 there had been the review of the National Curriculum Orders carried out by the Curriculum Council for Wales (CCW) and ACAC[14], in conjunction with Dearing's review in England. In 1995 and 1996 ACAC had a full and thorough review of the National Curriculum assessment arrangements. Between 1997 and 1999 ACCAC had carried out reviews of Personal and Social Education (PSE) and Work-Related Education (WRE). Despite all this, an *Interim Report: School of the Future* prepared for the Education and Lifelong Learning Committee in 2003 recorded that there was broad agreement that the National Curriculum had eliminated past inconsistencies in the quality of teaching and learning provided across Wales. Overall, the concept of a national curriculum was judged to be useful and should be retained.[15]

Almost from its inception there was a general feeling that the 1988 Curriculum Orders, which set out the content and structure of the curriculum, were too narrowly focussed on detailed subject knowledge rather than skills development. Between 1997 and 1999 ACCAC had undertaken a review of the school curriculum aimed at providing a single coherent framework for curriculum and assessment from the start of the new millennium. The resultant document attempted to draw together the increasingly disparate strands of the National Curriculum and its modifications. Skills were given a higher profile than might have been immediately obvious from the text of 1988 documents, but other than that there was little indication of the thinking that needed to be done in regard to curriculum development.[16]

In 2004 ACCAC had presented a far more comprehensive report to the then Welsh Assembly Government entitled *A Review of the School Curriculum and Assessment Arrangements 5–16*. The review had taken a great deal of evidence from experts and practitioners and organised a series of conferences. The aim of the review was to examine what was needed to establish a curriculum for the twenty-first century, that more appropriately met the needs of learners. It noted that 'the existing curriculum has placed greater emphasis on knowledge and content at some expense to the development of skills. The review's recommendations seek a more appropriate balance between these elements'.[17]

It was felt that while the National Curriculum had served many learners well, a considerable number had been alienated and ill-served by it. There was also a widespread perception that the curriculum was overloaded at Key Stage 2 and 3. Many were also concerned about the detrimental effect an overemphasis on literacy and numeracy was having on children's wider learning, to say nothing of the damage they believed was being inflicted by a culture in which 'teaching to the test' was becoming the norm. ACCAC pressed that 'the National Curriculum Orders are revised to develop a learner-centred, skills-focussed curriculum that is relevant to the twenty-first century and inclusive of all learners. The aim should be for the revised curriculum to be first taught in September 2008'.[18]

It is interesting to note that at one of ACCAC's conferences 'A more radical option describing the statutory requirement principally in terms of skills was also discussed. While many expressed support in principle for this option, there were reservations about moving to such a model in the near future … There was general agreement that this skills-based option, although currently too radical, might be seen as an aim for the future'. The sticking point seems to have been more about implementation than ideology, because 'while many schools and others saw a curriculum more firmly based on skills development as the ultimate aim, they argued that it was very important to support teachers in moving from the present system to that future. Retaining but revising a subject-based curriculum would do that'.[19]

In a bold move, the report recommended that 'the Welsh Assembly Government should consider, as a long-term goal, the vision of a radically revised curriculum that is more overtly learner-centred and skills-focussed, and not necessarily subject-based'.[20] It was to take another ten years before that consideration would inch towards reality. Overall the report urged a modification of the 1988 curriculum to make it more skills-focussed and to promote parity of esteem. Tellingly, the report's authors obviously knew what they were dealing with in the Department for Education and Skills: 'The implementation and change agenda needs to be coordinated by the Welsh Assembly Government as an ongoing and sustainable process. Such change cannot be achieved by an activity (for example, revising the subject orders or the assessment arrangements) nor can it be achieved by an event (for example, launching a revised curriculum and assessment arrangements). It needs to be multi-layered and supported at national, Local Education Authority (LEA) and school level if it is to bring about a real change in the experience of learners'.[21]

Concern about the skills deficit in the curriculum would not go away. In 2008 a *Skills framework for 3 to 19-year-olds in Wales* was published. This was one of the documents underpinning the revised, more skills-focussed curriculum that ACCAC had urged in 2004. The framework had been developed to provide 'guidance about continuity and progression in thinking, communication, ICT and number for learners from 3 to 19 and beyond. These are skills that will enable learners of any age to become successful, whether in school, the workplace, at home or elsewhere, and they need to be firmly embedded into the experience of learners across all their learning'.[22] The framework addressed the key concerns of thinking, communication, ICT and number. The document noted that 'skills' development is cyclical or spiral, rather than linear', and also that as 'progression in tasks moves from the concrete to the more abstract ... Learners progress from needing support to more independent working'.[23]

But any of the radicals who had hoped that such a document would signal a move away from the prescriptions of the 1988 National Curriculum were to be disappointed by the explicit limitations of the document: 'This framework is **not** intended to be a curriculum framework. It underpins the Foundation Phase framework, all the subjects of the National Curriculum, plus the [other] frameworks ... and aims to ensure a coherent approach to learning and to progression. Its greatest value will therefore be to support planning'.[24] It provided detailed sections, with complex fold-out grids charting the development and progression in the four skills areas of thinking, communication, ICT and number. The value of metacognitive research was acknowledged in the first, the different means of communication, especially oracy, in the second. The growing importance of ICT was discussed in the third section, while numeracy and related issues got an airing in the final section.

The Framework represented a measured attempt to push the importance of skills much further up the curriculum agenda. It also showed that skills development should be conceived as a continuum, illustrated in the fact that its scope was to be from 3 to 19. It tried to convey some of the thinking about curriculum, knowledge and skills that had occurred since 1988. However, there were some limiting constraints on the value of the Framework from the start. It was not statutory for starters, and so was all but ignored in certain quarters. Perhaps the greatest limitation was the well-intentioned but misguided attempt to bolt on a skills-based ideology to a national curriculum which was resolutely knowledge-based. All in all it was a bit like trying to play rugby union using rugby league rules.

The debate over the National Curriculum rumbled on. Other countries in the UK, such as Scotland and to a much lesser extent England, held national debates on the nature and purpose of the curriculum. In Wales change was piecemeal, ad hoc and fragmentary. Apart from the Foundation Phase no real attempt was made to develop an underpinning philosophy of the curriculum in its entirety. No one was happy, but no minister was prepared to launch a full scale review. Even the redoubtable Leighton Andrews was loathe to begin that process. In a conversation with him around the time of the launch of the Qualifications Review I pointed out that, while the political necessity of securing control over qualifications in the face of Gove's rather reckless attempt to reform GCSEs was sufficient for *that* review to take place then, we were putting the cart before the horse big time and a review of the curriculum was now essential. His response was illuminating: 'We love talking about the curriculum in Wales. We've done little else in the last ten years.'

His point would have been stronger if he himself hadn't fired up that debate by commissioning independent reports in several key curriculum areas. In the space of two years, review after review was ordered either directly by Andrews or in tandem with another ministerial colleague. In October of 2012 a report was commissioned into the *Cwricwlwm Cymreig*. Published in July 2013, it called for just 'one curriculum for Wales' into which the elements of the *Cwricwlwm Cymreig* would be fully integrated.[25] In the same month in 2012, a review of second language Welsh teaching had been ordered in response to concerns about standards. The resultant report, which saw the light of day in September 2013, was gloomy. Standards indeed were dropping, and it was now 'the eleventh hour for Welsh second language teaching'.[26]

In November 2012 Andrews called for a review of ICT. The resultant report, which recommended that computing be compulsorily integrated into the curriculum as the 'fourth' science, came out in September 2013.[27] Physical education was the subject of a report jointly commissioned in June 2012 with

John Griffiths, the Minister for Housing, Regeneration and Heritage in whose brief sport lay. Chaired by the formidable Baroness Tanni Grey-Thompson, the report, published in June of the following year, stood out by virtue of its single recommendation: physical education should become a core element of the National Curriculum.[28] In the summer of 2012 a similarly sponsored report was commissioned into the state of the arts in Welsh schools. This time it was the doyen of Welsh arts, Professor Dai Smith, that chaired the report steering group that delivered in September 2013.[29]

But as the thick and weighty reports thudded on to the ministerial desk across the summer and early autumn of 2013, their original commissioner was gone, having resigned in a fit of pique in June 2013 after being embroiled in a controversy over the closure of Pentre Primary School in his constituency. His successor, Huw Lewis, looked overwhelmed by the challenges ahead, not least in regard to the curriculum. But the civil servants had a cunning plan.

The Donaldson Review

On 12th March 2014, Huw Lewis announced a thorough review of the entire curriculum and assessment regime. In a statement, he clarified his intention: 'I want to see the development of a Curriculum for Wales, which will provide our children and young people with opportunities for learning that will support them in being able to think, do, prosper and adapt'.[30] The decades-long piecemeal adaption of the 1988 curriculum, with its unwieldy add-ons and adaptions, it seemed, was at an end.

In keeping with the new-found fervour for all things Scottish, Professor Graham Donaldson of the University of Glasgow would lead what was billed as a 'comprehensive, wide ranging and independent review of the National Curriculum and assessment arrangements in Wales'. Lewis was seeking his footnote in history by claiming that this was 'a historic step forward in Welsh Education history'. The review would 'articulate a clear, coherent vision for education in Wales, from Foundation Phase to Key Stage 4'.[31] It would closely consider all the recommendations from the reports which had landed on his desk the previous year. The report was scheduled to be with Lewis by the end of the year. Donaldson was either a fast worker or would bring with him much of the experience of the *Curriculum for Excellence* of his native land.

In the event, it was a combination of both. Just before the official publication of the report a very senior official had hinted to me that 'if one knows Graham's previous work, none of it will come as a surprise'. The report was a little delayed, finally being published on 25th February 2015. It was comprehensive and far ranging, covering all the key areas and articulating a vision for a future Welsh curriculum. Donaldson had done his homework, aided by a team of seconded civil servants. He had also ensured that he engaged with all the key stakeholders both via face-to-face meetings and through survey work. He had had over 700 responses to his call for evidence, 300 of which were from children and young people. As well as thanking the usual suspects such as Estyn, Donaldson went out of his way to thank the trades unions for their constructive engagement. It was a pleasant change.

Successful Futures: Independent Review of Curriculum and Assessment Arrangements in Wales was keen to situate itself in the wider debate about curriculum, which Donaldson noted was a highly contested area. He outlined the two polarities in the debate. Some saw it as 'a framework of subjects to be taught over a defined period [and] based on a belief that subject knowledge has stood the test of time and remains the best path to a sound and relevant education'. At the other extreme were those who argued that 'learning is shaped by much more than individual subjects and syllabuses, and that fulfillment of the purposes of the curriculum requires approaches which are more directly relevant to emerging personal, social and economic needs. In this approach, the curriculum is often framed in terms of the key skills, capacities or competences that will be developed in children and young people'.[32] Almost in a nutshell it summed up the increasingly bitter battle between government and unions in England, and also the rather limping approach to curriculum reform seen in Wales since the advent of the Assembly.

Donaldson neatly sidestepped such a pyrrhic dichotomy and avoided taking sides: 'A subject against skill/competence debate creates unhelpful polarisation. The curriculum, learning and teaching need to enthuse children and young people about learning in ways that include both the vital contribution of discipline-based learning and the knowledge, skills and dispositions that will help them to meet the needs of today and the challenges of tomorrow'. The first recommendation tried to state a common definition of the curriculum: 'The school curriculum in Wales should be defined as including all of the learning experiences and assessment activities planned in pursuit of agreed purposes of education'.[33]

The report contained sixty-eight recommendations in all, and touched on many of the debates about curriculum and assessment in Wales and beyond. Donaldson was keen to stress that the curriculum should have 'clear and agreed purposes', an indication that these were not there in the mish-mash that had arisen post-1988. He proposed four. These should be that children and young people develop as: 'ambitious, capable learners, ready to learn throughout their lives; enterprising, creative contributors, ready to play a full part in life and work; ethical, informed citizens of Wales and the world; healthy, confident individuals, ready to lead fulfilling lives as valued members of society'. These high level purposes would be delivered by a broad curriculum for 3 to 16-year-olds that would be organised no longer in terms of subject but rather into 'six Areas of Learning and Experience: Expressive arts; Health and well-being; Humanities; Languages, literacy and communication; Mathematics and numeracy; and Science and technology'. He was insistent that each of these would still have 'an identifiable core of disciplinary or instrumental knowledge'.[34] The Google extremists had not won the day.

So far the report was simply arguing for a more sensible division of the curricula cake – recommendation six was more radical. All teachers, at whatever level, should share three cross-curriculum responsibilities: 'literacy; numeracy; and digital competence'. These and wider skills were to be embedded within the Areas of Learning and Experience. The quest to break down the silo mentality, which the *Cwricwlwm Cymreig* and the other guidance over the years had desired, was now to be made a reality. As a sop to the status quo, however, Religious Education, now seen as part of Humanities, was to be kept as a statutory requirement from the age of three.

One of the more salient criticisms of the previous curriculum regime had been the sharp disjunctions experienced at each of its key stages. This was most marked in transition between the Foundation Phase and Key Stage 2, but it was there at other points as well. All too often there seemed to be an abrupt change in pedagogy as the child moved from one stage to another. Donaldson urged that 'The new National Curriculum should be organised as a continuum of learning from 3 to 16 without phases and key stages'. Instead 'Progression should be described in relation to a continuum of learning in each Area of Learning and Experience, from when a child enters education to the end of statutory schooling'. He then went on to argue that 'Progression should be signalled through Progression Steps at five points in the learning continuum, relating broadly to expectations at ages 5, 8, 11, 14 and 16'. How these 'Progression Steps' would differ from the Key Stages was not really spelled out in any detail beyond the fact that they 'should be reference points, providing a "road map" for each individual child and young person's progress in their learning and not universal expectations of the performance of all children and young people at fixed points'.[35] It will be interesting to see whether, apart from a change in nomenclature and a headline commitment to a more fluid approach, in practice there will be a great deal of difference in a child's experience or the organisation of learning in a school.

In a similar vein, in recommendation 17, Donaldson urged that we see 'achievement in a broad sense, rather than only narrower measures of attainment'. Furthermore, in recommendation 19, he argued 'All children and young people should make progress along the same continuum, regardless of any additional learning needs they may have, although they may reach and move between Progression Steps more slowly or more quickly than others'. All this would clearly, as indicated, require far more development in practice.

If any teenagers were reading the report, doubtless some of them would have been disheartened by recommendation 21: 'The Welsh language should remain compulsory up to the age of 16'. The professor picked his way very carefully through the recommendations of the two reports on the *Cwricwlwm Cymreig* and second language Welsh teaching which had arrived on the minister's desk the previous year. There was no reference to second language Welsh GCSE, but there were loud hints about the direction that needed to be taken.

Recommendation 22 stated that the teaching of the Welsh language should be construed 'primarily as a means of communication, particularly oral communication and understanding'. Above all, children should be encouraged to achieve 'transactional competence' by the age of 16. That a number of practitioners, parents and pupils were still dubious about the compulsion was tacitly acknowledged in recommendation 24, which urged that the value placed on the language 'should be enhanced by strengthening the focus on its commercial value for the jobs market, the suggested [a interesting nuance if ever there was one] cognitive benefits of bilingualism and its importance … to achieve a good understanding of the cultural life of Wales in the past and present'. After all the efforts to promote the language through carrot and stick, it seemed that some were still unconvinced. Reflecting one of the most recent fads of the Welsh Government in terms of delivery, recommendation 26 stated that 'Welsh-medium schools should act as hubs for the Welsh language'.[36] In a death blow to the current second language qualification, recommendation 29 of the report urged that 'The Welsh Government should realign Welsh language qualifications at 16 with the proposed focus on speaking and listening and application in the workplace'.

Choice, which, as we saw, had proved to be a contentious issue in regard to the Learning Pathways agenda, received but a fleeting consideration in recommendation 31: 'between the ages of 14 and 16, all young people should select courses or undertake activities from each of the Areas of Learning and Experience, hence maintaining breadth and meeting national priorities, including science and health'. The vagueness of this recommendation left the door open for the narrowing of the qualifications offer which the Welsh Government was concurrently planning as it revised its performance measurement for schools.

No fewer than eighteen of the recommendations related to assessment, nearly 25% of all those put forward. They will be examined and contextualised in the next section.

The concluding recommendations dealt with the process of implementation. Given the Welsh Government's track record, this is the graveyard of many a well-intentioned reform. In recommendation 54 Donaldson urged 'an agile change strategy that establishes understanding and support, sets a measured pace, builds capacity and manages dependencies, particularly accountability arrangements'. The phrase needs unpacking. Much of the implementation to date had been anything but 'agile'.

As we saw in the last chapter, the department's usual *modus operandi* was to pursue a course of action, often in the face of evidence and constructive criticism, until the wheels almost dropped off. It was anything other than 'agile'. The whole curriculum reform project obviously needs complete 'buy in' from the profession, and so the caveats about building 'understanding and support' should be carved in stone at the entrance to the department. The reference to 'measured pace' was also well chosen. There were those who were understandably eager to set sail, but experience in Donaldson's native Scotland had shown that the whole project could come to grief if rushed through. For such a seismic change to occur there would need to be a great deal of capacity building.

That capacity building is both essential and badly needed was rendered explicit in several recommendations, such as in recommendation 58: 'An extensive and sustained programme of professional learning should be developed to ensure that the implications of the Review recommendations for the skills and knowledge of teachers and other practitioners are fully met'. The recommendation was very welcome. It has become a commonplace belief that, in the words of McKinsey, 'The quality of an education system cannot exceed the quality of its teachers'. Yet in the years when England had been investing and focussing on up-skilling its workforce through initiatives such as the National College for School Leadership, established in 2000 to be the 'Sandhurst' for teachers, and producing National Strategies for Literacy, Numeracy, and other key areas, there was much rhetoric but little concrete initiative in Wales.

Quite whether the 'New Deal' for the education workforce, which was mentioned in recommendation 59, will come up with the goods remains to be seen. The project has really yet to get off the ground in any meaningful way. The need to build system capacity was also recognised, and for action alignment. Recommendation 61 noted that 'The Department for Education and Skills, regional consortia, Estyn, Qualifications Wales and universities will need to establish mechanisms for coordination and joint working that recognise the responsibilities and respective strengths of each'.[37]

Successful Futures was published in February 2015 to general critical acclaim.[38] On the 4th March, Lewis attempted to launch what he called a 'Great Debate' on Donaldson's report and recommendations. This caused confusion to some, who believed that Donaldson was the conclusion of a 'great debate' on the curriculum. Simon Thomas, the Plaid Cymru education spokesperson, asked for clarification from the Minister as to whether Donaldson was the 'blueprint or not'. The Minister's rather confused reply seemed to indicate that the 'Great Debate' was just another step along a decade-long process of reform.[39]

The 'Great Debate' consisted formally of three roadshow events, workshops, a webinar and an online survey, but other events were encouraged across schools and colleges.

Whether this was the start or the finish of the debate or just a stopping off point along the way, the fact is that this 'Great Debate' took two months. There were 639 responses to the questionnaire issued. The main findings were summarised in a report published in June.[40] The key messages were clear.

> The majority of respondents welcomed the overall emphasis and direction of the recommendations set out in *Successful Futures*. Respondents recognised and valued the purposes of education set out in the Review, which many thought provided a firm basis upon which to think about the curriculum. On the whole, respondents were supportive of the substantive content of the recommendations around curriculum and assessment arrangements. This agreement stemmed from, in part, the perceived limitations of the current curriculum and assessment arrangements, which respondents believe to be in need of reform. The current curriculum was seen by many to be content driven and over-crowded, and the purpose of assessment largely motivated by accountability, rather than for learning.[41]

However, if there was a high degree of welcome for the proposals, there was a great deal of anxiety about the Achilles heel of implementation:

> Across a number of recommendations, respondents sought clarification regarding the precise details of how the new curriculum and assessment arrangements would be implemented in practice. There was concern around the balance between subject knowledge and competencies contained within the proposals, and how the new curriculum would link to national assessments, such as GCSEs. To be effectively implemented, respondents felt that the new curriculum would require careful consideration, consultation and planning, as well as sufficient time, resources and support.[42]

One or two more cynical critics had worried, at least in private, that Donaldson's report had been a bit too much 'all things to all men'. Undoubtedly some of the recommendations, such as the ownership of the curriculum, would need a great deal of unpacking. (Advocates of a 'local' curriculum have never made completely clear, to my mind, how this stops being a parochial curriculum narrowly focussed on the perceived needs of local industries or, worse still, the hobby horses of individual practitioners. One of the key strengths of the 1988 reforms had been the establishment of a national entitlement over a postcode lottery.) One, a fellow Scot, going as far as to say to me that he thought that one 'could get what one wanted' out of it. While that is probably unduly dismissive, the inevitably generic nature of such a report does mean that clarification and the determination of meaning will play a key role in implementation.

In conclusion the summary report had noted:

> At times, it is possible that respondents had understood the aims and scope of a particular set of recommendations in ways that were not intended. There was significant variation, for example, in the way people had interpreted the recommendations around Areas of Learning and Experience and the role of subject disciplines. Clarification around these recommendations could be valuable to ensure that future discussion and debate centres on a common understanding of the proposals'.[43]

If the 'Great Debate' has ended, perhaps the real one has only just begun.

Donaldson implementation

The Welsh Government was quick to accept the Donaldson Review in full. On 22nd October 2015, at a conference in Cardiff City Hall, *A Curriculum for Wales – a Curriculum for Life* was officially launched.[44] The keynote speaker was the First Minister himself, Carwyn Jones. This was both an indicator of the importance of the new venture but also a tacit admission that Lewis, who was relegated to the graveyard slot after lunch that day, was not up to the job. As it was, the First Minister's speech was a very partial tour of Wales' successes in education since 2011. There was no mention of the decade before.

In his Ministerial Foreword to *A Curriculum for Wales – a Curriculum for Life*, Lewis announced that 'This is an exciting time for education in Wales'. Lewis was confident that the profession was both willing and able to take on the challenge of designing a new curriculum for Wales. So confident was he in this regard that he promised that the new curriculum would be available by 2018. There was an audible intake of breath in the City Hall when that had been announced.

The delivery plan was to be constructed around eight essential building blocks: Embedding the four purposes of the curriculum; Creating a new curriculum encompassing Areas of Learning and Experience; Extending and promoting learners' experiences; Developing cross-curriculum responsibilities; Enabling the Welsh language to thrive; Developing a new assessment and evaluation framework; Building the capacity of all practitioners and leaders; Establishing a constructive and robust accountability system.[45] It was to be supported by four enablers: working in partnership; strong school-to-school working; inspiring leadership; and inclusivity.[46]

Key to delivery of the new curriculum and assessment arrangements was to be a network of 'Pioneer Schools'. These would 'share thinking, test ideas and keep them up to date with latest developments as the curriculum and assessment framework develops'. The document promised that there would be 'Robust quality assurance processes...put in place to ensure we fulfil our ambition to develop a world-leading curriculum'.[47]

There would be four stages of development of the vision set out in *Successful Futures*. Stage 1, which would run from October 2015 to January 2016, would see the selection, induction and preparation of the Pioneer Network. Stage 2 would see the design of framework and principles for each Area of Learning and Experience, and include the fleshing out of progression reference points and achievement outcomes. Stage 3 would continue the development of each of the Areas of Learning and Experience in tandem with curriculum experts. The final stage would be concerned with further checking, quality assurance, and include international benchmarking.[48]

So, within two years a new curriculum will be designed and developed, and be ready by 2018 in time for adoption more widely by schools. By 2021 the entire system will have implemented it. From start to finish the whole project will take six years.[49]

To say that this timescale is ambitious would be an understatement. Scotland had taken nearly twice as long to bed down its *Curriculum for Excellence*, and it was coming from a much stronger place. Whether a demoralised profession, hit by repeated PISA failures and subject to a rapidly introduced draconian accountability regime after years of drift, will be able to come up with the goods is a moot point. Whether an Education Department with a chronic record of delivery failure can provide the necessary support is, unfortunately, far less debatable. Expect to see slippage in terms of delivery dates.

Assessment

Curriculum design and reform is only part of the story. A wonderful curriculum can exist on paper but not be delivered. A vital concomitant is assessment. The sharp eyed reader will already have noticed that a number of investigations were tasked with sorting out both assessment and curriculum. Indeed the very name of ACCAC – and acronym derived from Awdurdod Cymwysterau, Cwricwlwm ac Asesu Cymru (Qualifications, Curriculum and Assessment Authority for Wales) showed that the two things were very closely linked. Donaldson's report had been explicitly subtitled a review of the 'Assessment Arrangements' too.

Lying behind much of what follows is the fundamental tension between assessment of learning and assessment for learning. It is surprising how much turns on the addition of one letter to the preposition. Crudely put, this distinction can be boiled down to this. Assessment of learning is an accountability measure. It tells how much learning has taken place and pinpoints where a child or cohort of children are on their journey. It can obviously then be used to form relative judgments both on children and, more controversially, institutions. It is essentially a snapshot of past achievements. It tends to be loved by governments.

Assessment for learning is a pedagogical tool. It makes an assessment of a child's progress and understanding, but is used diagnostically with the clear intention of developing that progress. It is essentially future orientated. It tends to be loved by teachers. Assessment for learning has been defined by the Assessment Reform Group as 'the process of seeking and interpreting evidence for use by learners and their teachers to decide where the learners are in their learning, where they need to go and how best to get there'. It is therefore as much a tool for pupils as their teachers. Any halfway decent education system will need a combination of both approaches. But to confuse matters, they are often banded together and, depending on the concerns of the moment, one gets subsumed under the other. Almost from the very first, the National Curriculum and its roll-out were bedevilled by such a confusion.

SATs were introduced from 1991 through until 1998 for the purpose of testing 7, 11, and 14-year-olds at the end of the Key Stages of the 1988 curriculum. They recorded attainment in terms of National Curriculum attainment levels, numbered between 1 and 8. Whatever the actual meaning of the acronym, which have been variously interpreted as 'Statutory Assessment Tests', 'Standard Attainment Tests', 'Standardised Achievement Tests' or 'Standard Assessment Tests', one thing is clear: teachers loathe them. Many point to the stress that the tests generate in young pupils, and also the narrowing effect they have on the curriculum, as teaching-to-the-test becomes the norm. In England the tests for 14-year-olds were to be abandoned in 2008 and the tests for this stage and that for seven-year-olds replaced by levels derived from teacher assessment. But at 11 the national tests still remain.

At each Key Stage the data developed provides the fodder for the generation of League Tables which purport to show the relative performance of schools and thus generate a market. The League Tables are another reason for the

SATs to be loathed by teachers and others who dispute the suitability of a pseudo-market in education. Despite spirited interventions from educational academics, think-tanks and the unions, the New Labour government in England resisted pressure to abolish them, bowing more to the pressure of 'middle England', who wished to keep them. The coalition government that followed it at Westminster similarly showed little real interest in abolishing them.

Here was a chance to show how devolution could make a difference for Wales. In 2002, Davidson announced the abolition of the Key Stage 1 tests for seven-year-olds. Few lamented their passing. The writing was on the wall for the whole SATs regime. In its *REVIEW OF THE SCHOOL CURRICULUM AND ASSESSMENT ARRANGEMENTS 5–16: A Report to the Welsh Assembly Government* published in April 2004, ACCAC was upfront in its findings and recommendations. While 'the programme of testing has produced valuable, useful data on pupils' performance' it was clear that 'at Key Stage 2 in particular, there has been a negative impact on the curriculum because of "teaching to the tests" [and] there is a clearly emerging view that teacher assessment should be retained as the sole means of statutory end of Key Stage assessment'.[50] There was a perception that children were tested too early and too often. An allied perception of pressure to 'teach to the test' was believed to be narrowing the curriculum.

ACCAC also reported that 'Despite work to improve transition between Key Stage 2 and Key Stage 3, many teachers still have doubts about the reliability of test and teacher assessment information passed between the Key Stages. Therefore, a crucial aspect of future change must relate to improving communications between schools'. It does not seem to have occurred to anyone at this stage that these doubts might have had some foundation in truth. ACCAC was, however, aware of questions of public accountability. In regard to the data that SATs generated for League Tables, ACCAC was insistent that 'Any successor system must be able to demonstrate securely the accuracy and consistency of assessment judgments if it is to command public confidence and trust'.[51]

In the event, demonstrating 'securely the accuracy and consistency' of the new assessment judgments was easier to wish for than to achieve. ACCAC commended the Interim Report of the Daugherty Review, which suggested that 'secondary schools should be accredited as having in place effective procedures for ensuring that teacher judgments are comparable'. Perceptively, ACCAC argued that the accreditation should cover the *processes* for arriving at end of Key Stage teacher assessment judgments and for moderation of those outcomes (my emphasis) and, in an appendix, outlined what such a model could look like. It would be based on two main components: firstly, verification of schools' procedures and then, secondly, the moderation of portfolios compiled by schools.[52] The move to teacher assessment as the sole mechanism for gauging progression and performance would need to be carefully nuanced and managed.

Daugherty

ACCAC were not the only ones looking at assessment. In June 2003, Davidson initiated a debate about National Curriculum assessment arrangements at the end of Key Stages 2 and 3, obviously with an eye to their abolition. The review group was chaired by the eminent educationalist, Richard Daugherty, Professor of Education and Head of the Education Department at Aberystwyth University, and included big hitters such as the then Chief Inspector, Susan Lewis, and the CEO of the soon to be abolished ACCAC, John Valentine. It convened in September 2003 and reported in May 2004. The report argued for a 'revised assessment framework' but warned, ominously as it turned out, that there was 'further work to be done if the Group's proposals are to be translated into appropriate policies and practices [and its] design, development and implementation'.[53]

The report highlighted issues surrounding transition, especially that between primary and secondary schools, as a major issue. It also noted that many thought that pupils were over-tested. Interestingly, they didn't quite buy the teacher unions' argument that the SATs were alone responsible for this, noting that many local authorities used other tests *as well as* the SATs to provide what they felt was missing data or information about pupils. This was contributing to the 'over-testing' narrative in no small way.

To build up a better and more useful picture, the report recommended that at the end of Year 5 there should be a 'skills profile for each pupil, in order to give a picture of his/her learning strengths that is different from, but complementary to, end of Key Stage summaries of attainment levels in the core subjects'.[54] Significantly, it was suggested that the marking of the relevant skills tests should be undertaken externally.

The report homed in on the reliability of teacher assessment as opposed to external assessments. It noted that evidence suggested that the former could be as robust as the latter, *if* properly moderated. The report spent several pages highlighting what sort of moderation would be needed if the confidence of the two key users of the data – parents and secondary schools – was to be ensured.

Part of the remit for the group had been to seek ways in which the 'information on progress in improving educational standards in Wales is rigorously based and capable of international comparison'. After considering the alternatives, such as TIMMS (Trends in International Mathematics and

Science Study) and PIRLS (Progress in International Reading Literacy Study) run by the IEA (International Association for the Evaluation of Educational Achievement), the group put forward Recommendation 25: 'For the purpose of comparing standards in Wales in key aspects of learning with standards in other countries, Wales should participate in the PISA survey of 15 year old pupils from 2006'. (PISA, the Programme for International Student Assessment Organisation is run by the OECD, the Organisation for Economic Cooperation and Development.) The die was cast.

On 9th November, Davidson reported back to the National Assembly. Unsurprisingly, she was happy to accept the recommendations of Daugherty and ACCAC and so the statutory tests, at least at Key Stage 2, were laid to rest. She spoke of it as 'an historic day'. Her fellow Labour AM, Jeff Cuthbert, (successor of Ron Davies, the architect of devolution, as AM for Caerphilly) later to be a lacklustre Deputy Minister for Skills, predicted that 'these changes put Wales ahead of the game. In education, we are getting used to envious glances from educationists and parents in England'. The opposition parties concurred. Even David Davies, then AM for Monmouth and subsequently its MP, was in agreement, though he soured the pill by adding 'we need to ensure that the outside moderation, or whatever method you use to ensure that schools are not failing their pupils, works'. The motion to make the Key Stage 2 SATs optional in 2005 was passed unanimously.[55]

The general rejoicing within the profession can best be gauged by a vox pop article in the *Western Mail*, entitled *So what's so great about scrapping SATS*,[56] which interviewed ten headteachers. The abolition of Key Stage 3 SATs followed in 2006. The unions welcomed the move, though the NASUWT worried predictably about its implications for teachers' workload.

The guidance document which emerged in early 2005 outlined the timeframe and change management routine. It also noted that although 'there was also a good deal of support … for external marking being made available for a further year, i.e. in 2006 for Key Stage 2 and 2007 for Key Stage 3, [the] provision of such a service carries with it a significant cost and the Minister is not, at this stage, minded to extend its availability'.[57] One of the biggest changes in a decade was to be phased in quickly with highly limited funding. There was bound to be a price to be paid.

Both ACCAC and Daugherty had pointed to the reliability of teacher assessment. Neither had objected to the abolition of the SATs. But both had spelt out – ACCAC very forcefully – the moderation regime that needed to be put into place. ACCAC, as we have seen, was categoric. It had insisted that 'any successor system must be able to demonstrate securely the accuracy and consistency of assessment judgments'. It had endorsed Daugherty's suggestion that secondary schools should go through some process of accreditation based on two main components: firstly, verification of schools' procedures and then, secondly, the moderation of portfolios compiled by schools. Thus comparability, robustness and accuracy would be ensured.

Unfortunately it simply didn't happen. At the end of 2013, Leighton Andrews, sitting on the back benches, asked his successor, Lewis, a series of questions. They were answered on 6th January 2014. It's worth replicating the most salient of them:

> Leighton Andrews (Rhondda): How many secondary schools were given accredited status by ACCAC (Qualifications, Curriculum and Assessment Authority for Wales), following the Daugherty Review? (WAQ66145)
>
> Huw Lewis: While a process for the awarding of 'accredited status' was developed, our records do not indicate that any schools received an 'accredited status' for their teacher assessments.
>
> In 2004 ACCAC was asked by the Welsh Government to develop systems and procedures to ensure the quality and consistency of teacher assessment at the end of Key Stage 3. The model they developed comprised two elements: External moderation of sample evidence for all KS3 National Curriculum subjects and Verification visits to schools by external verifiers who focus on schools systems and procedures. It was intended that those schools meeting the required standard would be awarded an 'accredited status'. In 2005, ACCAC awarded the contract to deliver this model to the WJEC.
>
> During 2006/07 and 2007/08, schools were required to submit sample materials to WJEC showing attainment exemplifying the characteristics of National Curriculum levels 4, 5, 6 and 7 (covering all attainment targets) for moderation.
>
> During 2007/08 and 2009/10, schools were required to submit sample evidence to WJEC for moderation on a similar, but not identical basis as that undertaken for the core subjects.[58]

The implications of losing this important part of the jigsaw were to be wide ranging. As Andrews commented in his book, 'the steps recommended by Daugherty for implementation after the ending of the tests were not followed through ... the moderation process for teacher assessment was never introduced and accredited status was not given to secondary schools. This had clear implications for the accuracy of teacher assessments. The diagnostic test in Year 5 was not introduced, meaning there was no national system for measuring literacy or numeracy'.[59]

Omitting the crucial elements outlined by ACCAC wasn't careless – it was reckless in the extreme. From the middle of the decade it meant that teacher assessments were not anchored in a national context. As time went on it became difficult for those on the ground to get a true impression of what 'good' might look like. Comparisons of schools' performance became increasingly more difficult. With subtle cajoling from headteachers, themselves under the cosh from local authorities, the pressure on teachers to inflate grades was inevitable. There were almost Maoist leaps in some authorities. The alleged dip in performance between Key Stage 2 and Key Stage 3 became more pronounced. And, as we shall see, there were to be near catastrophic consequences for GCSE results. But the whole system was starting to believe the rhetoric peddled from on high that Wales was leading the world. Here in Wales, we were told, was the educational Garden of Eden but without credible, external, scrutiny the veracity of that claim was becoming increasingly suspect.

The botched implementation threw bones to the detractors of teacher assessment to gnaw over with glee. With hindsight, the omission of a key *ACCAC* recommendation is stunning. When I questioned David Egan, Davidson's Special Adviser at the time, he answered rather wanly that the civil service simply hadn't followed things through. That simply won't do as an answer. The whole process of the abolition of SATs had been milked by Davidson to portray herself as a radical reformer. Was there no ministerial oversight? Did she not grasp the integral nature of the whole ACCAC package? Where was she when implementation was taking place?

This new regime was not to last long. As we saw in Chapter 3, by the time that Andrews became Minister he and others were coming to the disturbing conclusion that, far from being paradise, the Welsh educational system was becoming increasingly dysfunctional. PISA had given some rude shocks to the system, confirming the growing gap in GCSE and other external exam results. But there was also growing disquiet about the reliability, accuracy and consistency of the assessment regime. Estyn was also reporting that standards in literacy and numeracy were hardly improving: 'Standards in primary schools are similar to what they were last year... Standards in secondary schools are more variable than those in primary schools. Fewer than half of secondary schools are good or better and the proportion that is unsatisfactory has increased from one in seven to one in four'.[60]

There were, as we have seen, particular concerns about the impact that a misinterpretation of the Foundation Phase pedagogy could be having on literacy and numeracy. Concerns were growing about the deepening gender gap being displayed between boys and girls. And, as ever, the department was not helping matters with its usual lack of coordination. Andrews recounts in his book having two meetings about literacy on the same day with completely different officials who were but dimly aware of their colleagues' work.[61]

Andrews' twenty-point plan speech, *Teaching Makes a Difference*, was riddled throughout with concerns about assessment. He was stark: 'We have kidded ourselves about measurement for too long... Abandoning SATs was not meant to be a signal for anything goes. As Ann Keane has said to me "I am concerned about the lack of robustness in the assessment of learning at the end of Key Stages, at transition points between primary and secondary schools and between secondary schools and post-16 education and training." She confirms that "In Year 7 at the beginning of Key Stage 3 or in post-16 provision, when all students are screened to identify basic skills needs, for instance, gaps in skills are identified that belie the level of attainment at the end of the previous stage" '.[62] One of the biggest elephants in the room had taken centre stage.

National testing re-introduced

Andrews could have dusted off the ACCAC recommendations about moderation. But he was a man in a hurry and increasingly strapped for cash. He short-circuited the whole debate by re-introducing national testing. It was now only a question of how SATs-like tests could be re-introduced. Points 4 and 5 of his groundbreaking speech had announced that 'As part of our National Literacy Plan, we will introduce a national reading test, which will be consistent across Wales ... By the 2012-13 academic year, we will have developed similar plans for numeracy'.

Part of the rescue package for education that Andrews had outlined in his February 2011 speech, was the establishment of a Schools Standards Unit which would collate data and drive change. Speaking in the Senedd chamber on 5th July 2011, Andrews updated AMs about progress.[63] The previous week, the National Literacy and Numeracy Framework had been published. In tandem with that had been a report by Professor Rhona Stainthorp of the University of Reading, who had been commissioned to provide an analysis of the validity, rigour and practicalities of the reading tests then in use across Wales. She had found, not surprisingly, that there were a plethora of inconsistent tests in place, with very little comparability across local authorities. In the autumn, a new national test would be required. It is notable that by now no AM opposed the re-introduction of national tests, indeed Andrews was 'worried by the consensus that is breaking out across the Chamber'.[64]

In June 2013, a full and comprehensive report was published by the Australian Council for Educational Research (ACER) about the state of teacher assessment in Wales. The review had been carried out across the previous year. It showed that Wales was not a complete basket-case when it came to teacher assessment. Indeed 'the picture that has emerged from this investigation is of a teacher assessment system that has the main components of successful systems elsewhere in the world. It has adequate levels of documentation ... However, the implementation of teacher assessment is an enormous task and there are many parts that must be functioning smoothly ... The system has not yet achieved that level of functioning'. One of the key issues was that there was no systematic gathering of data within clusters, and moderation was still too *ad hoc*. This meant that 'it is impossible to know how well the system is doing in regards to the consistency of teacher judgment'. This was one area to be tackled and it led on to another concern: 'the current system is already under threat because some schools have lost trust in the judgments made in the teacher assessment process'. Trust would only be restored once impact and operability were addressed.[65]

The new national literacy and numeracy tests duly arrived in schools for implementation in May 2013.[66] The tests were to be administered annually to all pupils in Years 2 to 9, although some limited disapplication was possible. The tests were to be administered by the National Foundation for Educational Research (NFER) on behalf of the Welsh Government. Given the abundance of information about testing, and the department's own debacle with the CDAP in the Foundation Phase, examined in the last chapter, one might have legitimately hoped that the new regime would bed down without too much problem.

The first results to parents were pushed out at the end of the summer term. Many felt confused by the 'information' they were being given. A web discussion on Mumsnet is typical. 'Jemima Muddled-up' commented that the 'age equivalent scores seem a bit strange, and some of the standardised scores aren't actually on the graph'. She also pointed to another frustration that many were feeling – 'School broke up today so we won't get the chance to ask the teachers until September'. A number of others expressed themselves similarly confused. The tests had been administered in the required timeframe and the raw scores collated and standardised by NFER, but had arrived back late at schools which were then under pressure to share them with parents. Again this was the sort of planning difficulty that by now any department with some strategic sense would have spotted a mile off.

The reaction of the unions fell into two broad camps. There were those, such as the NUT and NASUWT, who were ideologically opposed to this sort of testing, and others such as ASCL, NAHT, ATL and UCAC, who took a much more pragmatic approach. The NASUWT remained true to its role as 'denier' of any performance problems, as it had done with PISA and almost all other indicators that things were not rosy.[67] The more moderate unions, while understanding why the tests were seen as an option, and welcoming the Literacy and Numeracy Frameworks, were concerned about the narrowing effect that the tests could have on the curriculum.[68]

Worse was to come. Few were in any doubt that one of the key intentions behind the tests was to provide far more reliable data for the new accountability mechanisms that Andrews was introducing in wake of his twenty-point plan. We shall look at these in the next chapter. The data had to be reliable, in a way in which the previous teacher assessments were not, but it also had to be comparable across time as well as across the land. Without such comparability it would be difficult to show both the progress of an individual child, and also the progress of the system as a whole.

The following year the standardised scores were again late in arriving. It also emerged that year on year comparability would not be possible either. The Welsh Government's response was pathetic even by their own standards: 'It's disappointing that we've not been able to publish progress information this year as planned, but this is a complex process that has never been undertaken on this scale and the process has taken longer than expected'. The outgoing President of NAHT Cymru, Ruth Davies, spoke for practitioners when she said the whole process so far had been 'a complete and utter shambles. There's a simple end of term report for Welsh Government – "could do much, much better" '.[69]

Back to the successful future?

So, national testing was abolished amid much trumpeting and self-congratulation. It was then re-introduced amid much hand-wringing and soul-searching. What of the future? Are we to spin round through 180 degrees yet again? Donaldson's report was about assessment arrangements too, so what can we glean about the future? One thing is certain – the toing and froing has done nothing to enhance the Department's reputation for thought or delivery. It has also had a tremendously destabilising effect on the whole school system.

Donaldson had obviously watched the writhing of the Welsh system in regard to assessment, as well as being well acquainted with assessment regimes across the UK and elsewhere. Two key words governed his whole approach to one of the most inflammatory of issues. Assessment should be 'relevant and proportionate'. Moreover, he was clear that 'Assessment arrangements should give priority to their formative role in teaching and learning'.[70] Teacher Assessment should remain as the norm and should use a wide range of techniques. Tests were part of that armoury, but only a limited one. It is important to note that he was not of the 'comparison-is-odious' school of thought, manifested by some of the unions, but argued that: 'Where the results of assessment are to be used for purposes of comparison, issues of reliability in teacher assessment should be addressed through effective moderation'. He was also not advocating a return to the disastrous past, insisting that 'External, standardised testing provides important benchmarking information and should be used in combination with school tests and teacher assessment'. However, he was clear that 'its frequency should be kept to a minimum in view of its impact on the curriculum and teaching and learning'.[71] I suspect the interpretation of 'frequency' will become one of the key battlegrounds in the implementation of Donaldson's proposals.

Assessment was not to be the preserve of teachers either, self-assessment and peer assessment were other ways in which children could realise and plan their progress. Any reporting to parents should include contributions from the child themselves, recording both achievements and aspirations. In time, children should be able to develop their own e-portfolio which would record their achievement in a transferable way.[72]

Donaldson also charged the Welsh Government with two essential tasks. It should 'establish a comprehensive assessment and evaluation framework in line with the recommendations of this report'. Such a framework is badly needed to bring some coherence and sense to the rather confusing current arrangements. He also urged that the government 'establish an arms-length structure for day-to-day leadership and steering of curriculum and assessment arrangements'.[73]

Obviously one would not want constant government interference in the curriculum, but the point was deeper than that. By insisting that it was arms-length he was providing not just for its relative independence but also for far greater efficiency and effectiveness. The old ACCAC had not just been an exam regulator. It has also been responsible for developing the curriculum. Its absorption into the Welsh Government had proven almost disastrous in regard to its regulatory function, as we shall see in the next chapter, but the piecemeal and chaotic reform of the curriculum had also shown what a bad move its abolition had been.

Notes

1   ATL publication Teachers and Government: A history of intervention in education (2003) https://www.atl.org.uk/publications-and-resources/research-publications/teachers-and-government.asp

2   The actual terminology used varies from document to document and is either given in Welsh alone or a mixture of Welsh and English. This variation does not impact on the documents referred to.

3   I have found them. Them seems to be no confusion about what is being referred to in doing so.

4   ACCAC, Advisory Paper 18 'Developing a Cwricwlwm Cymreig' (1993)

5   Estyn, Y Cwricwlwm Cymreig, The Welsh dimension of the curriculum in Wales: good practice in teaching and learning (2001) P.5. I must note here the excellent service provided by Estyn. As it is not available electronically, Estyn scanned and sent me a copy of the

report on the same day as I requested it. A small organisation whose customer service puts many much larger ones to shame.

6   P. 8.

7   P. 9.

8   Originally an acronym for IN-SErvice Training day, sometimes known as Baker days, occur five times in the school year at least. It is a time during term but one which does not require pupils to attend school.

9   ACCAC, *Developing the Curriculum Cymrieg* (2003) http://www.wasacre.org.uk/publications/wag/E-developingthecurriculumcymreig.pdfp4

10 P. 5.

11 P. 6.

12 http://www.estyn.gov.uk/english/docViewer/176003.1/cwricwlwm-cymreig-phase-2-2006/?navmap=30,163,

13 https://www.tes.co.uk/article.aspx?storycode=2111738

14 ACAC soon gained another 'C' which stood for 'Cymwysterau', that is, qualifications.

15 Education and Lifelong Learning Committee, *Interim Report: Schools of the Future* (March 2003), http://www.assembly.wales/Laid%20Documents/Education%20and%20Lifelong%20Learning%20Committee%20Interim%20ReportSchool%20of%20the%20Future%20(pdf,%20753kb)%20-%20LD2069-01042003-25313/bus-GUIDE-N0000000000000000000000000009460-English.pdf p. 20.

16 ACCAC, The School Curriculum in Wales (1999)

17 ACCAC, REVIEW OF THE SCHOOL CURRICULUM AND ASSESSMENT ARRANGEMENTS 5–16: A Report to the Welsh Assembly Government (April 2004) P. 3.

18 P. 4 and p. 22.

19 P. 40.

20 P. 4.

21 P. 40.

22 Skills framework for 3 to 19-year-olds in Wales, p. 4. http://www.amdro.org.uk/SiteCollectionDocuments/Learning/Subjects/ICT/Skills_Framework.pdf

23 P. 5.

24 P. 6.

25 http://learning.gov.wales/docs/learningwales/publications/190920-cwricwlwm-cymreig-final-report-en.pdf

26 One Language for All: Review of Welsh second language at Key Stages 3 and 4 Report and recommendations September 2013 http://gov.wales/docs/dcells/publications/130926-review-of-welsh-second-lan-en.pdf

27 http://learning.gov.wales/docs/learningwales/publications/131003-ict-steering-group-report-en.pdf

28 Physical Literacy – an all-Wales approach to increasing levels of physical activity for children and young people http://gov.wales/docs/dcells/publications/130621-sports-and-physical-activity-review-en.pdf

29 An independent report for the Welsh Government into Arts in Education in the Schools of Wales http://gov.wales/docs/dcells/publications/130920-arts-in-education-en.pdf

30 http://gov.wales/about/cabinet/cabinetstatements/2014/assessmentcurriculumreview/?lang=en

31 http://gov.wales/about/cabinet/cabinetstatements/2014/assessmentcurriculumreview/?lang=en

32   http://gov.wales/docs/dcells/publications/150317-successful-futures-en.pdf p. 5.
33   P. 6.
34   P. 38.
35   Pp. 53 and 54.
36   We now have hub schools for Welsh, ICT and Oxbridge admissions. And certain schools
     will be 'Pioneer Schools' for Donaldson. As ever, the Welsh Government should learn
     that, as in decoration, 'less is more'.
37   P. 98.
38   http://www.walesonline.co.uk/news/wales-news/revealed-radical-education-overhaul-
     dramatically-8713170 gives a flavour of the union reaction, for instance.
39   http://www.yoursenedd.com/debates/2015-03-04-3-statement-on-the-donaldson-review-
     of-curriculum-and-assessment-next-steps
40   Wavehill, Successful Futures: Independent Review of Curriculum and Assessment
     Arrangements in Wales, A report on responses to the Great Debate (June 2015) http://
     gov.wales/docs/dcells/publications/150630-wavehill-e.pdf. A breakdown of respondents
     can be found on p. 2.
41   P. 3.
42   P. 3.
43   P. 17.
44   http://gov.wales/topics/educationandskills/schoolshome/curriculum-for-wales-curriculum-
     for-life/?lang=en
45   P. 6.
46   Pp. 6 and 7.
47   Pp. 10 and 11.
48   Pp. 10 and 11.
49   P. 28.
50   Successful Futures p. 4.
51   P. 30.
52   P. 31.
53   LEARNING PATHWAYS THROUGH STATUTORY ASSESSMENT: KEY STAGES
     2 AND 3 DAUGHERTY ASSESSMENT REVIEW GROUP FINAL REPORT MAY
     2004 http://217.35.77.12/archive/wales/papers/education/pdfs/daughety-final-report-e.pdf
     Section 1.6 (irritatingly, the report is not paginated).
54   Section 3.14 ff.
55   http://www.assembly.wales/record%20of%20proceedings%20documents/the%20
     record-09112004-41952/bus-chamber-n000000000000000000000000025732-english.
     pdf
56   http://www.walesonline.co.uk/news/wales-news/whats-great-scrapping-sats-2429943
57   Report on the Consultation on National Curriculum Assessment Arrangements for 11-
     and 14-year-olds Date of Issue: January 2005 (DfTE Information Document No: 002/05)
     http://dera.ioe.ac.uk/5338/1/nc-cons-report-e.pdf p. 16.
58   http://www.assembly.wales/en/bus-home/pages/plenaryitem.aspx?category=Written%20
     Question&itemid=2787 (Interestingly, Daugherty's diagnostic tests had suffered the same
     fate:
         Leighton Andrews (Rhondda): Will the Minister confirm whether the skills-based
     diagnostic test envisaged in Year 5 of primary school following the Daugherty report
     was ever introduced; and whether ACCAC was ever involved in designing assessments
     and ensuring their consistency? (WAQ66146)
         Huw Lewis: I can confirm the diagnostic tests envisaged following the Daugherty
     report were never introduced. ACCAC were involved with work to design and improve
     the consistency of teacher assessments. In 2004 the Welsh Government asked ACCAC

to develop systems and procedures to ensure the quality and consistency of teacher assessment at the end of Key Stages. They developed a model for Key Stage 3 which comprised two elements: External moderation of sample evidence for all KS3 National Curriculum subjects and Verification visits to schools by external verifiers who focus on schools systems and procedures. In 2005 ACCAC awarded the contract to deliver this model to WJEC.

59   Andrews, Leighton *Ministering to Education: a reformer reports* (Parthian; Cardigan, 2014), pp. 103 and 104.

60   The Annual Report of Her Majesty's Chief Inspector of Education and Training in Wales: 2012-2013.

61   Andrews, *Ministerting to Education*, p. 92.

62   Teaching makes a difference, p. 10.

63   http://www.assembly.wales/en/bus-home/pages/plenaryitem.aspx?category=Record%20 of%20Proceedings&itemid=748#cod

64   http://www.assembly.wales/Record%20of%20Proceedings%20Documents/The%20 Record%20(PDF,%20883KB)-05072011-219200/rop20110705qv-English.pdf

65   ACER An investigation into Key Stages 2 and 3 teacher assessment in Wales Prepared by the Australian Council for Educational Research. (June 2013), pp. xxi ff http://dera. ioe.ac.uk/18413/1/130718-investigation-key-stages-2-3-teacher-assessment.pdf

66   The Education (National Curriculum) (Assessment Arrangements for Reading and Numeracy) (Wales) Order 2013 http://www.legislation.gov.uk/wsi/2013/433/article/3/ made

67   This has been the consistent position of the NASUWT. The position was eloquently summarised by Rex Phillips, National Official for Wales, speaking at a forum on the reform of Initial Teacher Training: 'the NASUWT does not subscribe to the view that the standards of the education workforce need to be raised … These are myths borne out of the artificial crisis in education created by the former Education Minister around the PISA outcomes reported in December 2010.

68   For a balanced view of the unions' positions see Michael Dauncey, National Assembly for Wales Research paper, Literacy and Numeracy in Wales (June2013), p. 20 ff http:// www.assembly.wales/Research%20Documents/Literacy%20and%20Numeracy%20in%20 Wales%20-%20Research%20paper-03062013-246762/13-039-English.pdf

69   http://www.walesonline.co.uk/news/wales-news/wales-national-reading-numeracy-tests-7430313

70   *Successful Futures*, p. 75.

71   Pp. 78 and 79.

72   *Successful Futures*, Recommendations 41–48.

73   *Successful Futures*, 51 and 56.

5

Qualifications
'Holding Hands Around a Hole'

Wales shares a tripartite exam system with England and Northern Ireland. Youngsters sit GCSEs at the age of 16 and then proceed on to other qualifications. There are obvious differences in some of the qualifications sat. There are separate qualifications for the Welsh language, and others, such as history, take due note of the provisions of the *Cwricwlwm Cymreig*. The rapid growth of the Welsh medium sector also means that qualifications have to be offered in Welsh. Wales also had its own exam board, the WJEC (Welsh Joint Education Committee), but schools were not obliged to use it.

For much of the opening decade of devolution, qualifications were no more a controversial issue in Wales than elsewhere in the United Kingdom. As pass rates and grades got better year-on-year there were the rather empty debates about grade inflation and dumbing down. Similarly, employers frequently complained about the gap between youngsters' paper qualifications and actual ability. Any Welsh contribution to these debates got subsumed in the much bigger English debate. But there was no controversy in regard to the nature or value of Welsh and English qualifications. All that changed, with the advent of two big political beasts on the education scene.

Two GCSE fiascos

Michael Gove had made no secret of his unhappiness with the examination and qualifications system, even before he became Secretary of State in 2010. He was obviously a hawk when it came to the question of dumbing down. He made no bones about his complete hostility to modular exams, his drive for more traditional content, and his desire to return to some sort of O-level regime. His mixture of success and failure in regard to his proposed reforms would merit a book in itself.

We will focus on the acute controversy that came to a head in the summer of 2012 over the question of English language GCSE and its grading. But at the outset, the resultant pitched battle between him and Leighton Andrews should not be conceived as one of reactionary against reformist or liberal versus conservative. Andrews, as we have seen, was pushing a fairly traditional agenda in his quest for renewed rigour in the form of national testing, literacy and numeracy frameworks, and school banding. In his own book, Andrews clearly allies himself with those who believe that there is a cultural deposit that needs to be transmitted and states that, in line with the Marxist philosopher Gramsci, 'political progressivism requires educational conservatism'. Andrews goes on to say that 'We must recognise that the ideal of a democratic citizenship requires some endorsement of a common culture, alongside a recognition of the power and importance of diversity'.[1]

The issue was not one of old and new, left or right, trendy or trad. The explosion was one that only a tiny handful of officials could have seen coming – but did not. It was far more about the ownership and control of the tripartite examination system in a politically fractured world.

Schools spend hundreds of thousands of pounds on examinations each year. Qualifications are a big industry in the educational world. This industry is complex and parts of it are quite arcane. A key component of any exam system is to try to ensure that outcomes are comparable. It is quite clear that a grade awarded by one exam board needs to be comparable to that awarded by another, otherwise students will be unfairly penalised. But it is equally necessary that exam results are comparable year on year. There needs to be confidence that an A grade this year is of the same sort of level as that awarded five years before. Go to the extreme of fixed quotas for grades and you will never be able to reward better teaching and more industrious students. Go to the other, of a fixed mark, then year on year more and more students will leap over that hurdle as teaching to the test pays off. There is an unhappy medium that lies between these two extremes that tries to ensure equity between cohorts.

Herein lies the doctrine of 'comparable outcomes'. Very briefly, as summed up by the highly informed former *TES* journalist Warwick Mansell, this 'is a system whereby the regulator aims to keep national GCSE (and A-level) results roughly similar from year to year, so long as there are no changes in the characteristics of the cohort taking the exams. Statistics are used, with exam boards expected to ensure that roughly the same numbers of pupils of a given level of prior attainment …come out with each GCSE grade from year to year'.[2] So year on year, while there might be one or two localised, surprises, overall the system is going to show the same sorts of results. The rub lies in the qualifying clause, 'a given level of prior attainment'. The elision above contains the fateful words 'as measured, in England, by each GCSE cohort's Key Stage 2 test results obtained five years earlier'. The adoption of these test results as indicators was the seemingly minor change that resulted in a political explosion rarely seen in the education world.

In a tripartite system there are obviously three players. The regulators are Ofqual for England, CCEA (Council for the Curriculum Examinations and Assessment) in Northern Ireland and, until September 1st 2015, the Welsh Government. Of the three, the Welsh system is obviously the odd one out with the Government having also subsumed the regulatory role following the abolition of ACCAC in 2006. Meetings between the three national systems are held regularly and were, until 2010, uncontroversial. The advent of Mr Gove changed that. He clearly wanted an end to what he perceived as grade inflation, and was seemingly prepared to pay the price for any increase in rigour – i.e. lower results.

As usual it was in mid-August that the 2012 GCSE cohort received their exam results. For a number of students they were not what had been expected. In English Language, the news was particularly bleak. In England the rate had dropped from 65.4% to 63.9% for those obtaining the coveted A* to C. In Wales the story was even worse. The overall A* to C rate had dropped from 61.3% in 2011 to 57.4% in 2012. But it was not only the youngsters who were perplexed, angry and disappointed. In Wales, Andrews, briefed as customary the day before, was 'cross and depressed'.[3] He was also undoubtedly angry, because as his reformist agenda was biting in the form of literacy and numeracy frameworks, school banding and the like, the actual results seemed to be going in the opposite direction.

Andrews was apparently, initially completely unaware that there would be a problem until late in the long process of determining grade boundaries, long after the exams had been taken. Indeed his chapter on the whole debacle begins with these words, reminiscent of an opening line from one of Anthony Burgess's novels: 'I had no knowledge that anything was likely to go wrong with English language GCSEs in 2012 until, at the end of a routine meeting with the chief executive of the WJEC, Gareth Pierce, on 30th July, he made a reference to difficulties in the awards and the possibility that Welsh students in particular might lose out'.[4] The impact of this sentence never ceases to amaze me: his officials were either unconcerned or unaware of the bomb blast that was imminent. They had attended meetings with Ofqual, though on occasions, it later transpired, they were missing during vital discussions but should have had an understanding of the impact of Ofqual's proposals. Their colleagues in the WJEC would not have been slow to share their anxieties either. For some reason all this was ignored and not brought to Andrews' attention.

The blast rocked England as well as Wales. Ofqual came out of the whole affair very badly mauled. Some insinuated, unfairly, that it seemed as if they had bowed to political pressure and tried to tackle the issue of grade inflation in a very crude and unfair manner. After the results were published it became more and more apparent that it was the use or rather the abuse of the KS2 data as predictive of outcomes that had swung the results way out of what was expected.

Andrews ordered a rapid review on the day that the results were published, which confirmed this. The KS2 results in Wales were particularly problematic and unreliable and so the 'dip' in Welsh performance was more marked. The GCSE debacle was another legacy of the reckless way in which the SATs had been abolished a few years before. With the results of his rapid review on his desk, and after consulting some of the unions and others, Andrews ordered a re-grade, with 2,386 pupils receiving an unexpected present in the form of a better GCSE grade than that given a month before.

The exchanges between the Welsh Government and Ofqual are notably sharp in tone, but by this stage Tweedale, the civil servant in charge of the school side of the department and described as 'feisty' by Andrews in his twenty-point speech, had wrested control of the whole issue from the hapless officials in the regulatory section.[5]

In Wales Andrews was applauded; in England Gove described him as 'irresponsible and mistaken'. Later in the year, when questioned by the Select Committee at the House of Commons, Andrews put in a bravura performance justifying his actions. It confirmed him as a politician on a par with the best in Westminster.

So Andrews covered himself in glory. Here was a minister prepared to fight for Wales and to protect the interests of its youngsters. The media loved it. But had the upset been necessary in the first place? A closer reading of the situation might suggest otherwise.

In Gareth Evans' book, *A Class Apart*, a far more forensic examination of the whole saga is presented.[6] While praising the Minister, he rightly excoriates the officials involved. While Andrews writes from the inside out, Evans writes as an objective bystander looking in. One of the more level-headed commentators, his take on the whole issue can be found in a reflective piece he wrote in November 2012, once the dust had settled, and he made a number of telling points. It is worth reproducing at length:

> Let's start with what we knew already – the use of Key Stage 2 (KS2) predictors to set grade boundaries was the root cause of Wales' woes.
>
> Students this side of the border were wrongly disadvantaged because England's exams regulator, Ofqual, insisted on a change of methodology. Cue problem.
>
> Banding Welsh pupils according to prior attainment in England is an accident waiting to happen. After all, learners in Wales are subject to locally moderated teacher assessments – and external tests (SATs) no longer exist.

But Mr Andrews met with his own regulatory officials – who first discussed the use of KS2 data in January – twenty-four times before the GCSE grading fiasco played out in the media. So why wasn't he made aware of the potential pitfalls in Ofqual's plan?

Mr Andrews says he was only alerted to the possibility of results being down by WJEC chief executive Gareth Pierce during 'a previously scheduled meeting on other matters' on July 30.

And then there's the Qualifications and Learning Division which, by its own admission, 'would never support the use of one sole indicator to determine grade boundaries'. Only it did. The model may have been 'untried and untested', but it was still considered by the Welsh Government to be fit for purpose.

Someone, somewhere was holding a bomb. They helped construct it; they helped deliver it; and only after it blew up in August, did they take steps to clean it up.[7]

The metaphor of someone holding a bomb is priceless. At no time did they alert the Minister to the possibility of the explosion. Perhaps they did not know themselves what they were carrying, but that is even more worrying than the thought that they did but were unconcerned. Twenty-four meetings later (as unearthed by an FOI from Gareth Evans at the *Western Mail*) it is a chance comment from another source that alerts the Minister, who is after all responsible for the regulatory function of the government. The civil service comment that they would never support one sole indicator is blown apart by the very fact that that this is exactly what they did. The lead 'bomb carrier', who one could legitimately expect to have been alert to the consequences of these decisions and should have alerted the minister, was promoted in due course.

Examining the debris after the bomb explosion I had started to formulate one of the key recommendations of this book: the Education Department must be fundamentally challenged, radically changed and irrevocably reformed. The potential damage done to youngsters' life chances had been immense. But like the Bourbon monarchs, the officials had 'learned nothing and forgotten nothing'.

In January 2014, another GCSE fiasco hit the press, as hundreds of youngsters found that the interim grades they were receiving bore no relation to those predicted. The new English GCSE examination had been hastily introduced in part to ensure that as a 'made and regulated in Wales' examination, the grade boundaries would no longer be subject to any external interference. ASCL called for an urgent inquiry. The Welsh Government argued that comparisons with previous years could not be made because of record numbers of early entries, and also attacked Robin Hughes, the ASCL

Director. The WJEC tried to defend itself by pointing to Welsh Government insistence that 'accuracy' was to be rewarded more, but was confident that all would be alright in the end.[8]

In the event, the WJEC was largely correct, but not before considerable stress had been caused to youngsters, teachers and parents. There was a mop-up investigation carried out by the Chairman of the Review of Qualifications group. All stakeholders were invited to give evidence. I told them that it was like watching an educational version of groundhog day. My jaw hit the ground when I was told that the relevant officials had not considered the new GCSE in English a 'high risk' area. Given that it was new, and given the debacle of 2012, I commented that in that case I did not know what would be so considered. This was an area which had a huge red flashing neon sign reading 'Danger' above it, but the new Head of Qualifications apparently could not see it.

The Review of Qualifications

Looking back, the GCSE fiascos have tended to colour the general perception of qualifications development in Wales. This is a shame, as the decade had opened with some promise. One of the perennial concerns that besets politicians is the relevance of the qualifications that youngsters are studying. These anxieties are not new and not confined to one particular party. One of Gove's first acts had been to commission the immensely respected Professor Alison Wolf of King's College, London to reflect critically on the vocational qualifications then on offer to England's 14 to 19-year-olds. Her seminal report was published in March 2011. It was scathing about the quality and usefulness of many of the courses that youngsters pursued post-16, and equally emphatic about the absolute need to get their literacy and numeracy skills up to speed. It was clear that big changes would be under way in England.

In September of the same year, Jeff Cuthbert, the Deputy Minister for Skills, announced Wales' own review of qualifications, which would ensure both value for government money but also, mirroring Wolf, that what was on offer actually met the needs of learners and the economy. A simplification of qualifications had been a Labour manifesto pledge in the 2010 Westminster election. The review was centred around three main themes: the identification of the most relevant qualifications; the promotion of understanding and trust in those; and ensuring that they remained fit for purpose. Cuthbert, or at least his speech writer, was alert to the bigger debate: 'We often hear it said that some qualifications are more useful to learners than others. Likewise, we hear that some Vocational Qualifications prepare young people more effectively for employment than others. We want to find out which qualifications have greatest value; which qualifications are most relevant and should be encouraged'.[9] The Review would be chaired by the combative Huw Evans, OBE, recently retired Principal of Llandrillo FE College.

The Review was delivered fourteen months later in November 2012. It was thorough, comprehensive, and refreshingly independent. It did not confine itself to vocational qualifications but looked at the qualifications economy in the round. Without doubt, events that summer had proved a mind-sharpening experience, especially in regard to the ownership of the qualifications system. The opening paragraphs set out the stall:

> The central conclusion of the Review is that the time has come to develop a high-quality, robust and distinctive national qualifications system for 14 to 19-year-olds in Wales, and to support divergence between Wales and other parts of the UK where this is in the interests of learners in Wales ... [While] a large proportion of qualifications will continue to be shared between Wales and England ... decisions about which qualifications should be accredited and approved for use in Wales, how these should be assessed, and how performance of providers in Wales should be measured, must be taken in Wales on the basis of what is best for our learners and economy.
>
> The national qualifications system for Wales should be developed in a strategic and evidence-based way ... It should not be allowed to simply emerge through a series of reactions to events or decisions in England.[10]

The report made forty-two recommendations.[11] The first four were the flagship ones for the entire document. As well as the recommendation that there should be 'a coherent, high-quality, robust and distinctive national qualifications system for 14 to 19-year-olds in Wales', the others that followed were aimed at ensuring that distinction and robustness. The second recommendation asked that the 'Welsh Government should establish a revised and more rigorous Welsh Baccalaureate model at the heart of the qualifications system for full-time learners at 14 to 19'. But although it was to be more rigorous, the model itself was retained. This in itself was not uncontroversial, as we shall see later. The third recommendation brought centre stage one of the concerns that many had with the development of a distinctive Welsh identity and insisted that 'the Welsh Government should ensure that qualifications in Wales are of a standard comparable with the best in the world, so that they offer portability'. This would require 'a substantial, long-term, UK-wide communication strategy to promote and explain the qualifications available in Wales'.

As we have noted before in 2006, in a specious 'bonfire of the quangos',

ACCAC, the independent regulator, had been subsumed into the Department for Education. There had been little debate about the wisdom of such a move. In the summer of 2012 when the Review of Qualifications report was being written, the folly of such a policy had come back to bite the Welsh Government with a vengeance. The fifth recommendation dealt with the fallout of that debacle head on: 'The Welsh Government should establish a single body (Qualifications Wales) that is responsible for the regulation and quality assurance of all non-degree level qualifications available in Wales'. The folly of having the government itself as regulator was writ large. Yet another Davidson initiative was about to bite the dust. More contentiously, the report went on to outline that 'In time, Qualifications Wales should take responsibility for developing and awarding most qualifications for learners at 14 to 16' and cited the 'model in operation in Scotland' as an example. Qualifications development was not to be exempt from educational tourism, it seemed.

Recommendations 7 and 8 tried to expand the horizon. The value of qualifications should be judged more by their outcomes 'such as progression to further learning or to employment' rather than just as an end in themselves. This would require close cooperation with the newly reformed careers service, Careers Wales.

The flagship qualification, the Welsh Baccalaureate (WBQ), was addressed next. It needed to be 'more rigorous', suggesting that, to the Review board at least, the concerns of teachers, pupils and universities had at last carried some weight. To this end the 'Bacc' should now be graded at least at Advanced level in the first place, be awarded at 'National Foundation, National, National post-16 and Advanced levels' and be universally adopted by schools and colleges.

By now the problems associated with bilateral GCSEs were obvious. The sticking plaster revisions that had been applied in 2012 to avoid another debacle were clearly inadequate, indeed a few months later they were to be shown to be destructive, and so the review urged that 'the Welsh Government should review GCSE English Language and GCSE Welsh First Language in order to introduce revised GCSEs in these subjects for teaching from September 2015'. These would build on the Literacy and Numeracy Framework (LNF) and should be strengthened 'by placing significantly more emphasis on the quality and accuracy of writing and on core writing skills such as spelling, punctuation and grammar, than the specifications that were taught from September 2010'. Without highlighting it, the Review was again showing how inadequate the development of qualifications had been under the auspices of the Education Department. A greater surprise than urging yet another reform of English was the report's recommendation that 'the Welsh Government should introduce, for teaching from 2015, two new mathematics GCSEs, one covering numeracy and the other covering aspects of mathematics techniques'.

There was a debate to be had about how successful the whole GCSE concept had been, given the fixation on the magical A* to C grades. But, given the confusion that was engulfing qualifications in England – a proposed return to O-levels abandoned in favour of entirely new qualifications, which were themselves quickly shelved – the Review of Qualifications opted for the safest ground. It urged that 'The Welsh Government should retain GCSEs as the main Level 1 and Level 2 general qualifications at 14 to 19'. In fairness, it was indicated that new GCSEs needed to be developed, which placed 'a greater emphasis on the application of knowledge and understanding to real-life contexts, learning from the style of questions employed in PISA tests'. Similarly, 'The Welsh Government should retain A-levels as the main Level 3 general qualifications at 16 to 19... [and] maintain the same A-levels as England and Northern Ireland where possible'. You could only take distinctiveness so far. Tampering with the A-level regime could fatally damage portability.

No review of qualifications would be complete without yet another attempt to secure the holy grail of parity of esteem between vocational and academic. The Evans' Review could not resist. It called, in its thirty-first recommendation, for the Welsh Government to 'ensure that the qualifications system for Wales recognises appropriate vocational qualifications on a par with equivalent general qualifications'. The WBQ was to have a key role in this. But the Review also sought to provide some clarity on the sort of vocational qualifications that 14 to 16-year-olds should be studying: 'only IVETs (Initial Vocational Education and Training) should be available'.

The plethora of qualifications on offer was perplexing to government and students alike. The Review urged that the 'Welsh Government and Qualifications Wales should develop a new and significantly stronger gatekeeping process for the accreditation and approval of all qualifications for use by 14 to 16-year-olds and 16 to 19-year-olds in Wales'.[12] Various hoops should be installed so that the qualifications on offer were of sufficient quality but also lead somewhere afterwards.

The Review then proposed a change to the performance measures for schools and colleges, in an attempt to move away from the perversities of the 'C grade' gold standard. The Welsh Bacc should become the key measure and this was to be introduced from 2017. In addition it argued that the government should: 'continue to collect Level 2 (inclusive) threshold and capped points score data and use these as the headline measures in the medium term; report separately on English Language/Welsh First Language and Mathematics (and, from 2017, Numeracy) to align with its priorities and the secondary school banding indicators'. Schools were to be measured as never before in Wales.

The report also sought to close off some of the niggles that had bedevilled proper comparisons between schools, advocating that there should be 'a limit of two GCSEs equivalence in performance terms per qualification and introduce a limit of 40 per cent on the contribution of non-GCSEs to the Level 1 and Level 2 thresholds'. Similar moves were already under way across the border.

This would enable another longed-for aim that 'Estyn should report separately on outcomes in sixth forms and tertiary provision in FE colleges, enabling comparisons to be made between the school and FE sectors'. The different structural options inaugurated by the 14–19 Pathways would finally be open to evaluation. The Welsh Bacc should also be the lead in planning and funding post-16 provision.

On 29th January 2013, Cuthbert announced that 'the Welsh Government broadly accepts all of the Review's recommendations. The recommendations form a coherent package which provides a strong and sustainable basis for developing a world-class qualifications system for Wales'. The change was to be phased in over five years. He was aware that this would mean divergence from England in certain key regards and promised 'a major, long-term, UK-wide communications strategy in late 2013, to raise the profile of qualifications in Wales, especially with universities and employers in England'.[13] How far this strategy worked will be seen in future years. Huw Evans and his team certainly travelled a great deal, trying to charm English universities and major employers.

Although there would be no rush to implementation, a significant development was the fact that 'At the heart of the system will be a revised, more rigorous, Welsh Baccalaureate'. He acknowledged that there were 'some serious concerns over the rigour of the current model' and promised that the Bacc would be graded. Unable to resist the party political dig, he also announced that Wales 'will retain GCSEs and A-levels. Unlike Mr Gove, we and our stakeholders have confidence in these well established and recognised qualifications, which command respect with employers and universities around the world'. Turning to qualifications development, the Deputy Minister promised 'new GCSEs in English Language and Welsh First Language and two new Maths GCSEs covering numeracy and mathematical techniques... for teaching from September 2015'. He claimed that 'having two Maths GCSEs will reflect the importance of the subject for progression and employment. We will expect most learners to take both Maths GCSEs'.[14]

This 'extra' maths, the requirements to study not one but two sciences to be phased in by 2017, and the promotion of the Welsh Bacc were sowing the seeds for a very significant narrowing of the curriculum before Donaldson had even set sail!

So as the dust settled, the landscape had not changed a great deal for pupils. Wales retains GCSEs and A-levels and the Welsh Bacc will become all but compulsory. But I suspect that all is not quiet on the qualifications front. Questions about the role and purpose of GCSEs, which the review had ducked, become ever more pressing.

As well as ATL and some of the other unions, the CBI has recently come out in favour of GCSE's being scrapped. John Cridland, Director General of the CBI, urged that they be abolished within five years. Cridland believed GCSEs to be an irrelevance when most pupils stay in education or training until the age of 18. As Cridland put it 'We have to face the uncomfortable truth that – internationally – we're the oddballs'. He argued that the Westminster Government only retained them so as to allow measurement of schools through League Tables.[15] The Welsh Government's categorisation regime would be similarly in tatters if they were to go.

Perhaps most tellingly of all was the trenchant criticism of GCSEs given by Lord Baker, the Secretary of State for Education who introduced them nearly thirty years ago: 'Not many have woken up to the fact that education now stretches to 18 years old. If education has moved up to 18, you have to ask yourself what are we testing at 16? Sixteen is no longer a departure for youngsters and very few go to work at that age. GCSE is no longer assessing performance at departure and over the course of the next ten years it will disappear because it won't have much of a purpose...It will wither on the vine. It won't have much of a purpose'.[16] I hope Welsh Government officials are thinking about what needs to be done, but on past performance I doubt it.

Welsh Baccalaureate

The idea that the post-16 regime undertaken by youngsters is too narrowing is not a new one. There have been constant cries down the years that we learn from our European rivals, especially Germany, about producing an offer which is broader and bridges the academic/vocational divide. Down through the years there have been several attempts to do so by providing qualifications which are less subject based. In England the last abortive attempt was the proposed Diplomas, launched in the dying days of the New Labour regime, to bridge the divide and establish the Holy Grail of 'parity of esteem' which has been eluding policy makers for decades. They quickly died a death once the Conservative-LibDem Coalition took power in Westminster in 2010.

In Wales the outlook for innovation was much brighter. The development of a Welsh Baccalaureate had been signalled in *The Learning Country*, and along with the Foundation Phase is often hailed as one of its flagship policies. It was dogged by criticism from the start. Some of the problems arose over the understanding of what a baccalaureate should look like. The original idea predated the arrival of devolution. In a report in 1993, *Wales 2010*, the Institute of Welsh Affairs had argued for a baccalaureate style qualification.

The proposals had been worked up at the start of the millennium by Colin Jenkins, former principal of Atlantic College, an independent residential Sixth Form College in the Vale of Glamorgan offering the International Baccalaureate and John David, suggesting that any Welsh Bacc should be modelled on the highly respected International Baccalaureate qualification. It was not to be. The Welsh Bacc was to take a different route and be primarily a 'wrap around' qualification *in addition* to the others on offer. At its inception Jenkins and David criticised the Welsh Government's proposals as 'missing a huge opportunity', a 'feeble quick fix' and 'not a baccalaureate'. Davidson's response was predictable. Her more modest proposal was 'a significant innovation [and]... distinctive, modern and proudly Welsh'.[17] It is interesting to note that a decade later similar rhetoric was to be used to defend the so-called English Baccalaureate, which was even further removed from any international model.

The pilots of the Welsh Bacc were launched in 2003 and then rolled out to a number of schools and colleges. From 2007 it became universally available to any institution in Wales who wanted to offer it to students. Originally it consisted of a 'Core' engaged by all students alongside the other academic or vocational qualifications being studied. The Core comprised five components: Key Skills; Wales, Europe and the World; Work-Related Education; Personal and Social Education; and an Individual Investigation. It was offered at Foundation, Intermediate, and Advanced levels. Initially offered on a pass or fail basis, the award is now gradually being graded, with the Advanced level being graded since September 2013. By 2015 the total number of Advanced Level Welsh Baccalaureate Diploma entries was 10,529, a similar figure to 2014. At the Intermediate Level numbers had crept up from 13,491 in 2013 to 14,307 in 2015.

But questions about the validity and value of the Welsh Bacc have continued to dog its roll-out. Even at the time of writing there is disagreement about its real currency with universities, especially the better ones outside Wales. The whole debate ignited again in 2011 when Jeff Jones, quondam leader of Bridgend Council, former chair of the WJEC and something of a national curmudgeon, labelled the qualification as 'nonsense' with 'Mickey Mouse additions', adding for good measure, 'If I were a student I wouldn't touch it with a barge pole'. Mr Jones alleged that the WJEC had felt compelled to bid for the development contract solely because it was the Welsh exam board. Both David Evans of the NUT and I backed up the government's claim for the value of the Bacc as something that showed a broader base being offered by Welsh applicants to university.[18]

Far more nuanced criticism was to be found in a report commissioned by the Welsh Government from WISERD, considering the role that the Welsh Bacc was having on students once they were in Higher Education. The report,

Relationships between the Welsh Baccalaureate Advanced Diploma (WBQ) and Higher Education did what it said on the tin and its findings were mixed, in fact positively perplexing: 'The evaluation reports two key, but interrelated, findings. The first is that there is strong evidence to suggest that the WBQ is enormously valuable in helping students to enter higher education. This benefit would appear to be largely due to the weighting given to the Core component of the WBQ as the equivalent of an additional A-level qualification (at grade A) for (some) university admissions. However, the evaluation also finds evidence to suggest that students with the WBQ Core find they are less likely to achieve a 'good' degree result than equivalent students without the WBQ Core, once they are at university'.[19] If the second finding were true then the advantage outlined in the first would quickly be lost.

The report was blunt: 'low-achieving students appear to have the most to gain from having the WBQ in terms of university participation. Although overall levels of HE participation for relatively high-achieving students do not appear to be affected by having the WBQ, it does confer some advantage in terms of entry to Russell Group universities'.[20] It was not surprising then that one of the key recommendations of the report was that the Welsh Bacc be made more challenging, and that grading might be a limited step in achieving that aim. The Review of Qualifications was happy to endorse this plea and inaugurate some other step changes.

In response to trenchant and sustained criticism, the Core has now been radically reformed. Since 2015 a Skills Challenge Certificate has been introduced which aims to enable learners to develop and demonstrate an understanding of and proficiency in the essential and employability skills of: Communication, Numeracy, Digital Literacy, Planning and Organisation, Creativity and Innovation, Critical Thinking and Problem Solving, and Personal Effectiveness. As well as the Individual project, there will be three 'Challenge Briefs' covering enterprise and employability, global citizenship, and a community challenge.

There has been some change in that the new Bacc focuses far more on the seven essential employability skills: Literacy, Numeracy, Digital Literacy, Critical Thinking and Problem Solving, Planning and Organisation, Creativity and Innovation, and Personal Effectiveness. There has been some change in nomenclature associated with the Bacc too. It is still offered at three levels but while the Foundation and Advanced levels remain so called, the Intermediate one has been confusingly relabelled the 'National' level. To add to confusion, the Foundation level will be graded as 'Pass' or 'Fail', while the National will run from A* to C, and the Advanced Level from A* to E.

In terms of results, the vast majority of students who take it are awarded the WBQ. In 2015, at Advanced level 92.2% of candidates achieved the Core certificate with 87.4% also receiving the full Advanced Level Welsh

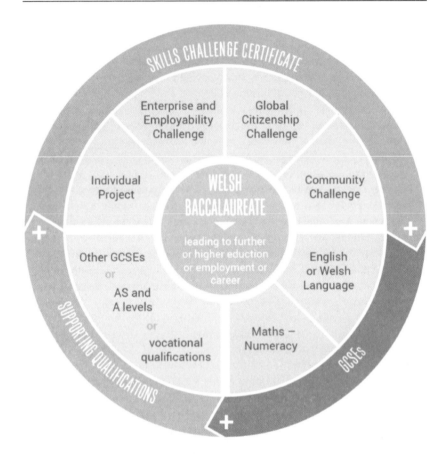

Baccalaureate Diploma, up from 82.7% in 2013. In the core certificate, 12.2% achieved a grade A*. At the Intermediate Level 89.4% achieved the Core Certificate, a dip from a high of 91.6% in 2014, and those being awarded the Intermediate diploma dipped from 85.7% in 2014 to 82.2% in 2015.[21]

It is obviously early days for this new Welsh Bacc. It is also equally obvious that this new qualification is substantially different, especially in terms of rigour, than its predecessor. These developments may well help the reception of the WBQ at English universities. Although the Welsh Government blithely claims that the qualification is worth 120 UCAS points, therefore the equivalent of an A grade, there is clearly a wide difference in practice.

In any case, the WISERD Report threw cold water on the Welsh Government's jaunty assertion of value. After noting some blunt criticism from students themselves, WISERD highlighted the uncertainty that surrounded the Bacc's actual reception in practice:

This uncertainty as to the WBQ's appropriateness for universities that made offers in terms of grades and subjects largely came about because universities did not always regard it as the equivalent of an A grade at A-level; 'I was also told it was an A grade, but to all the universities in London it's seen as a B or C, and some only take it as an AS not an A-level. So whereas I came into it and was told it would be an A, when you actually look into it it's not' (Sixth-form student, School B).

This was further compounded by some universities not being entirely sure themselves whether they accepted it or not, or how they regarded it if they did; 'some of the universities I went to weren't sure if they were taking it. That made me uneasy about it and made me wonder whether to keep working on it or put it on the back burner in a way' (Sixth-form student, School A). WBQ Coordinators were very explicit about the lack of consistency or clarity in how the WBQ was regarded for university admissions; 'different universities are offering different things [...] the biggest thing we can do is give them the advice that it might not be an A' (WBQ Coordinator, School B); 'Within the same university they can look at two courses – one will offer [the WBQ], one will not, which could disadvantage them' (WBQ Coordinator, School C).[22]

The confusion over the value and nature of the Welsh Bacc is still with us. Behind closed doors there is far more frank talking about current problems with the qualification than the Welsh Government would like to admit. Heads and college principals share many of those concerns. Many teachers are still not convinced of its worth. At the grand conference held to launch the new 'Donaldson' curriculum in October 2015, the 'pupil panel' was noticeably tepid in its response to a question about the Welsh Bacc. This is not to say that the qualification is no good, far from it, it's just to note that there's a lot more work to be done.

There are obviously some questions that will not be answerable for a few years to come, until comparable data becomes available. These include: What real value will employers and universities put on the grades awarded? Will the C grade, for example, suffer the fate of grades D to G at GCSE and be regarded as a failure? Will future cohorts show similar levels of attainment? But perhaps the greatest question of all will be the real value that universities, especially those outside Wales, actually put on the WBQ. The answer to that last question will not be given by helpful Admissions Tutors responding to Welsh Government requests for endorsement, but by a survey of actual destinations.

Qualifications Wales

The other great reform of the Review of Qualifications was the re-instatement of the independent regulator for examinations. The GCSE fiasco had shown the danger of the Welsh Government being invested with this function. But the quality of qualifications and assessments was also a cause for concern. We cannot know how things would have developed if ACCAC had stayed in existence, but my gut feeling is that the GCSE row would not have taken place – or would have taken place far earlier. I also think that the quality of qualifications development, especially in regard to the Welsh Baccalaureate, would have been of a superior quality. The advent of Qualifications Wales gives us some chance to judge those counter-factuals.

Qualifications Wales could not simply be magicked into existence. It required legislation. And that required scrutiny. From the start it was clear that there were two main issues at stake: the independence of the new body, and its future role in awarding qualifications.

The danger of too quick a progress to the second issue was apparent to most, though Andrews' rather dyspeptic hostility towards the WJEC and its Chief Executive, Gareth Pierce, blinded him to this. As we had just narrowly averted a disaster because of the confusion of the roles of poacher and game-keeper it was hardly wise for the new body to try to undertake them both. When the Qualifications Review had recommended that 'Qualifications Wales should take responsibility for developing and awarding most qualifications for learners at 14 to 16' it had importantly qualified this hope with the phrase 'In time'. As the process for setting up Qualifications Wales unfolded it became increasingly obvious that this 'golden era', was was receding further and further into the distance.

In its pre-legislative scrutiny of the proposed Bill, the Children and Young Peoples' Committee was clear: 'The Qualifications Wales Bill should be limited to establishing Qualifications Wales as a regulating body only. Future changes to its remit, including its role as an awarding body, should be brought forward in a subsequent Bill'.[23] The original proposal of the Qualifications Review that Qualifications Wales should be both regulating and awarding had already been watered down, as the WJEC had refused point blank to roll over and die. Although Huw Evans, whose tone and manner before the Committee struck one as someone confident of being the new Chair of the Qualifications Board, stuck to his guns that regulation and awarding should go together, the threat of a legal challenge from the WJEC to protect their operational independence meant that he proposed a commissioning model as a face saver. This too bit the dust as the committee was 'unconvinced that there is yet sufficient clarity in terms of how the proposed commissioning model will work in practice'.[24]

The Committee had other concerns in this area. The recently announced Curriculum Review had the potential to throw everything up into the air again, and there were substantial changes under way to GCSEs which would need time to bed down. Off the record, a number of its members expressed their concern about the way in which the GCSE fiasco had been handled. It had certainly not enhanced their esteem for the Department's proposals.

During the Committee's scrutiny, ACCAC had been discussed. Huw Evans was content that curriculum development should be a future role for Qualifications Wales. The Committee echoed the view of many that since its abolition there had been a noticeable gap in curriculum expertise and direction. Gareth Pierce of the WJEC was laconic and to the point: 'It seems as if the Welsh Government and WJEC are holding hands around a hole, and the hole is ACCAC'. Doubtless there are those in the Welsh Government who would be content for Qualifications Wales to take the whole responsibility for curriculum development off their hands.

With unusually trenchant recommendations from the Committee, substantial lobbying by stakeholders of various hues, and the realisation that unacceptable proposals would be fought hard by the WJEC, it was hardly surprising that on the day that the Bill was introduced into the Senedd, Huw Lewis had reluctantly stated that: 'My long-term ambition remains for Qualifications Wales to become an awarding body, but that needs to be at the right time'. When politicians, whose time span is usually governed by the need for the next headline, speak of long-term ambitions, you know that this is really a hefty kick into the long grass.

I suspect that we are a long way from Qualifications Wales undertaking any 'developing and awarding' function. Apart from the obvious conflict of interests which would have to be very carefully negotiated – and the GCSE English fiascos have laid a long trail on landmines in that regard – there is also the vexing fact that the GCSE regime is currently not a Wales-only preserve. This was one of the fundamental differences between Wales and Scotland (the latter's qualifications regime is stand-alone and uncontested) that Andrews' dyspepsia and the officials' wilful ignorance refused to take into account.

It proved relatively easy to ensure that the poacher and gamekeeper functions were not confused. It was more difficult to ensure that the independence of the new body would be a fact and not a fiction. The Welsh Government has a long history of setting up allegedly independent bodies which it then seeks to control. In education the most notorious recent example has been the establishment of the Education Workforce Council (EWC). Its predecessor body, the General Teaching Council for Wales, had at least some semblance of democracy and independence in that twelve of its twenty-five members were elected. The EWC by contrast is a pure quango appointed solely by the Minister in some guise or other. The EWC may or may not survive; it is currently little regarded by the profession, and of little importance to them. Qualifications Wales by contrast holds the future of generations of youngsters in its hands. If it were to be susceptible to government interference, or even given the impression that it could be, then the situation would be far graver. It was essential that its independence was enshrined and its accountability made manifest.

The Qualifications Wales Bill was laid on 1st December 2014.[26] The Stage 1 scrutiny undertaken by the CYPEC threw up a number of pertinent questions. By Stage 2, which commenced on 25th March, it was clear that a far more nuanced approach would have to be taken if relevant qualifications were still to be available in Wales. Seventy-six amendments were tabled, fifty-five of them from the Minister. The original intention on the face of the Bill was that any publicly funded qualification had to be approved by Qualifications Wales. This presented immense practical problems for Qualifications Wales in terms of time and resource. The Minister now had to propose a new category of 'designated qualifications' to facilitate continuity during the early years of Qualifications Wales. Unpicking the mess made by the abolition of ACCAC was never going to be easy.

The original proposals had been vague about the nature of the independence of the new body. Obviously any independent organisation funded by government would need checks and safeguards so that the piper could not call the tune. Lobbying by key stakeholders, especially ATL and ASCL (whose Director at the time had a long history in qualifications development) and forensic scrutiny by the education committee ensured that Qualifications Wales now has a duty to engage stakeholders. It will also be subject to the scrutiny of an annual debate in the Senedd, in much the same way as Estyn. The only opposition amendment to make it into the final Act was that of the very able Liberal Democrat educational spokesperson, Aled Roberts. The original wording had provided only that Qualifications Wales should report 'whether, and if so how' on any engagement with stakeholders. Amendment 68 strengthened the requirement on Qualifications Wales to include in its annual report details of *how* it had consulted with stakeholders that year.[27]

Not that the battle in terms of independence is over. The appointment of Philip Blaker, the then Director of Operations at Universities and Colleges Admissions Service (UCAS), and a veteran of the qualifications world, gave some hope that independence would be promoted and maintained, but appointment of the new Chair raised some eyebrows.

Most commentators had expected the redoubtable Huw Evans, who had so effectively undertaken the Review of Qualifications, to have been the obvious choice. Evans had also been instrumental in ensuring that the path taken by Wales in regard to qualifications has been understood, especially in

England. The progress and publicity of the main finding of the Review had been exemplary compared to many other botched initiatives by the Welsh Government, but it appears likely that despite Huw's expertise, his manifest independence ensured that he was overlooked as Chair.

In the event it was Ann Evans who has been on the original steering group of the Review of Qualifications who got the job. Before gaining operational independence in September 2015, the website for Qualifications Wales was run by the government. When consulted over the summer of 2015 it stated that 'Ann Evans has been an independent education consultant since 2012, following four years as Chief Executive of Careers Wales, Mid Glamorgan and Powys. Her earlier positions include Assistant Chief Executive of ACCAC (Qualifications Curriculum and Assessment Authority for Wales), a school Science teacher and a lecturer and manager in Further Education'.[28]

Interestingly there was no reference to the time when she worked at the Department of Education and Skills as Head of Qualifications and Learning, from 2005 to 2008, during which time she was a colleague of the GCSE 'bomb carrier'. Some qualifications veterans wondered, in private, about the potential for a considerable conflict of interest. They also wondered if, when the inevitable crises come, the Board of Qualifications Wales would be prepared to take a strong line with the Welsh Government.

Notes

1   Andrews, *Ministering to Education*, p. 234.
2   http://www.naht.org.uk/welcome/news-and-media/blogs/warwick-mansell/ofqual-to-ditch-comparable-outcomes/. I recommend Mansell's writing on this confusing and somewhat arcane issue for its clarity, and also for spelling out the mess the system gets into when politicians try to have their cake and eat it.
3   Andrews, p. 208.
4   Andrews, p. 207.
5   Andrews, p. 213 ff.
6   Evans, G *A Class Apart: Learning the Lessons of Education in Post-Devolution Wales* (Welsh Academic Press; Cardiff 2015). See especially Chapter 6.
7   http://www.walesonline.co.uk/news/local-news/gareth-evans-chance-hurt-leighton-2016808 10 November 2012.
8   http://www.bbc.co.uk/news/uk-wales-26464441 and http://www.walesonline.co.uk/news/wales-news/the-system-itself-trial-pupils-7639873.
9   http://gov.wales/newsroom/educationandskills/2011/110929qualifications/?lang=en
10   Review of Qualifications for 14 to 19-year-olds in Wales: Final report and Recommendations. P. 18.
11   These can be found on pp. 7 and following.
12   Recommendation 35.
13   http://gov.wales/about/cabinet/cabinetstatements/2013/1419qualificationsreview/?lang=en

14   http://gov.wales/about/cabinet/cabinetstatements/2013/1419qualificationsreview/?lang=
      en

15   http://www.bbc.co.uk/news/education-33190028

16   http://www.telegraph.co.uk/education/further-education/11803801/GCSEs-are-outdated-
      and-will-wither-on-the-vine-says-the-man-who-introduced-them.html

17   https://en.wikipedia.org/wiki/Welsh_Baccalaureate_Qualification

18   http://www.walesonline.co.uk/news/wales-news/row-ex-exam-chief-says-welsh-1833733

19   Relationships between the Welsh Baccalaureate Advanced Diploma (WBQ) and Higher
      Education (Summary) http://gov.wales/docs/caecd/research/130325-relationships-between-
      welsh-baccalaureate-advanced-diploma-higher-education-summary-en.pdf p. 3.

20   P. 4.

21   Statistics from briefings provided by the WJEC. Available on their website.

22   WISERD, p. 35 http://dera.ioe.ac.uk/18417/1/130325-relationships-between-welsh-
      baccalaureate-advanced-diploma-higher-education-en.pdf

23   Children, Young People and Education Committee: Pre-legislative scrutiny of the proposed
      Qualifications Wales Bill (July 2014) http://www.assembly.wales/Laid%20Documents/
      CR-LD9833%20-%20Children,%20Young%20People%20and%20Education%20
      Committee%20Report-%20Pre-legislative%20scrutiny%20of%20the%20proposed%20
      Qualifications/CR-LD9833-e.pdf

24   P. 13.

25   P. 20.

26   http://www.assembly.wales/laid%20documents/pri-ld10026%20-%20qualifications%20
      wales%20bill/pri-ld10026-e.pdf

27   An excellent and understandable account of the process can be found at http://www.
      senedd.assembly.wales/documents/s40411/Research%20Service%20Summary%20of%20
      changes%20at%20Stage%202.pdf

28   http://www.qualificationswales.org/news/2015/03/17/appointment-of-chair-of-qualifications-
      wales-shadow-board/ (Accessed 21st August 2015).

6

The Hour of Reckoning

League Tables, Banding, Categorisation and PISA

No one can doubt that since devolution Wales has taken a very different course in education policy to that being pursued in England. Indeed, one of the foundation arguments for devolution had been the freedom it would bring to do just this. But it is one matter to make things different and quite another to make things better. In this chapter we will look at various judgments that have been passed on the effectiveness of the reforms since 1999. At the outset I want to make it absolutely clear that the judgments under discussion are ones about the situation in Wales. They should not be read in any way as an endorsement of policies pursued in England. That would require another evaluation which is way beyond the scope of this book. Some of the measures we will examine are internal, such as the debate about the abolition of the League Tables and their subsequent re-introduction in another guise. Others are external, such as the comparative performance of Wales in terms of exam results and, of course, PISA. All affect little Megan profoundly.

In another League: the abolition saga

School League Tables have become such a part of the education topography in England that it is salutary to remember that they are of relatively recent origin. Even during the Thatcher years the relative performance of schools was a closed Pandora's box. There were many guesses as to which were the better performing schools, but little usable hard data was in the public domain. All that began to change in 1992 when information started being made available by John Major's newly elected government. The logic was deceptively simple and, as with all such seemingly simple logic, deeply flawed.

The mantra of parental choice had been deeply embedded in Conservative policy for decades. It had been one of the factors bringing Thatcher to power.

(I well remember Conservative posters in windows in my home village of Gelli in the Rhondda in 1979, because the Tories were offering parents the right to choose which of the local comprehensives their children would go to, rather than the local council's determination to allocate them as it saw fit.) But choice is of limited value in the absence of data. By giving parents the hard data about local schools, so the argument went, they could then opt for the one that was best for their child. The flaws are obvious. What if geography effectively curtailed any realistic choice? What data should be used? What perverse behaviour would schools start to practice to improve their data? And above all, what parent in their right mind would not choose the highest performing school in their neighbourhood?

But logic has never been a strong suit with governments of any hue, and the League Tables were introduced. The Westminster Education Department weakly claimed that it was publishing data rather than publishing League Tables. But the way in which the data was portrayed, by LEA and in alphabetical order, was simply a cover. Local and national journalists had an easy time of comparing schools in their area and showing where the best and worst schools could be found. The most significant data set, the one which dominates reporting and discussions to this day, was that which gave the A to C GCSE grades. The clear intention was not simply to produce usable statistics but also a mechanism whereby some pseudo-market would reward the good and drive out the bad suppliers.

From the start the League Tables were controversial. Their initial form, which consisted only of raw data such as the percentage of pupils gaining five or more GCSEs, or those reaching level four in KS2 tests in primary schools, saw the selective schools and state schools in middle-class areas topping the tables. In many ways these simply served to show where the wealthy lived. They showed little about the school's effectiveness but much about its catchment. Since 2003 the tables have included a 'value-added' measure, which purport to show the progress pupils made during their time at school in an attempt to capture the 'school effect'. Other tweaks and modifications have also been made.

Their critics, as well as pointing out the unfairness of using of raw data for which schools were not responsible, also pointed out the dangers of 'teaching to the test' which such a measurement could cause, not to mention the stress they caused to pupils and teachers alike. Others also cited surveys which showed that parents often didn't look at the information before choosing their child's school, and even those who consulted it frequently could not understand the data confronting them. From the start, the education unions, as might be expected, were bitterly opposed to the whole project. Despite rumblings, the Blair government made no attempt to stop the League Tables, and it remains the case that in England, unlike the rest of the UK, the hated League Tables are still in force.

Devolution opened up yet another possibility for Wales to be different, and Davidson wasted no time in seizing the chance. A consultation in the opening months of 2001 had indicated overwhelming support for abolition. Geraint Davies of the NASUWT spoke for many when he said: 'We don't want these school League Tables – let's do away with them. They have been a pointless bureaucratic exercise which pits one school against another'. The NASUWT also highlighted the workload they produced for teachers. The NUT similarly insisted that even proposed value-added measures would be insufficient and that the whole setup was unfair to schools as 'Performance tables encourage crude comparisons between schools, based on narrow measurements of achievement influenced by factors beyond the control of schools and teachers.'[1]

On July 20th Davidson grabbed headlines throughout the UK by announcing that the League Tables for secondary schools would be abolished immediately by cancelling the scheduled publication of the relevant data in the following November. It wasn't quite a first as Sinn Féin's Martin McGuiness had announced a similar course of action in Northern Ireland earlier that year. Primary schools had never been subjected to the League Table regime in Wales. Davidson claimed that secondary school League Tables in Wales were scrapped following a consultation which showed that neither teachers nor members of the public supported them. She went on to say 'That does not mean we will hide the information from parents or the public. Schools will continue to publish their own results'. What it did mean was that school-to-school comparison was made well neigh impossible, and any parent so minded would have to apply for a prospectus for each school in an area.[2]

The unions were delighted. Gwen Evans, Deputy General Secretary of ATL, called the move 'bold' and wondered 'How long will it be before England follows this excellent example?' The NAHT endorsed the call for England to follow suit.[3] But it didn't, and anger over the League Tables continues unabated to this day.

But there was a narrow path to tread between abolishing the publication of the data required to construct the League Tables, and publishing data that could be legitimately expected as an indicator of the performance of a school, LEA, and the whole system. In early April 2007 the Welsh Government published a consultation document *Review of Secondary School Performance Measures*, which attempted what it called a 'zero-based review... [seeking] to find a solution that actually serves stated objectives by starting from the premise that nothing should be included just because it was included in the past'.[4] It looked *inter alia* at what should be included in the measures of school performance in terms of GCSE results and other key indicators, and was particularly keen, in line with the then direction of travel, that vocational qualifications should feature more highly in 'the scores on the doors', and in setting targets for schools and colleges. The Review acknowledged that the promulgation of the Freedom of Information Act in 2005 had caused something of a headache in terms of the data and information that could now be demanded from government sources. Indeed, we were reassured that 'the Minister gave considerable thought as to how to meet obligations under FoI without reneging on her commitment to schools that there would be no publication of 'League Tables' in Wales whilst she is Minister'.[5]

The document contained an interesting résumé of the Welsh Government's position on League Tables. It asserted that:

> performance information that can be ranked in the form of 'League Tables' is not the most effective way of presenting this information to schools and parents, and the wider public domain. The Assembly Government remains committed to this principle.
>
> This is because 'League Tables':
> * focus on examination results ... and do not reflect the 'value-added' by the school to pupils' performance;
> * do not show the year-on-year improvement achieved by each school;
> * fail to take account of the differing socio-economic factors that prevail throughout Wales;
> * do not recognise the possible impact that Special Units or Classes may have on a school's results;
> * can be divisive, and demoralising to staff and pupils;
> * encourage schools to focus on examination results at the expense of the wider curriculum and other educational experiences for young people;
> * contain a limited range of information; and
> * encourage parents and others to make unfair and simplistic comparisons between schools.[6]

Under Davidson at least there would be no rowing back from the abolition at the start of the new decade. Few would have wanted it at that stage, in any case.

Looking back it is difficult to remember how optimistic many in the Welsh establishment were, myself included. It seemed as if we had cracked the performance nut without having to have recourse to methods which seemed to narrow the curriculum, cause undue anxiety, and promote an unhealthy competition in what should be a collaborative exercise. Even Professor David Reynolds, whose mild criticisms had made him a *persona non grata* to the Davidson regime, shared that outlook. In June of 2007 the *Western Mail* was confidently predicting that England would be under pressure to follow Wales' lead and scrap the SATs tests. Reynolds commented that: 'When Wales began to abolish the external SATs there was a degree of concern in English policy-making circles that standards would suffer. But Wales does not appear to have performed worse than England in the early years of primary because of this. A lot of people now are feeling the courage of their conviction that they can go the Welsh way and standards will not suffer. There are a lot of things which, in the next six months, England may start picking up on if it is abundantly clear that the Welsh way works'. But Reynolds was no fool. The paper went on to note that 'Professor Reynolds believes the results of the international PISA survey in the autumn, which assesses Welsh children against their English counterparts for the first time, could be a turning point'.[7] The caveat was an important one. The first result from the Programme for International Student Assessment (PISA) was to show that all was far from well. Wales was noticeably behind the rest of the UK.

Examination by Bristol

In October 2010, just two months before the publication of the second PISA survey, a final body blow was given to any hopes that the Welsh way was one to follow. The Centre for Market and Public Organisation of the Bristol Institute of Public Affairs, based at the University of Bristol, published *A natural experiment in school accountability: the impact of school performance information on pupil progress and sorting.*[8] The paper was an attempt to test a simple hypothesis: 'that the publication of school performance tables raises school effectiveness'. The data available was an educational sociologist's dream. It was now possible to compare two very similar systems – one with, and one without a major accountability mechanism. The paper's conclusions were stark and damning: 'We find significant and robust evidence that this reform [the abolition of League Tables] markedly reduced school effectiveness in Wales'. And to put the boot in a little further, the paper also set out to 'test whether the reform reduced school segregation in Wales, and finds no systematic significant impact on either sorting by ability or by socio-economic status'.[9]

The alleged reduction in effectiveness was sizeable. It was claimed that it amounted to 'a fall of 1.92 GCSE grades per student per year'.[10] As shown in Figure 2.

The report was far from crude. Its authors had obviously done their homework on some of the excuses that might be trotted out to show that it was other factors which had caused the comparative underperformance. The report discussed, examined and controlled for factors such as changes to the inspection regime, differential reporting of GCSE results by schools, local government involvement, Free School Meals, poverty, and differences in

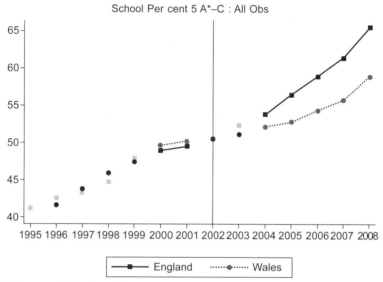

N.B. Connected points indicate the before and after periods in our analysis

Figure 2: School Percent 5A*–C in England and Wales over time.[11]

GCSE equivalences. They also accounted for and dismissed the clear funding gap that was by then emerging between Welsh and English Schools. It was difficult for the Welsh Government to know how to respond.

Late in the evening two days before the publication of the report I was tipped off about its content. The tip off also indicated that the Welsh Government had apparently decided against making any official observation on the report, and I was urged to push myself forward into the media glare to try and calm the whole situation down. I agreed because ATL and the other unions had called for the abolition of the League Tables. I was also increasingly aware that our problem wasn't so much the abolition of the League Tables as the absence of any accountability system whatsoever. The media interaction wasn't easy. I remember two consecutive outings to *Good Morning Wales*, BBC Radio Wales' flagship news programme, to discuss the ensuing hue and cry. On the second I was pitted against the late Chris Woodhead, one time Ofsted's Chief Inspector, and a man whose name made many teachers' blood boil. It was a bad tempered exchange.

I had ignored poor and superficial advice from a London source to try and rubbish the report by playing the deprivation card but my late night perusal of the report and its findings had convinced me that this was a non-starter. Others were of a different opinion. Chris Keates General Secretary of NASUWT fulminated that 'This appears to be an ideological theory in desperate search of evidence to back it up. It conveniently fails to highlight the fact that overall school performance in schools in Wales increased during the period covered by the report'. (The report had actually acknowledged this, as can be seen in the graph.) She demanded that: 'The Assembly must not cravenly accept this report. It is entirely wrong implicitly to criticise the commitment and hard work of teachers and schools in Wales on the basis of such a questionable piece of research. No definitive conclusions about the effectiveness of performance League Tables on educational standards in Wales or anywhere else can be drawn from this report'.[12]

Others, who *had* read the report, were more nuanced. Reynolds wondered if there needed to be a reassessment of position on League Tables. He was obviously impressed by the quality of the research: 'This is a slap in the face with good data. League Tables were abolished for the best possible reasons but now they should have another look'.[13] I claimed that 'The vast majority of headteachers, teachers and pupils would not welcome the reintroduction of League Tables', but while I praised the Welsh Assembly Government for stating that there would be no return, I acknowledged that the findings of the report were disturbing. While arguing that 'Naming and shaming is too crass' I concluded that 'a new system of accountability must be sought'.[14]

The thought was not unique to me. A Welsh Government spokesperson said that they had 'a commitment to learning and benchmarking against those near and far away and the use of data at all levels in the system to promote continuous improvement'. The concrete manifestation of that commitment was shortly to be unveiled.[15]

Professor David Egan, who had been Davidson's Special Advisor, was far less aggressive than Keates in his rejection of the report. Writing on the Bevan Foundation website a month later, Egan commented that he thought the research had some 'interesting, but unconvincing, statistical modelling and analysis', and rejected any 'single cause' theory. He also castigated the report for choosing 'to ignore that exactly the obverse situation applies in relation to academic achievement by 11-year-olds in the two countries, where Wales consistently achieves better outcomes than England. Why, if the existence or not of League Tables explains outcomes at age 15, do they not at the age of 11?' Unfortunately, the robustness of the KS2 data in Wales was by that stage being seriously undermined. He concluded that 'The decision taken by the Assembly Government in 2001 reflected the widespread view that the publication by the print media of League Tables was unfair, inaccurate and an inappropriate way of reporting on student and school performance. There is no evidence to suggest that this no longer remains the overwhelming view of public and educational opinion in Wales'.[16] The last claim, at least, was true.

Leighton Andrews had perhaps been the most nuanced of all in his response to the report. Quoted in the *Western Mail* he said: 'In Wales over the decade of devolution we have implemented most of the changes the profession wanted to see. So we don't have League Tables. We will see in December, when the international comparisons of school performance are reported in the Programme for International Student Assessment (PISA) survey, whether that approach has paid off'.[17]

The problem was it hadn't. The second PISA survey showed that Wales was falling further behind. In the summer of the following year, Professor Burgess of Bristol returned to the attack. He noted with some glee that: 'Responding to our research, the Welsh Assembly Government said "wait for the PISA results". These results are now in and do not make happy reading. No doubt there are many factors underlying the relative performance of Wales and England, but the diminution of public accountability for schools in Wales is surely one of them'.[18] By that stage the development of a new form of public accountability was well under way. School Banding was about to hit the scene.

School Banding

Andrews had signalled his intention to introduce a school grading system in his 2011 speech, Teaching Makes a Difference. The word 'Banding' was later used in place of 'Grading' to try to soften the blow. The move was still controversial. Secondary schools were put in provisional bands in September 2011 by the newly established School Standards Unit, another commitment from the February speech. It was not well received. By December 2011 the new scheme was unveiled in its entirety and some tweaks made to the provisional placings.

The opening bullets of the final document for stakeholders set out how Banding was meant to work as part of Andrews' improvement agenda. It was keen to stress that 'The Minister has stated categorically that Banding is NOT about labelling schools, naming and shaming or creating a divisive League Table'. Critics would argue otherwise. Banding was rather about grouping schools so that they could receive an appropriate 'framework of support and challenge that will be developed over time to accompany each band'. Ominously it was left to 'local authorities and consortia to agree the detail of how they will use Banding to help target support and raise standards for all'. This last caveat was to prove one of the weak points of Banding and its successor, as the quality of support brokered by local authorities and consortia ranged so widely. It could be argued that this should have been sorted on a national level before the Banding process began, but Andrews was a man in a hurry.[19]

The model was keen to reflect the newly enunciated ministerial priorities of literacy, numeracy and narrowing the gap in pupil performance caused by deprivation. It tried to combine data in such a way that schools would be given credit for the difference they were actually making rather than just receiving a reward for being in the right place at the right time, as the cruder versions of school League Tables had tended to do. It used groups of data around Level 2 threshold, including English/Welsh and mathematics, capped points score, English/Welsh and mathematics average points scores and, more controversially, attendance. These elements were then scored according to the quarter in which the school fell, with quarter 1 representing performance in the top 25% of schools in Wales and quarter 4 representing the lowest 25%. These had equal weighting in the overall score with the exception of attendance, which had a comparative weighting of 50%.

Progress was measured relative to the Free School Meal levels in the school, in an attempt to account for the well known correlation between these and underperformance. It was also measured according to the overall performance of the school when all the four elements were combined. The Banding boundaries were then set by looking at the best and worst possible scores, which were 11 and 44 respectively. This gave a range of 33 which was then divided by 5 to give the band boundaries.[20]

From the start the Banding regime was dogged by difficulty. There were obviously those who were opposed to any sort of system which ranked schools. David Evans, Secretary of NUT Cymru, was unconvinced by the semantics surrounding the denial that this was a reintroduction of League Tables under another guise and quickly labelled the whole scheme as 'Branding'. Even those who were more open to the realisation that something needed to be done were uneasy about what was put in place. Frank Ciccotti, a leading light in NAHT Cymru, labelled the banding system a 'fiasco'. He warned that in regard to the final calculation 'the way it is added up is foolish and this leads to extremely unstable results. The good statistical work is undone by a crass final calculation, clearly not well thought through in terms of its capacity to take small differences and magnify them into unacceptably divergent judgments'.[21] That chicken would soon come home to roost.

Often the Banding judgment sat curiously ill with that of Estyn. Treorchy Comprehensive in Andrews' own constituency found itself in Band 3-despite receiving the highest grades in its very recent Estyn inspection. On the ground the promised support often failed to materialise, schools in the lower bands just felt stigmatised, and staff morale fell. This was not necessarily a fault of the Banding process itself but more because of the fact that help and support was to be delivered through the new consortia, the groupings of local authorities, which were functioning with highly variable effectiveness on the ground.

In his February 2011 speech Andrews had promised that Banding would be visited on primary schools too. On 2nd December 2011 Andrews announced plans for the 'Banding' of primary schools, stating that it was important to 'consider the whole passage of children through the education system' and ensure quality.[22] This was not simply a restoration of League Tables to the *status quo ante* but an even more fundamental rejection of the Davidson regime. Primary schools had never been subject to League Tables in Wales, even before devolution.

But to promise – or rather threaten – Banding was one thing, it was quite another to deliver it. Andrews was both sufficiently versed in the unreliability of the primary data and in the art of politics to risk it. I had put it to him that the data was so dodgy that anyone could have a field day driving a coach and horses through any such ranking scheme. On 20th February 2012 he shelved primary Banding until 2014. He cited as definitive a conversation with Ann Keane, the shrewd and wise Chief Inspector of Schools, who had shown him the magnitude of the problem with inconsistency in teacher assessment.

With over a quarter of the assessments judged to be insufficiently reliable, Andrews pulled the plug. 'On the basis of all this evidence I do not feel we currently have sufficiently robust data to be used in the calculation of bands for primary schools. We need to wait until we have data sets which are based on more consistently standardised, and therefore more robust data. We are in the process of introducing new reading and numeracy tests. These will all be in place in all schools on a statutory basis from 2013'. ATL and most of the other teaching unions praised the Minister for listening to the profession. Anna Brychan of the NAHT said that 'This is absolutely the right decision. We congratulate the Minister on his willingness to listen to teachers' and school leaders' concerns about this and hope that we can now work with him to construct a genuinely powerful school improvement and support model for Wales'.[23]

The real Achilles heel was the inherent volatility of the Banding system itself. Because it used no floor targets, each year there would inevitably be schools in each of the five bands. The only way in which equilibrium could be established was if all schools were in Band 3, otherwise there would always be Band 5 schools, whatever the uplift in the system overall. The rather crude progress measure also meant that schools could bounce around within bands. As Ciccotti had pointed out, the final scoring could be distorted by a very small statistical shift. The whole edifice was unstable. In the second year of Banding some of the top schools found themselves near the bottom. Ysgol Tryfan in Gwynedd, for example, plummeted from Band 1 to Band 4. I called the whole thing the 'Banding yo-yo' and the metaphor stuck. Owen Hathway of the NUT summed up what many felt when he Tweeted: 'Last year's Banding was ominous, this year's is ludicrous'.

In fairness to Andrews, he had always been clear that Banding was not set in stone and, as one senior official confided to me, its real purpose was meant to be more of a short, sharp shock. In that regard it worked, as it certainly succeeded in focussing attention on outcomes as never before. If Gove developed a reputation for getting things done then Andrews was not far behind. Despite Andrews' public protestations that there were simply a few minor difficulties with Banding, behind closed doors the officials were quick to admit that the system was badly in need of an overhaul. Over the next few months, during which Andrews resigned to be replaced by Huw Lewis, the Department worked on sorting out the Banding system.

Categorisation

In January 2014 these deliberations were subject to unexpected public scrutiny when the *Western Mail* secured a considerable coup in getting hold of leaked documents which showed that a 'Categorisation' scheme was being developed to replace the Banding regime. It was clear that Banding's volatility was severely undermining its effectiveness. Schools would now be divided into four cohorts and a traffic-light type system used to show their achievement and progress. To get the 'green light', top schools would have to show how they were helping those stuck on red. The Department was thrown by the media glare, confusingly insisting on the one hand that 'Banding is here to stay' but conceding on the other that they were 'looking at it to make sure that it's effective …That work is ongoing. As and when we're in a position to make an announcement we will'.[24] By May, Huw Lewis, the Minister, was conceding that work was well under way but confusion still remained about the future of Banding and the Department was still not giving a clear line on future developments.[25]

As well as volatility, any new system would have to address several other concerns. The delivery of support had been very patchy. The Hill Report on 'The future delivery of education services in Wales' had forced a public commitment from the Welsh Government and the Welsh Local Government Association that there was now a need for a national model to ensure delivery of support across the country. There was also a pressing need to introduce more qualitative data into the process which would allow those on the ground to introduce professional judgments about a school's ability to improve. And finally there was the problem of how primary schools were to be classed.

In due time the official announcement of the new system confirmed in large part what the *Western Mail* had ferreted out. There would now be four new categories of school: green, yellow, amber and red. I remember being at a meeting called in late September to brief the unions about it and wondering if anyone else was thinking of the scene in Evelyn Waugh's *Decline and Fall* where Mr Levy, the dubious proprietor of what we would now call a teacher supply agency, was outlining his school rating system. 'We class schools, you see, into four grades: Leading School, First-rate School, Good School, and School. Frankly ... School is pretty bad'.[26]

In his Ministerial statement on the new National School Categorisation System on 25th September 2014, Huw Lewis coded schools slightly differently. Green were the 'best schools', yellow were the 'good schools', amber schools were 'in need of improvement', while red were 'schools in need of greatest improvement'. He was clear that Banding had impacted on results. In Band 5 schools the improvement was particularly impressive, albeit starting from a low base: 'Band 5 schools in 2012 have seen the overall percentage of pupils achieving the Level 2 threshold including English/ Welsh First Language and Mathematics increase from 35% in 2012 to 45% in 2013'. Progress was more limited in Band 4 schools where the threshold achievement had risen from 45.8% to 49.5% in 2013.[27]

The new Categorisation system would not be 'purely data-driven but also takes into account the leadership, teaching and learning that goes on in our schools'. The new system would be built on three steps: 'a range of performance measures provided by the Welsh Government; robust self-evaluation from schools on their ability to improve in relation to leadership, learning and teaching; and corroboration of the school's self-evaluation by education consortia Challenge Advisers'. These last had been employed consortia-wide to drive improvement. To ensure consistency across consortia and nationally, and if truth be told to ensure that local authorities took the whole process far more seriously, Lewis announced that his officials would attend the moderation meetings which decided into which category a school fitted.

The Education Department now felt sufficiently confident to secure the elusive categorisation of primary schools as well. Performance data would look at such things as the 'Proportion of pupils achieving the Foundation Phase Indicator at the end of the Foundation Phase and the Core Subject Indicator at the end of Key Stage 2' for literacy and mathematics. Attendance too would be factored in, as would Free School Meal (FSM) measures.

Crucially Lewis promised that Categorisation, unlike Banding, would be 'an absolute model. This will mean that schools that can demonstrate improvement against their own baseline can move up in the system and will not mean that another school will have to move down in the system'. One of the major flaws of Banding had gone.[28]

The new Categories were published on 29th January 2015. There were some surprises. Whitchurch High, regarded as one of the best performing schools in Wales, in terms of academic results, was categorised as red. Out of 1,332 primary schools assessed (considerably fewer than the total as very small primaries had had to be excluded because of the statistical impacts one or two children could have in them), 207 were given green status while fifty-eight were put into the red. Out of 211 secondary schools, thirty-one were green support category and twenty-three were judged to be red.

There were the predictable comments from those who were ideologically opposed to any form of public data publication, but more damaging was the row brewing between the government and the new consortia. The Central South and South-east Wales consortiums (covering most of the south Wales local authorities between them) sought to distance themselves from a last-minute decision to exclude schools from the green zone if they failed to meet the 27.2% Wales average of FSM pupils gaining five A*–C grades at GCSE including English or Welsh and Maths (Level 2+). This late change had been at Lewis' own instigation, given his long-term commitment to the poverty agenda. Two key players were furious. Dr Chris Howard, acting Director of the NAHT, derided the new system as 'very little better' than Banding and stated that 'The new school Categorisation system will anger many schools in Wales at a time when the Minister should be recognising the hard work that's been done to raise standards. It will do nothing to encourage schools and teachers working with the most challenging communities'. ASCL claimed that the change was 'at odds with government policy' and gave those in areas of high deprivation 'more hoops to jump through'.[29]

At the time of writing it seems as if Categorisation is here to stay. Although Donaldson has quite emphatically put the horse before the cart in terms of assessment, he did not call for the abolition of Categorisation. Recommendation 67 simply notes that: 'The school categorisation system should, in due course, be adjusted to reflect the recommendations of this Review'. So far, so bland but it will take a real act of faith by the government to implement Recommendation 69 in any meaningful way, I fear: 'The Welsh Government should no longer gather information about children and young people's performance on a school-by-school basis but should monitor performance in key aspects of the curriculum through annual testing on a sampling basis'. The lessons from the recent past may be too difficult to unlearn.

It would be too crude to accuse Andrews of reintroducing School League Tables *per se* to Wales. There was never any hint that the market would be relied upon to provide the solution by driving underperformers to the wall. But some of the rhetoric about the difference between Banding and League Tables was thin and there was an element of 'naming and shaming' in making the Banding judgments public. It is interesting to note that Andrews' self-defence of at least putting accurate information in the public domain and not leaving the whole thing to the vagaries of journalism was almost the exact same one that Blunkett had used in publishing school performance data at the start of the millennium. What was abundantly clear was that yet another ill thought-through and badly implemented policy from the Davidson years, the abolition of publicly available comparable data about schools, had decisively bitten the dust.

GCSEs

So if the Welsh Government's own re-introduced 'League Table' clearly showed that, even allowing for salient differences, the huge variations in school performance noted in some of the opening debates of the first Assembly were far from tackled, what about the news coming from other performance indicators? We will examine the PISA scores shortly but before that it will be useful to compare and contrast the 'scores on the doors' for the GCSE results.

As we saw in Chapter 6, until comparatively recently the GCSE regimes in Wales and England (and indeed Northern Ireland) were not vastly different. Schools were free to choose which exam board they wanted to use and, despite a media frenzy to the contrary, investigations in both countries had proved inconclusive as to whether or not some boards were more lenient than others. Even after the GCSE debacle in 2012, valid comparisons could still be made between the relative performances of youngsters in both systems. Those comparisons were even more valid the further back one goes, and they tell an interesting tale about the performance of both systems, as is shown in Figure 3.

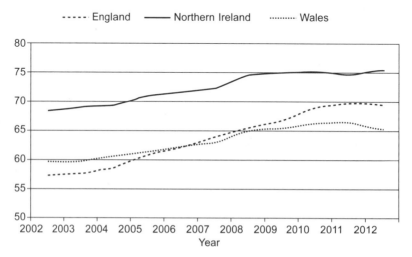

Figure 3: Percentage of Pupils with 5 GCSEs (Grade A*-C) [30]

In 1999, apart obviously from the Welsh language, the offer and take up of GCSEs in both countries was not different in any significant way. Comparisons between the two regimes were still possible without major caveats until 2012. What is initially clear is that at the dawn of devolution the Welsh system was performing better in terms of outcomes than its English counterpart. Any gap was in Wales' favour and was worth about 3% points. By 2006 the English results were starting to pull away and even though this could have been considered statistically insignificant, and possibly a blip, by 2010 it was clear that the gap was widening in England's favour. It's also important to realise that it is not the case that Wales' performance dipped. Overall the rise in pass rates and achievement is on a constantly rising trajectory. What actually happened was that the English rise was of far greater momentum. The results from Northern Ireland should add a note of caution to those who too quickly want to use the relative deprivation of Wales as an excuse.

Drilling down deeper into the data also makes one realise that these headline figures need to be treated with some caution. The excellent work done by Professor Gareth Rees and WISERD shows that the English ascendancy is not all it seems. Much revolves around the use of equivalences for GCSEs in any official counting, as Figure 4 illustrates.

If we compare what could be called 'pure GCSEs' then the gap between England and Wales is significantly less and the performance of the two countries is much more similar. It is also the case that Wales shows a significant increase in the numbers taking equivalent qualifications from 2007/8 onwards. Historically this take up had been noticeably behind

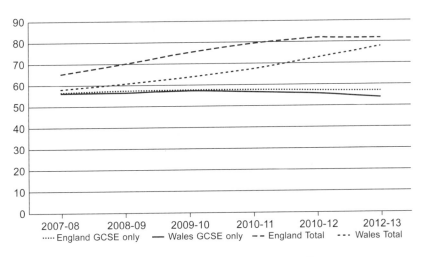

Figure 4: GCSE and Equivalences[31]

England's. But, nevertheless, the gap is still there on both indices and the direction of travel seems to be showing a dip in Wales' performance on the 'pure GCSE' measure. The lower take up of equivalent qualifications in Wales also raises other questions. Is their greater use in England just a cynical attempt to manipulate the League Tables, or is it the result of a deeper desire to marry qualifications to the needs of the learner?

So even though the gap may not be of the magnitude that it appears at first sight, all the data points to the fact that it exists. As we saw in Chapter 3, Andrews was very concerned to narrow the performance gap with England and part of his analysis relied on assuming that the gap was real and not apparent. At the time he was speaking, relatively watertight comparisons could still be made. After the new specifications to English Language GCSE, hastily introduced in Wales in 2013, and also changes to the regime in England, robust comparisons became more fraught. The Director of ASCL Cymru, Robin Hughes, who had worked for the exam board OCR and therefore could be relied upon to have some grasp of these matters, put it well when he warned in 2014 that future comparisons would be like trying to compare 'apples and pears'.[32]

The desire to close the gap was understandable and a major part of Andrews' programme. As Figure 4 shows, from 2011 that gap did seem to be shrinking. However, only fools have rushed in to predict that it would close completely.

At a conference in November 2014, after a gratuitous and ill-informed attack on the media, Lewis reiterated a claim that he had already made several times before: 'The historic gap with England is now down to less than 1% and I promise you this – if we manage to overtake our colleagues across the border next summer, you may well see an Education Minister who is rather the worse for wear the following morning'.[33] Quite why the delegates should rejoice in the promise of a ministerial hangover was not clear, but the claim that the gap was conquerable was.

In 2011 the performance gap was a staggering 8.9%; it had seemingly tumbled to just above 1% by 2014. Superficially it did seem as if things were going Wales' way. But deeper analysis showed that the words of caution about comparability should have been ringing in the Minister's head.

In 2014 England announced its first ever dip in GCSE performance. In some ways that was to be expected as Gove had made no bones about his disquiet with grade inflation. The mood music and changes to the exams regime were meant to make things tougher and a dip in results was regarded by the Tories as a sign of success. The sorts of qualifications that would be allowed to count towards the final scores were also being curtailed.

A statistical release issued by the (English) Department for Education in 2015 highlighted two major changes affecting the way in which the Key Stage 4 data had been calculated. The recommendations of the Wolf Review of Vocational Education had been implemented. This meant that there were restrictions on the qualifications counted, a prevention on any qualification from counting as larger than one GCSE, and a cap on the number of non-GCSEs included in performance measures at two per pupil. In addition there had also been a change to early entry policy which meant that for performance measures, only a pupil's first attempt at a qualification could be counted. Other changes, such as the exclusion of IGCSEs (International GCSEs) from the calculation (which bizarrely meant that Eton was shown as having a 0% pass rate) had also served to depress the English results.[34]

So if the English methodology had been so drastically changed it was by no means clear that any purported narrowing of the gap had either taken place in reality or owed more to Welsh Government policy than Westminster's decisions. The wisest option would have been to focus on the clear improvements in the results of Welsh youngsters and avoid any claim about comparative performance. For instance by 2014/15 57.6% of Welsh youngsters were achieving the Level 2 threshold including a GCSE grade A*–C in English or Welsh first language and Mathematics. This was notably higher, by 2.1%, than in the previous period and a truly remarkable 13.2% higher than when the measure was first introduced in 2006/07. I was concerned that by focussing obsessively on the 'gap', Lewis could make youngsters in Wales a target for the right-wing English press who could claim that our GCSEs were in some ways 'easier' to obtain than those across the border. My understanding is that senior civil servants concurred.

In the Senedd chamber, Lewis was mauled repeatedly by the opposition spokespeople. The formidable Angela Burns, Conservative shadow minister, lost no time in highlighting the possible effects that changes in the English methodology could have had on the Minister's repeated claims to have narrowed the gap. In a debate on 16th September 2015 she commented scathingly:

'Everyone will be familiar with the Education Minister's grandstanding on how Wales would, this year, not only match but beat England in this summer's GCSE exams … However, as we approached results day, panic struck … It was time for Labour to try and limit the damage. We received an e-mail – the Welsh Government called it a technical note – offering us excuses for why we should not compare our GCSE results with those of our neighbours … if we shouldn't compare the summer results, why has the Minister been making so much noise about the summer results? Has there been a lack of communication between him and his officials? … the Minister told us how he had closed the Level 2 attainment gap with England, from 8.9% in 2010-11, to 1.4% in 2013-14. Now, that's a dramatic decrease, and one the Minister tried to make us think was all his own doing. We now know, from both the Labour

Government and the Department for Education in Westminster, that the drop was mainly due to England's changes in exam structure, as well as England's decision to stop factoring international GCSE results into their figures. So, the gap closed artificially.[35]

Knowing she was on to a winner she pressed home the same points in Ministerial Questions a few weeks later. Lewis' response was shambolic even by his standards and he lurched from attacking Burns for not accepting improvements to describing the situation in England as beyond his grasp. He had to concede though that 'my ambition to close the gap between Welsh and English GCSE attainment will actually be very difficult to prove statistically'. Burns was in no mood to spare his blushes and retorted that 'You, Minister, have stood in this Chamber over the last six to eight months and said that you are going to close the gap between England and Wales; that your policies are going to make that difference for our children. And, yet, when we actually looked at the figures, the reason why the statistical releases show that there was a closure in the gap had nothing to do with you, Minister; nothing to do with your policies, but everything to do with the changes that the English have made to their exam'. Lewis could only reply lamely that she was 'attempting to play the man and not the ball' and then, typically, blamed the media for being obsessed with comparisons.[36]

The trump card in Burns' hand was that by then the Welsh Government's own statistics department had conceded that comparison with England was no longer possible. In the notes accompanying the release about Welsh examination performance in 2014-15, it was stated that:

Following the Wolf Review of Vocational Education in England, GCSE reform in England and other changes introduced by the Department for Education in England, data on Key Stage 4 attainment in England and Wales are *no longer on a comparable basis* (my emphaisis). The main differences are: Data for England limits the size of vocational qualifications to a maximum of one GCSE. Currently in Wales there is no limit on the size of vocational qualifications, with many of the popular ones being equivalent in size to four GCSEs... Data for England only allow the first entry in any examination to count, regardless of grade. The best grade is taken in Wales. England have changed the way they discount qualifications so that similar general and vocational qualifications cannot both count in their statistics. This restriction does not currently apply in Wales'.[37]

All these changes were in the public domain. The Welsh Government officials had been well aware of them but Lewis had chosen to ignore their advice and had thus ensured a humiliating and major defeat for himself, whereas focussing on the results themselves could have provided a modest victory.

Given all these caveats one would either have to be brave or foolish to draw any hard and fast conclusions about whether or not the historic gap has narrowed in reality. Commenting in the *Western Mail* I said that 'the blunt truth is that comparisons are no longer possible ... so it's good to see that our Education Department has now acknowledged that fact. The verdict of history has to be that the gap narrowed but never closed'. And I still think that is the safest conclusion.

My hunch is that the gap is now less than at its widest and that the reforms and refocussing of Andrews have been effective to a significant degree. But of course all this means is that our children are *now* on a more level playing field with their English counterparts in terms of jobs and higher education. For several years they were not and their life chances have been affected accordingly. Little Megan may achieve almost as much as little Charlotte across the border but her older siblings will have paid the price for badly thought-through policy and the neglect of the standards agenda.

PISA

If the arguments surrounding the more recent comparisons of Wales and England in terms of GCSE results were inconclusive, another, wider set of comparable data has unfortunately left no one in any doubt about the underperformance of the Welsh system.

Every three years over seventy of the world's education systems, and nearly all those within the OECD group, are subject to the rigours of the Programme for International Student Assessment (PISA). The PISA survey aims to evaluate education systems worldwide by testing the knowledge and skills of 15-year-olds. PISA purports to administer tests which are independent of any particular school curriculum, focussing rather on assessing to what extent students can apply their knowledge to so-called 'real-life situations'. Since 2000, every three years, students take the tests in key subjects of reading, mathematics and science, with a primary focus on one subject in each year of assessment. The tests last two hours and are a mixture of open-ended and multiple-choice questions. To avoid bias, and in an attempt to compare like with like and rule out extraneous factors, headteachers also provide information about the background of students.

Before we move on to examine the data surrounding Wales' performance in the three PISA tests that Welsh youngsters have taken so far it is important to flag up that the whole endeavour is not without its trenchant critics. These range from some of the teaching unions, to whom the very idea of making comparative judgments is anathema, to rather more nuanced approaches which are concerned about the presumptions, methodologies and inferences that lie behind the PISA endeavour.

Some, such as Dr John Jerrim, a lecturer at the Institute of Education in the University of London, have pointed out that the apparent fall in England's performance was flatly contradicted by the rival scores provided from PISA's rival, TIMMs (Trends in International Mathematics and Science Study). Others, such as Professor Harvey Goldstein from the University of Bristol, have attacked the 'snapshot' nature of PISA, arguing in favour of a more longitudinal approach. More trenchant criticism has come from Professor Svend Kreiner of Copenhagen who criticised the Rausch model at the heart of PISA which gives 'plausible values', which are calculated from test scores but are not the scores as such. It is also important to note that PISA itself is promoted by the OECD as providing deep and nuanced analysis which goes far beyond the mere 'scores on the doors'.[38]

Keeping these caveats in mind it does seem as if the PISA world is here to stay, and it would be a brave or foolish politician who would advocate abandoning these tests, especially from a position of weakness. I suspect these discussions have taken place at the highest levels of Welsh Government with the current consensus being that it's best to stick on in there than be faced with yet more attacks for abandoning targets. There is also no consensus among stakeholders about abandoning them. Some argue that the money could be better spent elsewhere. My worry is that if we took away this last vestige of external scrutiny we would quickly run back into the wonderland of the decade before.

The results for the three PISA tests that Wales has taken part in are shown in Figure 5.

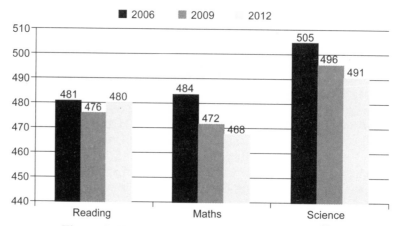

Figure 5: Wales' PISA Outcomes (2006-2012)[39]

As is immediately apparent the overall trajectory is downward. Students in Wales did worse in 2012 than they did in 2006. With the exception of Reading, which saw a slight rally, the other two components show quite significant drops in performance. Figure 6 shows this decline:

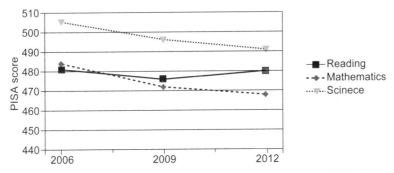

Figure 6: The Trend in Welsh PISA Performance (2006-2012)

Irrespective of comparisons with the other UK nations, these trends should be seriously worrying in themselves. We are not seeing here a coasting system or one suffering minor blips but rather one that is in serious decline.

Figure 7: Wales' PISA Rankings (2009-2012)[40]

Such falling performance has obviously affected Wales' place in the international rankings, as illustrated by the *Western Mail* in Figure 7.

This decline needs to carry a minor health warning, as a country's ranking obviously depends on the number of countries participating. The OECD issued a rebuke to Michael Gove for sensationalising the English fall, from 7th to 25th in Reading and 8th to 27th in Maths over the period from 2000 to 2009, because only the 2006 to 2009 data were directly comparable.[41]

The other nettle to grasp is while PISA may have some difficulty comparing radically dissimilar systems, its findings *vis a vis* the countries of the British Isles, three of whom (Wales, England and Northern Ireland) have had very similar educational topography until recently, are more reliable. The judgments are grim. The decline in Wales' performance was even more stark when compared to the other nations of the UK.

The other countries might be static on the three measures, but Wales is in steep decline in both maths and science.

When one factors in the OECD average we can see how poor the performance of Wales is compared to both the other UK nations and also to the OECD average. In 2012 the OECD average stood at 496 for reading, 494 for maths, and 501 for science.

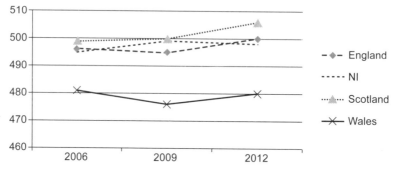

Figure 8: PISA Performance – UK – Reading

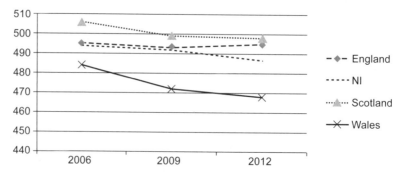

Figure 9: PISA Performance – UK – Maths

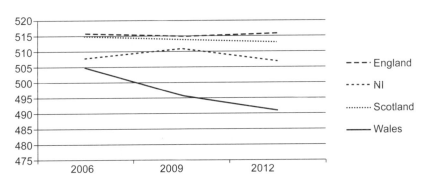

Figure 10: PISA Performance – UK – Science

With the exception of Northern Ireland's maths scores, all the other UK nations were above the OECD average for the three measured components. Wales was 16 points behind the average in reading, 10 points behind in science and a shocking 26 points behind in mathematics.

Much ink and angst have been poured in response to these worsening figures. In 2007 Jane Hutt had dismissed the results a 'valuable snapshot' in helping to analyse where to go next. A Welsh Government spokesperson was more candid, acknowledging that while 'Wales compares well with the other OECD countries in terms of science achievement … we want to improve our performance in both maths and reading'. Another, unnamed, source close to the government had added that 'There was a firm belief that Welsh education policy changes over the past decade would lead to impressive improvements'.[42] Professor David Reynolds laconically commented that 'We are round about countries like Azerbaijan and Croatia and this should be some kind of joke but it is not'.[43]

By 2010 the results were starting to be no laughing matter and Andrews, as we have seen, describing those results as 'A wake-up call to a complacent system', used the PISA shock to initiate a bold *volte face* on the *Learning Country* agenda and introduced his own drive for standards. Those had barely had time to bed in when the next earthquake hit.

In 2013 Huw Lewis looked dazed, as if he'd done 10 rounds in the boxing ring. After noting that 'The previous results in 2009 were a real eye-opener' he denied that other countries in the UK could celebrate as there were 'signs of stagnation across the UK'. In a final act of bravura he stood by the 'top twenty' target: 'I've been asked many times whether I stand by our target to be in the 'top twenty' Pisa countries in 2015. To limit our ambitions now would be the wrong response to these results. The 2015 target was always going to be a challenging one for us but you've got to be ambitious when delivering the best for our young people'.[44] A few months later the target was dropped.

The verdict

There may still be those who think that the Welsh education system is world-leading. There were certainly many more who thought so in 2006 when Wales first entered the PISA assessment, not least the then Minister, Davidson. As the years have progressed, PISA has become something of an albatross around the neck of successive Ministers. It has indeed showcased Wales to the world, but in the worst possible way. My argument is not that PISA is the only thing that matters, nor that it is flawless or indisputable, but simply that it reinforces on the world stage what the GCSE results are showing at a UK level, and the Welsh Government's own Categorisation system is showing on a Wales level. This is a seriously underperforming system. When one adds in the Annual Reports of the Chief Inspector it is quite clear that we are in a far from ideal place when it comes to the education our children receive. All these things are in the nature of what has been called 'cumulative probability'. There is no one killer blow or indisputable fact, but as we look at the evidence it starts to stack up in one direction. The need now is not to dispute that evidence and its inevitable conclusion but to see what can be done.

Notes

1   https://www.tes.com/article.aspx?storycode=348747
2   http://www.telegraph.co.uk/news/uknews/1334783/Wales-scraps-unfair-school-league-tables.html
3   http://www.lgcplus.com/league-tables-scrapped-in-wales/1335912.article
4   http://dera.ioe.ac.uk/7700/8/A9R5BA9_Redacted.pdf, p. 1.
5   P. 6.
6   P. 5.
7   http://www.walesonline.co.uk/news/wales-news/england-considers-scrapping-sats-2242324
8   Burgess, S, Wilson, S and Worth, J, *A natural experiment in school accountability: the impact of school performance information on pupil progress and sorting* CMPO Working Paper Series No. 10/246 http://www.bristol.ac.uk/media-library/sites/cmpo/migrated/documents/wp246.pdf
9   From the abstract.
10   P. 2.
11   P. 26.
12   http://www.walesonline.co.uk/news/wales-news/school-league-tables-abolishment-hitting-1883571
13   http://www.bbc.co.uk/news/uk-wales-11669714
14   http://www.walesonline.co.uk/news/wales-news/school-league-tables-abolishment-hitting-1883571
15   http://www.walesonline.co.uk/news/wales-news/school-league-tables-abolishment-hitting-1883571
16   http://www.bevanfoundation.org/commentary/the-abolition-of-league-tables-did-not-cause-a-decline-in-educational-standards/

17   http://www.walesonline.co.uk/news/wales-news/school-league-tables-abolishment-hitting-1883571

18   Research in Public Policy, summer 2011. http://www.bristol.ac.uk/media-library/sites/cmpo/migrated/documents/burgess14.pdf

19   Welsh Government, School Standards Unit 'The model for banding secondary schools Paper for information for stakeholders (December 2011 v1.0)' http://gov.wales/docs/dcells/publications/120118bandingpresentationen.pdf

20   If the reader is still interested in the nuances of Banding then the above document gives a full and detailed account.

21   http://www.westerntelegraph.co.uk/news/9420134.SCHOOLS_BANDING__Headteacher_says_process_is__lunacy_/

22   http://www.dailypost.co.uk/news/north-wales-news/welsh-education-minister-leighton-andrews-2674602

23   http://www.walesonline.co.uk/news/wales-news/schools-banding-primaries-delayed-until-2036322

24   http://www.walesonline.co.uk/news/wales-news/wales-set-abandon-school-banding-6650791

25   http://www.walesonline.co.uk/news/wales-news/questions-raised-over-new-grading-7090269

26   Waugh, E, *Decline and Fall*(Penguin; London, 1928), p 17

27   http://gov.wales/about/cabinet/cabinetstatements/2014/natschoolcat/?lang=en

28   http://gov.wales/about/cabinet/cabinetstatements/2014/natschoolcat/?lang=en

29   http://www.walesonline.co.uk/news/wales-news/row-over-wales-new-colour-coded-8546113

30   Graph from ATL Annual Lecture given by Prof Chris Taylor, Cardiff University. 16 June 2015.

31   The same.

32   http://www.walesonline.co.uk/news/wales-news/we-must-stop-comparing-english-7597074

33   http://www.walesonline.co.uk/news/news-opinion/gareth-evans-wales-bracing-itself-8112760

34   Department for Education, Statistical First Release Revised GCSE and equivalents results in England, 2013 to 2014 (January 2015).

35   http://www.assembly.wales/en/bus-home/pages/rop.aspx?meetingid=3427&language=en&c=Record%20of%20Proceedings (16.05)

36   http://www.assembly.wales/en/bus-home/pages/rop.aspx?meetingid=3432&assembly=4&c=Record%20of%20Proceedings#239056 (14.34)

37   Statistics for Wales, Examination Results in Wales 2014/15 (Provisional) http://gov.wales/docs/statistics/2015/150924-examination-results-2014-15-provisional-en.pdf

38   For an excellent – and accessible – article on the issues here see William Stewart 'Is Pisa fundamentally flawed?' TES magazine (26 July, 2013) https://www.tes.com/article.aspx?storycode=6344672

39   OECD, Improving Schools in Wales, p.20. http://www.oecd.org/edu/Improving-schools-in-Wales.pdf

40   http://www.walesonline.co.uk/news/wales-news/now-tories-attack-welsh-labours-8557991

41   https://fullfact.org/factchecks/school_standards_oecd_pisa_data_media_conservatives_education-2423

42   TES, 7th December 2007 https://www.tes.com/article.aspx?storycode=2483333

43   BBC 5th December 2007.

44   http://www.walesonline.co.uk/news/wales-news/huw-lewis-everybody-working-around-6381668

7

So Where Do We Go From Here?
'For the Sake of Our Children'

This concluding chapter outlines some of the key issues I think that the Welsh education system must now confront in the next few years if we really are to make things not just different but better for the children of Wales. In the latter part of the chapter I will outline seven key questions that we need to answer. Before that, summarising the previous chapters, I will outline where I think we are now and how we have got there. If we do not learn the lessons of history then we are destined to repeat them. But first of all it is imperative that we address the problem of PISA.

PISA meltdown?

As we saw in the last chapter, while Categorisation may be showing some improvements in school performance, and individual pupil achievement at GCSE seems to be getting better, albeit very slowly, it seems as if the system's performance as a whole, measured internationally, is going from bad to worse. The PISA results, however imperfect that measure, show us incontrovertibly two very unpalatable truths: first, we are nowhere near as good as the rest of the UK; second, and even more disturbing, we seem to be declining rather than improving.

Responsibility for GCSE achievement at the end of the day comes down to individual students and staff. Responsibility for the category a school is placed in comes down to its head. Responsibility for the PISA scores comes down to the national government. PISA gives us a snapshot of the *entire* system. The Welsh Government is responsible for Wales' poor performance to date and the Welsh Government has failed to tackle the deep rooted problems connected with vision, delivery and resource. PISA is a judgment on them.

In December 2016 we will know the results of the PISA tests that our youngsters have sat in the autumn of 2015. We hope for the best but fear the worst. With hope we will see that the corner has been turned and that the results are slowly edging upwards. A study by the respected scholar John Jerrim of the impact of the on-screen tests, which showed a narrowing of the gap between the performance of 15-year-olds from the highest and lowest socio-economic groups, shows that such an improvement is not beyond the bounds of possibility.[1] There will be a collective sigh of relief but there can be no complacency. We fear that the results have stalled or become even worse.

If they have worsened then we are at a watershed in the history of Welsh education in particular, and of the devolution project in general. It will simply not be enough for the Welsh Government Minister to appear on the TV screens, wringing their hands and promising that things will get better. We have seen it all before. It will not be acceptable to appear like Madam Acarti in the séance scene in Noel Coward's *Blithe Spirit*, promising that if we simply put our backs into it then all will turn out alright. The demons of poor performance will not be so easily exorcised. More radical action will be needed, along the following lines.

A Recovery Board should be set up to take charge of a strategic reform programme for Welsh education over the next six years. This Board should be comprised primarily of those with a proven record of delivery in education from across the UK. These could be academics, teachers and heads. They could also be those in charge of high performing local authorities. It should contain some civil servants from the other UK nations with a demonstrable record of delivery and of turning dysfunctional government departments around. Two or three members of the Board should be respected and capable independent figures from the Welsh educational scene. They would root the Board in the Welsh context but, being in a minority, there would be no room for special pleading or the pulling of punches, a perennial problem in Wales.

The focus needs to be on delivery rather than policy. The Recovery Board should aim to get the Welsh education system properly focussed and properly functioning. It should not be concerned to import experiments from other parts of the UK unless these are universally acclaimed as successful. There need be no introduction of Academies and Free Schools, neither of which have been proved to raise standards of themselves. The current comprehensive system would be kept but just made to work much better.

The Board should be appointed by and responsible to the National Assembly, not the Welsh Government. Candidates should be vetted in much the same way that Supreme Court Justices are vetted in the United States. This will ensure that we don't simply get yet another gathering of the great and the good, Ministerial cronies, or 'friends of friends' that can all too often bedevil the life of a small country. Estyn and the Wales Audit Office should carry out the mechanics of the selection process.

The Board should not concern itself with policy unless it can clearly be shown that certain policies are inimical to reform. It should be relentlessly focussed on delivery. To this end it should have complete power to re-order the Education Department itself if necessary. Just as failing schools have governors and senior management replaced, and failing local education authorities have their functions removed and senior management replaced by an interim board, the same approach has to be considered at the national level within the Welsh Government's Education Department. It goes without saying that shuffling the deck chairs has been something of a perennial response in the Welsh Government. It is a counsel of the last resort but it might well be necessary though to break down the silo mentality that still inhibits much government activity and delivery.

The Board should develop a six-year strategy whose overriding aim would be to ensure that Wales was performing at least as well as the other UK nations in the PISA tests of 2021. The target set in *Qualified for Life* would then be met. It would need initially to commission a quick and rapid review of what the results are really revealing about Welsh education. It would then need to outline a clear strategic plan to implement the lessons learned both about Welsh underperformance, but also about the comparative successes of the other UK nations. There needs to be no wide-ranging policy tourism. If Wales can do as well as England, Scotland and Northern Ireland then the Board will have fulfilled its remit.

Obviously there are tremendous costs involved in this proposal. As well as the obvious financial cost there is the cost to national pride: we would effectively be admitting that we cannot get out of the hole ourselves. There would be the total loss of face suffered by the Welsh Government in owning up to this fact. The other nations would have to be persuaded that our common interest as a *United* Kingdom is advanced by such a proposal.

There are two other alternatives. The first is that eventually the UK government will step in and remove the Welsh Government's control over education. This is not as unlikely as it might seem. In the run up to the 2015 Westminster election there were serious calls from some in the Tory party for responsibility for health to be taken away from Cardiff Bay. The situation in Northern Ireland shows that direct rule remains a distinct possibility when all other avenues have been judged to have failed. There is little doubt in my mind that in such a scenario, in which Welsh education was controlled from Westminster once more, we would quickly see the imposition of ideas such as Academies and Free Schools as the 'answer' to problems.

If that seems grim then the second alternative is even worse: nothing changes. There would be the hand-wringing and the furrowed brows, the apologies and the shouting, but when the dust settles the same tired old team with its same tired old ideas would still be in place. As Einstein said 'Insanity is doing the same thing over and over again and expecting different results'. The costs of such a course are immense. There are financial ones as Wales eventually becomes less and less economically viable as we continue to send out the clear message every three years that our potential workforce is less able than those found elsewhere. But the real cost of this strategy is the heaviest: our children suffer irrevocably.

Lessons from the past

Let's hope for now that none of the nightmare scenarios presented above are necessary. Let's hope that the PISA results towards the end of this year show marked improvement. Let's hope that we are, finally, on the right track. Can we then sit back and rest on our laurels, confident that we need no major changes? I think not.

We need to learn the lessons from the past so that we do not repeat them again. It's important that we are clear where we've been and how we got here before trying to move on. A big part of this book has been an attempt to set out where the Welsh education system is at present and what formed it. We cannot shy away from making judgments on the past.

Jones and Roderick's *A History of Education in Wales* remains a magisterial account of Welsh education from the collapse of the Roman Empire until the dawn of devolution. It stops where this account starts. The first seventeen years of the devolution project have been something of a roller coaster ride. Two big political beasts, Davidson and Andrews, have cast a long shadow over that period. Although they are both from the same party their analysis and policies could hardly have been more different. Chapter 2 brought out their fundamental contradictory narratives. Davidson portrayed Wales as some sort of educational Garden of Eden. Andrews did not buy that portrayal. The value and validity of the policies pursued by these polar opposite approaches have divided opinion. They are the product of very different understandings of the role and nature of education. Other chapters have shown how the difference played out on the ground.

The wrong vision

I think it will be clear on which side of that debate I fall. My own personal experience convinces me that a rigorous focussing on the 'standards agenda' offers working-class children one of the best starts in life. But for nigh on ten years, while most of the rest of the world was upskilling its workforce, introducing demand side mechanisms to correct provider capture and rigorously focussing on standards, Wales was elsewhere. The removal of almost all accountability mechanisms meant that few within the system had any idea how good or bad their bit of it really was. Virtually no one had any idea of the system's performance over all. The first set of PISA results, coupled with evidence from GCSE comparisons, started to show that the Garden of Eden narrative really was a fable.

Elsewhere I have made no bones about describing Davidson's legacy as 'toxic'. A combination of mistaken evaluation, deformed and partial delivery, and chronic underfunding was hardly a recipe for success. There were many indicators that Wales was out on a limb and falling behind. Looking back over *The Learning Country* fifteen years on, realising that many of its targets still need to be met, shows how ludicrous some of it really was.

As a piece of blue-sky thinking, *The Learning Country* would have made a good discussion document. As a ten-year blueprint it was woefully inadequate. The absence of clear delivery mechanisms is apparent. Most startling of all is the almost complete absence of anything resembling a standards agenda. The targets were there but the delivery mechanisms were not. This is not cheap point scoring. It matters to those children who achieved far less than they would have in other parts of the UK. Results did improve. GCSE pass rates in 2010 were noticeably better than they were in 2000. But when one compares these to the increases seen in England it would be ludicrous to attribute these to *The Learning Country*.

Rhodri Morgan was keen, after the narrow referendum win and shaky start of the fledgling government, to show that devolution was making a difference. It would have been a more secure legacy for devolution to have made things better. Part of the problem was a deep seated reluctance to learn from anything that England was doing. This became a mania once the Tories and Lib Dems were in power after 2010 but it was quite clearly there beforehand. National literacy and numeracy frameworks arrived in Wales ten years late. The rejection of anything like a national college for leadership was a grave mistake. Initiatives such as Schools Challenge were similarly delayed. The damage done by stripping out any demand side accountability mechanism has been clearly outlined in Chapter 6.

The lack of research and analysis of policy in the opening years of devolution was also noticeable. As I've indicated in the preceding chapters Davidson was keen to speak about 'evidence-based policy' (I'm not quite sure what the opposite would be, perhaps an indication of this being one of those dummy phrases that politicians love) but all too often the evidence was not cited. The move to reduce class sizes was a clear example of this. Where contradictory evidence was forthcoming it was greeted with hostility. David Reynolds, one of the first to realise that everything was far from rosy, has told me how apparatchiks from the Department repeatedly tried to keep him off the BBC.

The cost of short-changing the system

But the biggest legacy left by Davidson and her longest shadow over the whole enterprise is that of funding. Rumours are that her unpopularity with her own cabinet colleagues made it difficult for her to convince them that more should be spent on education. Year on year from 1999 the gap between what was spent in Wales and over the border grew and grew.

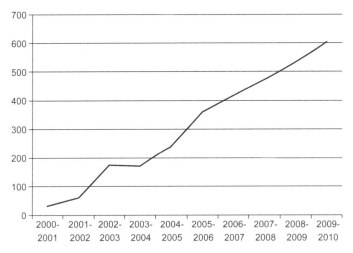

**Figure 11: Gap in Per Pupil Funding between Wales and England
(Welsh Government figures)**

The per capita sums perhaps hide the magnitude of the problem. If one thinks of a reasonably sized primary school as being about 200 pupils, then a funding gap of £604 per pupil translates into £120,800 per year, every year. For secondary schools the sums are considerably larger. A modest sized secondary of 1,000 pupils is losing £604,000 per year, every year. I suspect that these are now conservative estimates and that our schools are even more underfunded compared to their English counterparts. When one takes into account the fact that the biggest part of any school's bill is staffing, and that those staff costs are set on an England and Wales basis, then it is quite clear that schools in Wales simply didn't have enough money to spend on infrastructure and training. Many of the good innovations in England were never affordable in Wales and that has left a permanent scar on the system.

As the finance of the Welsh Government is allocated according the Barnett formula, in principle at least Wales should have been spending as much per pupil as England. Obviously the whole point of devolution is that Wales can determine its own spending but as to where that block grant money went, theories abound. One of the clearest hints was given in a Teach First seminar when David Egan, Davidson's Special Advisor, and myself were speaking. When I was telling the assembled 'teach firsters' about our financial plight and the impact it was making, Egan defended the decisions made. He pointed out that Wales could determine its own spending and acknowledged that other key priorities had benefitted from the education slice of the Barnett block grant. He singled out the Welsh language as one of these.

Obviously it has suited Government ministers to hide behind the cloak provided by the OECD when they show that spending and outcomes are not correlated. Even Andrews drew comparisons with Poland and New Zealand in his famous twenty-point speech. But two thoughts should be entertained. First, does anyone seriously believe that spending more money would have produced poorer results? Secondly, and more important, Wales might actually prove a nuanced counterfactual to the OECD's overall claim about spending. Perhaps it does matter after all. The best comparisons are between the most similar. It would be difficult to find two education systems as similar as those of Wales and England, at least in the first twelve years of devolution. One spent considerably more on education than the other. One has better GCSE results and a far better PISA performance and it's not the country that spent £604 per pupil less. When I travel around Wales and see the dilapidated school buildings, depleted facilities, aging IT kit, and staff desperate for quality professional development, the startling thing is not that Wales underperforms England but that the situation is not a whole lot worse!

Where we are now

LP Hartley said that 'The past is a foreign country: they do things differently there'. As we look back over the last fifteen years or so we can see some successes but also a number of unnecessary detours, cul de sacs, and blind alleys on the devolution journey. *The Learning Country* took us along the meandering B roads when much of the rest of the world was speeding along the motorway. Andrews at least got us to the correct junction and we started to deal with the things that really matter. But Andrews was a man in a hurry and like many reformers was impatient with the pace of change. Huge enterprises like an education system take time to turn around. It's interesting to note that a number of Andrews' initiatives have now bitten the dust, at least in the form that they were first mooted. The Banding system, as we saw in the last chapter, needed a severe overhaul; his plans to make Qualifications Wales an awarding as well as a regulating body have been effectively ditched and other initiatives such as the Masters in Educational Practice (aimed at newly qualified teachers) have been abandoned.

Perhaps most disappointing of all is the fact the department he labelled as 'dysfunctional' continues to be so. The appointment of a trusted stalwart as its Director was only at best a partial solution. The real culture change has not taken place. The appointment of that same Director, during the summer of 2015, to be Deputy Permanent Secretary responsible for part of the education brief *and* local government, housing, regeneration and tackling poverty, does not bode well for focus. The fact that skills, further and higher education now lie in the brief of another Deputy Permanent Secretary lead one to believe that silo working is not going to disappear any time soon.

The past is important because it forms the basis for the present and the future. This book has shown that there are key lessons from the past that must be learned. They must also be owned. In a number of pronouncements it is clear that recent Welsh Governments have tried to distance themselves from the legacy of the opening decade of devolution, even though the majority ruling party has remained unchanged since the heady days of 1999.

Andrews was a keen Cardiff City supporter so it's not surprising that he used a football metaphor to account for what had happened before his time in office. His predecessors had simply 'taken their eye off the ball'. In his book he notes, 'That phrase – "took our eye off the ball" – came to be the settled consensus of Carwyn Jones' governments about the first decade of educational policy in Wales. Huw Lewis used the term after the 2012 PISA results … and the First Minister used the same term in early 2014 on the BBC Radio 4 *Any Questions?* programme'.[2] Continuing the football metaphor, over the opening decade of devolution, educational policy could be more accurately described as a Welsh Government 'own goal'.

There has been a none too subtle attempt to portray 2010 as Year Zero. If another party had been in power before then there might be some credibility in that strategy. But that is not the case. Wales has been a one party state since 1999. The Labour Party should own up to its record across the *whole* of that period.

We need to wait for the PISA result to know where we really are at present. Are we now well on the way to being a good system? Are we getting better or are things getting worse?

The key questions to ponder

In this final section I want to pose seven key questions for all those with the betterment of Welsh education at heart. They seem, to me, to be the key ones we need to answer if we are now to move forward and build a better education system for our children. Some are obviously more important than others.

(1) Have we got a convincing narrative?

One of the most stinging criticisms in the OECD's report on the Welsh education system was that it lacked a coherent narrative. The grand narrative of *The Learning Country* was not alluded to at all and the report seemed to be drawing attention to the rather *ad hoc* reforms that were then under way in the wake of Andrews' 2011 speech. The subsequent response of the Department, *Qualified for Life*, fooled no one. It was a 'cut and paste' job hastily cobbled together to rebut the criticism. I doubt that one practitioner in a hundred can remember it or has referred to it in the past year.

A biblical phrase has come back to me again and again when looking back over the past seventeen years: 'If the trumpets give an uncertain sound, who shall prepare himself for battle'. During that period, the trumpet of the Welsh Government has given off a number of tunes for education. Some have been stirring but quite a number of them have been distinctly off key. It has been difficult to detect a leitmotif running through the whole, despite the continuity of party. Standards were once a minor part of the agenda, then became the only agenda, and now they seem to be slipping down the agenda once more. Teacher assessment was *the* way to improvement, then had nothing to do with it, and now is being touted once more as the way forward. No wonder many in the profession feel as if the goalposts are moving in an ever whirling carousel of directives, guidance and interventions.

We need a shared common narrative about the purpose of our education system. I suspect that we are some way off it at present. This impression was confirmed in a conversation with Graham Donaldson when he said that he had found no consensus on what schools should be about. The implementation of his curriculum reform gives us a golden opportunity to examine and debate what we think the answer to that question should be. All that takes time. It also takes openness on the part of the government, the profession, and those surrounding them to challenge some of the sacred cows, entrenched positions, and vested interests that we all have.

Any narrative must be formed by the government in dialogue with the profession and key stakeholders. Each constituency in that debate will have its own perspectives, prejudices and proposals. The narrative needs to be constructed after real debate which pulls no punches and probes all the options. The consensus that emerges has to be one in which all players have moved out of their comfort zones. The narrative needs to be high level and something that parents and pupils can understand and actively engage with. It then has to remain in place for at least a decade, protected from undue tinkering by politicians. To repeat, one of the sad aspects about our current state is that despite political continuity, policy continuity has been lacking.

We have had something of a debate about the narrative in the discussions over the curriculum but it has not been nearly as large or as deep as it needs to be. Perhaps it will occur as the Donaldson reform gets under way. If it doesn't then once again the system will be internally dissonant and fragmented.

(2) Are we prepared to pay the price for a properly funded system?

Good education cannot be done on the cheap. Period. If we really want a world-class system, or even one that is average, then we must leverage more money into our schools and colleges as a matter of urgency. We've seen how the funding gap opened up at an alarming rate under Davidson and what that gap means in practice for schools on the ground. The chronic underfunding has done untold damage to our education system and to our children. It has hampered their life chances. All that needs to change and it needs to change rapidly. We don't need so much a quantum shift but a quantum leap in funding.

There are about 460,000 children in the school system in Wales at present. The funding gap between Wales and England was last estimated at £604 per pupil per year. That was in 2010. Since then, most commentators believe that gap has got greater, with some putting it at nearer the £900 mark. But let's stick with the £604 figure. Let's also assume that some of that gap is accounted for in the pouring of extra money into projects such as Academies in England. Let's also assume that some of that money was wasted or not well spent. Let's assume that two thirds of that figure is what is needed to make a step change. Providing £400 per pupil per year extra would cost the Welsh Government £184 million per year.

No one would deny that this is a considerable sum, especially when budgets are shrinking. But it is possible if the hard political choices are made. That's what it comes down to at the end of the day. I have grown weary of Ministers in Cardiff Bay blaming Westminster austerity plans for the choices they are making. The chronic underfunding of Welsh schools long predates the financial crash of 2008-09 and was the result of policy choices in the earliest years of devolution. It's also a bit of an 'own goal' to suggest that radically different choices cannot be made. That, I thought, was one of the points about devolution in the first place. When one considers that over £20 million was spent on proposals for a relief road around Newport before a single foot of it was laid or even its very future secure then one starts to get an inkling that such a boost to education funding would not be impossible. Obviously other areas of the Welsh Government would be squeezed but politics is about choices. By spending on our children we are spending on the future of us all.

The extra funding would need to be wisely spent on interventions and programmes that really make a difference. Extreme caution would need to be exercised in making sure that this happened. It should not just be passported to schools without clear directions and guidance.(I vividly remember talking to one primary headteacher about the funding gap. I asked him what he would do with £604 per pupil more. His reply was not inspiring: 'Paint the boys' loos'.) Aids such as the Sutton Trust Tool Kit would be invaluable in this regard, as would clear, independent and impartial advice from WISERD and other respected institutions and researchers.

Extra funding is a necessary but not sufficient prerequisite improvement to the system. Real improvement will not take place without it but money alone is not all that matters. The other key questions need to be addressed too.

(3) Are we prepared to learn from others, wherever they may be?

As well as dialogue within Wales we need news from elsewhere. There are better performing systems than ours in the world, as PISA and a whole host of other data shows. We can and need to learn from the best on offer.

Three words of caution are appropriate at this juncture. Firstly, we must beware the perils of 'policy tourism'. There is a tendency for politicians and policy makers to travel to high performing countries to 'learn the lessons'. After Finland's unexpected success in the PISA tests of the early 2000s it became *de rigueur* for any politician or policy maker worth their salt to visit Helsinki. These sorts of visits are highly enjoyable for those who take part in them; they may or may not have some value. It is difficult to tell. Flights back and fore to Edinburgh, for instance, seem to have done nothing to alert Welsh Government officials to the salient differences between the Scottish qualifications system and our own tripartite one when they plotted to make Qualifications Wales an awarding as well as a regulating body. Educational tourism is not necessarily horizon expanding. Sometimes it can simply be used as a mechanism for confirming prejudices.

Secondly, learnings from educational outings, like poor wines, do not travel well. An education system is not something that can be bought off the peg. It exists in a certain culture and has grown up, usually, across several hundred years. There are deep seated cultures, practices and assumptions which simply cannot be replicated elsewhere. A more thorough analysis of Scandinavian countries might have paid dividends when the Foundation Phase was being formulated.

Finally, the systems most akin to ours, and from which we can learn good lessons, are closer at home within the United Kingdom. When one looks at the GCSE achievement of Northern Ireland, it does seem as if their system has something to teach us. In more recent years Scotland has been the first port of call for the Welsh Government. The major reform of the curriculum now under way is being led by a Scot. His report, *Successful Futures*, draws heavily on Scotland's Curriculum for Excellence which has been rolled out there over the last ten years. I have noted the mesmeric effect that the Scottish Qualifications Authority had for those contemplating Qualifications Wales. There are other examples too, such as literacy initiatives, where Scotland has been mined for good practice.

However, we need to look at Scotland with less rose-tinted spectacles. It has its own problems. Earlier this year, Nicola Sturgeon, Scotland's First Minister, announced that national literacy and numeracy testing was to be introduced to Scottish schools. Some have speculated that some sort of League Tables will be the next step.[3] A cursory reading of Scotland's performance in PISA might also give pause for thought. Between 2000 and 2012 Scotland had dropped from 522 to 513 in science, 526 to 506 in reading, and a staggering 533 to 498 in maths. Between 2006 and 2012 results had plateaued in science, slightly improved in reading but continued their downward trajectory in maths. This was also the period that saw the development of the Curriculum for Excellence, which was finally introduced into Scottish schools in 2010.

If we need to look with less rose-tinted spectacles to Scotland we need to remove the blinkers that stop us learning from England. All too often Welsh Government policy has seemed to be determined by *not* doing what England does. This prejudice was there from the start and accelerated once Labour was ousted from office in Westminster. As mentioned before Davidson's reluctance to establish anything like a National College for Teaching was a missed opportunity. Her refusal to adopt a national strategy approach to literacy and numeracy was also a huge mistake. This is not to say that everything that England has done should be imitated. The colossal amount of time, effort and cash expended on Academies and Free Schools does not seem to have paid off. The botched attempt at qualifications reform has left the system there demoralised and confused.

But there are some things we can learn. One, and this will be very unpalatable to Labour administrations who've majored on the rhetoric of poverty and deprivation, is the immense strides that have been made in England to tackle the effects of those two evils. Their policies have been far more effective than ours. Pupils eligible for free school meals in England are 50% more likely to obtain five good GCSEs than their counterparts in Wales. That's the conclusion of the former Labour Cabinet Minister Alan Milburn. His report on social mobility states starkly that 'Wales performs less well than all regions in England, including comparably deprived regions like the North East'. It's time to think again.[4]

(4) Are we prepared to reform the entire system, not just part of it?

From Andrews' February 2011 speech, *most* of the education system has been on what Elaine Edwards of UCAC has described as a 'white knuckle ride' in terms of reform. We have seen the introduction of national literacy and numeracy frameworks, national testing, and school Categorisation. In the space of three years we had moved from a system in which accountability was almost absent to a situation in which it is omnipresent. The human casualties have been clear to see as some heads and teachers have been eased out. Minds are focussed on outcomes as never before and general anxieties about performance have increased. The same has been true of local authorities who again have received unheard of scrutiny, with six in special measures at one stage. But one part of the system has escaped relatively unscathed: the Education Department itself.

There have been some minor shufflings of the deck chairs, it is true. Some personnel have moved on, but the culture, tone and output of the department is virtually the same as it was ten or more years ago. Davidson refused to tackle any of these problems, Andrews tried to but left the job, at best, half done.

Outside of Cathays Park, the seat of the Education Department, the Welsh education system has, in the last three years, undergone the most profound scrutiny and challenge in its post-devolution history. Some leading figures in schools and local authorities have been 'moved on' in response to concerns about their performance. Given the department's track record one might have expected to see a similar pattern there. Andrews had been bullish when it came to other organisations. In his book he boasts that in regard to local government he had clearly stated that 'when failure happens, heads should roll'.[5] A good example would have been better than tough talk. He could have started in his own department. After the debacle over Foundation Phase funding and the CDAP, the GCSE fiascos and the collapse of other programmes, some heads should have rolled, but they didn't, with just the occasional individual being 'promoted' away from the department.

A good performance management system would ensure that targets were met and deadlines observed. If the Welsh Government now wants to stress 'accountability' as never before then its first port of call might best be its own bureaucracy. How far has the new 'accountability' culture been applied to the Department?

In July 2013, a FOI request lodged with the Welsh Government which, *inter alia*, asked a number of searching questions including:

5. How many staff in DfES and its predecessors have faced disciplinary action for capability since devolution?

6.   How many investigations of capability of DfES staff and predecessors have taken place since devolution?

7.   How many staff at DfES and predecessors have been dismissed for incompetence and capability since devolution?

The response was illuminating:

'In relation to questions 5–7, we do not hold records of underperformance before 2006, when Education and Learning Wales (ELWa) merged into the Welsh Government. In accordance with our data protection policies, we do not release sensitive information on staff in a format which might enable individuals to be identified. We only provide information on data sets amounting to ten or more staff. I cannot therefore provide a further breakdown of figures'.[6]

It is hard to find anyone outside it who thinks that the culture of the Department has changed much in the last decade. But change it must if the challenges we now face are to be addressed. Three key reforms seem necessary.

Firstly, there has to be an influx of those with recent, relevant experience of the education system. It needs experienced practitioners who know how the system actually works on the ground. One of the first, of the many, reports commissioned by Andrews was one emanating from the Structure of Education Services Review Task and Finish Group in 2011. It was led by the highly respected Viv Thomas, former Director of Education in Neath Port Talbot. It found that out of nearly 750 staff at the Department of Education just two (yes, two!) had been employed in a school or college setting within the last two years. Since then, the number of secondees has increased. Talking to quite a number of them over the years, they have all reported the same sort of experience: a warm welcome but also a clear indication that civil service process and culture will always take precedence over any expertise or challenge they bring. If the Education Department is to be of use to the system it is meant to serve then it needs far more people who 'know' the core experience of schools and colleges from first hand.

Secondly, some of the arrogance of the Department has to be challenged. Most of the civil servants that I have had dealings with over the years have been polite and courteous. Off the record they have also been more open than their official positions would allow. Their openness to advice has varied, depending on their own grasp of the issues and the prevailing culture at the time. By and large those with the deepest insight have been the most open and honest. However, there is inevitably a collective mind-set and that does fluctuate. Ironically it seems to be in inverse proportion to the perceived strength of the Minister. When Andrews was in charge, the dialogue with officials was the most open I'd ever known it. Under Lewis the wagons were drawn in ever decreasing circles.

My third point is allied to the second. The civil service is keen to peddle the myth of its own neutrality. One does not have to be a Postmodernist or a disciple of Durkheim to realise that this claim is questionable *a priori*. Any government department has its own agenda and aims, irrespective of government policy. This holds true of our Education Department as of any other. It is *part* of the problem of education as much as any other part of the system. When this is forgotten, and the view from the centre is taken to be the only one that matters, the situation is fraught with danger. In a one-party state the dangers are amplified. The proper boundaries between the government and the bureaucracy become blurred and on occasions broken. Fiefdoms develop in which jobs, positions and contracts are seen as gifts. A closed culture emerges at the top which regards any criticism as an act of treason.

The normally mild mannered Jenny Rathbone, Labour AM for Cardiff Central, stated in October 2015 that 'there is an unhealthy culture at the top of the Welsh Government which does not allow for rigorous debate and reflection on the best use of public funds. Independent thought is not tolerated by AMs and if someone does step out of line, they are ruthlessly dealt with. This is not a good way to make difficult decisions'.[7] The same holds true for all others engaged in the political process. Doors are closed, funds for research fail to materialise again, counter-briefings are given in an attempt to win by stealth what cannot be won by argument. All these are inevitable in any system. The presence of a one-party state, however, makes them particularly pernicious.

We have to be especially vigilant to promote a culture in which decision making is based on evidence and not on self-interest. The Education Department needs independent scrutiny. Estyn should inspect its workings and delivery for starters. But it also needs to establish other mechanisms whereby feedback from all stakeholders is enabled and genuinely taken on board.

(5) How do we encourage 'heretics'?

Allied to the need for a culture of openness at the centre is a similar one to create more 'heretics' throughout the system. These are people who contest the accepted orthodoxies. They throw up unpalatable facts and suggest radically different approaches. They ensure that education remains a contested discipline. Newman, the great nineteenth century Catholic thinker, was unusual in seeing a positive value for heresy. He argued that those who opposed the Church's teaching made it think more closely and effectively about what it believed. The same is true in other spheres as well. It is sometimes the case that the minority view is the correct one. The irritating dissenter can pose fundamental questions occluded by 'group think'.

Education needs heretics. The *status quo* needs to be constantly challenged and probed. As the Webb Review noted 'small countries can slip into a cosiness that limits ambition'. That has happened all too often in Wales. Looking back over *The Learning Country* years, what the project most needed was challenge from outside by those who were proposing a different alternative. The Foundation Phase too could have benefitted from some sharp criticism.

Again and again we have been promised debates which turn out to be rather badly managed attempts to corral discussion along certain lines. We have seen consultations where key decisions have already been made. I worry that the overwhelming public consensus on Donaldson is not doing us any real favours. In private one hears concerns not just about implementation but about substance.

Nowhere in the 'Great Debate' have I heard any real discussion of the 'common culture' a curriculum should exhibit and the limits of choice. Both of those are from Andrews' discussion of curriculum in his book.[8] Those and many others need full and frank discussion if we are to build a curriculum that stands the test of time and not just one that papers over the cracks.

Heretics are needed at every level. The universities, through agencies such as WISERD, provide an invaluable resource in that regard. Our sadly shrinking media in Wales has provided this service way beyond the call of duty. But heretics should not be confined there. We need heretics in schools and local authorities who are prepared to challenge and critique. This challenge should be based on evidence and analysis. There is a world of difference between a heretic and old curmudgeon who simply doesn't like change.

(6) How do we train our teachers to teach?

Allied to this is the question of how we train our teachers. No one is happy with the current teacher training arrangements. We have had several reports, of varying value, which have sought to address the problems of training and formation, and the number and quality of those entering the teaching training institutions. We have cut the numbers and raised the bar. We have also trialled what might be called non-traditional routes into the profession such as Teach First and graduate training programmes. Estyn has produced a series of reports which have shown that a number of providers are underperforming.

But I don't think we have yet sufficiently articulated what exactly is wrong with the current setup, far less what we would actually like to see in its place.

Part of the problem lies with the rapidly changing nature of schools and education in general. Student teachers often feel ill-equipped to deal with the challenges they face, and older members of staff often agree with their analysis. We need to be more realistic. Newly qualified teachers are just that – *newly* qualified. They need to be ready to cope with the demands of the classroom but it is absurd to think that they are fully formed. It is not sufficient to put them through an initial teacher training programme, plonk them in a classroom, and tell them to get on with it for the next forty years. A career progression should be mapped which will enable them to grow into the role they have undertaken.

Current teachers are very unhappy with the level of professional development on offer to them. They too face the challenges of a rapidly changing society. Given the myriad of changes it is not surprising that many feel reform fatigue. There is now a lack of dynamism in the teaching workforce which is palpable. In a word we need to allow our teachers to 're-professionalise'. The Education Workforce Council could have a lead role to play in this but not in its current form. A body which is appointed completely by the Minister will never be credible. Teachers want and need something more than a governmental poodle. If the EWC were reformed and made more representative, if it were truly independent, then it could help restore dynamism and professionalism to a demoralised workforce.

In terms of professional development we know that the older model of attending courses to inform teaching no longer works. We know from international studies that a professional-to-professional approach pays far better dividends. Teachers learn best from other teachers. If the New Deal, promised in the wake of Donaldson, means anything it has to try to capture this model. It will require trust in the profession. It will also require some serious resourcing.

(7) How do we strike a fruitful balance between producers and consumers of education?

One of the most striking things, looking back over the opening decade of devolution, is how the education landscape in Wales changed in almost a completely different direction to that of the rest of the world. During that period, as in the decade before it, most economies were opening up their education systems to ever greater consumer demand. This demand side capacity was seen in initiatives such as League Tables, ensuring that schools were engaged in greater reporting to government and parents, and an explosion of publicly available data.

On the supply side there were reforms which sought to upskill teachers through prescriptive national programmes often connected with literacy and numeracy, and to enhance leadership through national models. The general public also became more suspicious of the professions *tout court*. High profile misconduct cases such as that of Harold Shipman, for example, initiated a raft of reforms to the medical profession.

The days of 'teacher knows best' are over. Anyone entering the profession now knows that they will be subject to scrutiny, internally from their senior managers, and externally from government and Estyn. Parents now have access to data on the performance of schools and inadequacies can no longer be hidden. That data is also readily available to the media and others to do with as they will. While some may not like this, no politician is likely to try to do again what Davidson did in the opening years of the millennium and put that data beyond reach. It is here to stay.

The demand side mechanisms have come to Wales late but since Andrews they have come with a vengeance. What England has done in nearly fifteen years we have been forced to do in two or three. Scotland's reluctant introduction of national testing shows that we are not the furthest behind the curve. Thankfully, Wales has been spared the crasser attempts at demand drive reform that have been seen in England. We have not constructed some pseudo-market or wasted money on the various schemes that have tried to give parents some sort of 'purchasing' power in terms of vouchers or the like.

One group of 'consumers', though, still seem to be under-developed. Ironically these are the pupils themselves. Although one of the successes Wales can boast of has been the development of school councils and a student voice, that has still to be translated into mechanisms that can enable real change. The Sutton Trust Tool Kit notes that 'feedback' is one of the most powerful drivers for student improvement. That's true at the micro level but it could also be true at the macro level. We don't want to get some state-sanctioned 'Rate My Teacher' but more feedback from pupils on the quality of their learning is to be welcomed. After all, they are the ones best placed to know if they have learned or not.

There is one fundamental question, however, which takes precedence over all the rest. It comes back to my first point: what is the fundamental narrative we want to tell? What is the ultimate aim for our schools, in fact, for our children? It boils down to this: are we aiming for excellence or mediocrity? My strictures about *Qualified for Life* show where my thoughts lie. That bland document let the cat out of the bag in its last section. Is 'Aiming for Average' our real aim? It is hardly an inspiring vision. While the original

PISA target was absurdly ambitious, it did suggest that we were not going to give up on *The Learning Country*'s aim for Wales to be world class in terms of education.

The policies and focus of *The Learning Country* in the opening decade of devolution did not help that aim. The abandonment of vast sections of the accountability regime has cast a long shadow that will not be easily dispelled. The piecemeal delivery and chronic underfunding have all played their part in weakening our education system. The statistics about achievement show that in the '90s, Wales was not the wooden spoon holder in the UK education league that it now appears to be. At the end of the day parents expect schools to educate their children. That has to be the core purpose of any school system. Other aims, however laudable, have to play second fiddle to that primary one. Other countries in the UK, notably England, learned that lesson better than we did.

Obviously we have a mountain to climb, but it can be done. Many of the PISA countries who have leap-frogged us have had far deeper problems than ours. Some of them have weaker economies and some, such as Croatia, were fighting bloody wars while we were still debating the devolution settlement. We cannot use our relative poverty in UK terms as a complacent fig leaf to cover our underperformance. I fear that we are too quick to resort to victim status as a nation and to seek to blame others for our woes. To be blunt we have been too quick to accept golden mediocrity in education as the best we can achieve. Some have even suggested a trade-off between excellence and equity as a given. Other countries give the lie to such life-reducing, horizon-narrowing, lazy complacency. It is ultimately our children who have suffered from such views.

We voted for devolution. We believed it would make things different. We had better start proving that it can make things better – for our children's sake.

Notes

1   http://www.walesonline.co.uk/news/education/leading-survey-suggests-girls-falling-10900865

2   Andrews, p 114

3   http://www.scotsman.com/news/education/national-testing-to-be-introduced-in-scots-schools-1-3874668#axzz3ojl8QNdq

4   Milburn, Alan State of the Nation 2014 Report (Social Mobility and Child Poverty Commission), and see http://www.bbc.co.uk/news/uk-wales-politics-24567287

5   Andrews, p. 142

6   ATISN reference 7516 (This will be found on the disclosure log of the Welsh Government)

7   http://www.bbc.co.uk/news/uk-wales-politics-34533424

8   Andrews, p 233

Index

welsh academic press

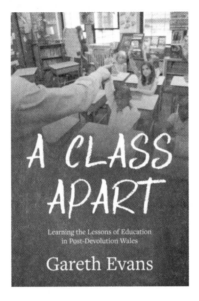

"Evans should be praised for revealing the personalities and politics behind key policy developments in an accessible, uncompromising, but fair style ... essential reading for anyone involved in the Welsh education system."
Dr Julian Skyrme, Agenda (Institute of Welsh Affairs)

"This is a trailblazing book. Political and educational partisans will hate it, but the open-minded will love it ... compulsory reading for senior civil servants in the Department of Education and Skills [and] compulsive reading for the rest of us."
Philip Dixon, Western Mail

"Gareth is Wales' most incisive commentator on education. He has built a reputation for fair and fearless analysis that gets beyond the spin."
Lee Waters, Director, Institute of Welsh Affairs

"Gareth is distinguished and trusted because he is a master of data mining and data, basing his reporting only on evidence rather than belief."
Sir John Cadogan, former Director General of the UK Research Councils and inaugural President of the Learned Society of Wales

"Gareth provides the perspective of an analytical, insightful, bold and fearless writer whose primary motivation is to see the Welsh education system become increasingly successful. I am convinced that the issues raised in A Class Apart are applicable internationally. There are many lessons which we can all learn from the Welsh experience and the strategies that they have employed."
Dr Avis Glaze, former Chief Student Achievement Officer of Ontario

978-1-86057-123-7 · £16.99 · 247pp · 4pp of photographs